The United States Of North America

Achille Murat

THE

UNITED STATES

OF

NORTH AMERICA.

BY ACHILLE MURAT,

CI-DEVANT PRINCE ROYAL OF THE TWO SICILIES, AND CITIZEN
OF THE UNITED STATES.

WITH

A NOTE ON NEGRO SLAVERY,

BY JUNIUS REDIVIVUS.

SECOND EDITION.

LONDON:

PUBLISHED BY EFFINGHAM WILSON,
88, ROYAL EXCHANGE;

W. F. WAKEMAN, DUBLIN; WAUGH AND INNES, EDINBURGH.
BANCKS AND CO. MANCHESTER.

1833.

CONTENTS.

LETTER FIRST.

GENERAL VIEW OF THE UNION.

LETTER SECOND.

ORIGIN AND HISTORY OF PARTIES.

LETTER THIRD.

DESCRIPTION OF THE NEW SETTLEMENTS.

3

LETTER FOURTH.

ON SLAVERY.

LETTER FIFTH.

ON RELIGION.

LETTER SIXTH.

ON THE ADMINISTRATION OF JUSTICE.

LETTER SEVENTH.

OF THE LAWS.

LETTER EIGHTH.

OF THE ARMY, THE NAVY, AND THE INDIANS.

LETTER NINTH.

OF THE FINANCES.

LETTER TENTH.

OF MANNERS, FINE ARTS, AND LITERATURE.

ERRATA.

Page 12, line 9, *for* the state, *read*, an individual
13, —— 16, omit the word *own*
44, —— 9, } *for* capital, *read* capitol
58, —— 20, }
73, —— 12, *for* government, *read* governments
78, —— 17, *for* factories, *read* forges, (*usines*)
83, —— 10, *for* every body, *read* some persons, and *for* terms, *read* term
85, —— 3, *for* right, *read* rights
94, —— 8, *for* old age, *read* on the brink of
99, last line, *for* let, *read* take
113, line 25, *for* were, *read* was
138, —— 22, *for* cannot, *read* could not
158, —— 16, 17, *for* court, wigs, *read* court-wigs.

TRANSLATOR'S PREFACE.

In submitting the following Work to the British public, the Translator deems it unnecessary to detain the reader by many prefatory remarks. The subject is one of acknowledged interest just now; and, therefore, information respecting it, which comes recommended by long experience, amidst diversified opportunities of observation, can hardly fail to be acceptable, particularly when, as in the present instance, those qualifications are further enhanced by considerable talent in the communication, and as much impartiality as is consistent with a just appreciation of what is excellent.

Our Reform Bill has opened the door to improvements in our social condition, but it comes to us so late that, in relation to its immediate consequences on the fortunes of many, it must be considered as the seed rather than the crop; the means to an end, not the end itself; and that end even yet so distant that

they cannot wait for it.   Accordingly, there is
a restlessness among the middle portions of the
community; and many eyes, familiar with disappointment here, are turned to distant regions,
in search of an eligible spot to which they may
transport themselves and families.   To such,
the United States, from affinity of institutions,
manners, and early associations, have necessarily considerable attractions.

But there is another respect in which the
United States is still more interesting to us
as a people; and that is in the working of the
machinery of their government.   We are now
looking at our institutions with a view to
their amendment, and we are sensible of the
advantages of comparison in the formation
· of a sound judgment.   People do not trouble
themselves, as they used to do, about the
abstract preferableness of this or that form
of government, but they inquire by what means
the greatest happiness can be diffused among
the greatest number of people at the least cost.
Few of them are any longer the dupes of that
vaunted prosperity in which a nation may be
called rich and flourishing, while the majority
of individuals who compose it, with difficulty
find the means of subsistence.   Diffusion, not

accumulation, is now regarded as the true test of prosperity, and a flushed head with paralytic extremities is, whether in the body politic or the individual, held to be symptomatic of disease and dissolution. To what extent the institutions of the United States are deserving of imitation is an inquiry too extensive to be at present entered into; but as the country is now feeling the evil consequences of long-continued profusion in expenditure, we are not likely to increase our troubles by keeping their example before us, when our civil and pension lists come under discussion.

The author's opinions on some of the subjects discussed will not meet with universal assent, but he is entitled to hold and utter them, and truth cannot lose by investigation; moreover, the age is favourable to it. Let us glance at an instance or two.

The subject of Slavery is discussed in a Note at the end of the volume, and an opposite view presented to that of the author, whose reasoning thereon, however ingenious, will be generally thought, in this country, to give a dangerous prominence to that law of the strongest which casuists have agreed to consider untenable, because destitute of support from moral considerations. Can that reasoning be sound to which the weak and defenceless cannot assent but to their injury?

Religion, according to our author, is abundant in the United States, but not without a plentiful infusion of secular feelings. It is difficult to say how much of the latter ought to be tolerated in our present state of existence; but, certainly, the American mode is of all modes the least exposed to censure, since the expenses of any religion are wholly and voluntarily paid by its members. Let us hope, too, that there is more sincerity of devotion than he supposes, and that an unattractive and distasteful form of speech is not necessarily indicative of hypocrisy.

The author describes Mr. Owen's system as undisguised atheism. This assertion must surely have been hazarded on purely negative grounds. Mr. Owen, in his lectures, does indeed generally confine himself to the concerns of this world, considering them to come most properly within his sphere of usefulness; but it seems not a necessary inference that he does not therefore believe in another. There are numerous examples everywhere of one world being on the lips, and the other in the thought.

Law proceedings in the United States resemble our own, and with little abatement of
their cumbrousness and uncertainty; this, connected with the comparative cheapness of law
there, tends to feed a spirit of litigation, which
the author acknowledges and good-naturedly
endeavours to extenuate.

After so much has been said, by Mrs. Trollope
and others, in disparagement of the manners
of the Americans, there is something humili-
ating in the acknowledgment, which nevertheless must be made, that the Americans, as
a people, are free from those meanest of all
idolatries, so continually obtruded upon us in
England, the worship of wealth and title,
apart from all worthier distinctions. There is
a spot or two of the sort in America, but the
general texture of society is free from it.

It is unnecessary to extend remark farther;
the reader is referred to the author's Dedication,
a part of the work which ought not to be
passed over, as it illustrates his general views,
and the grounds upon which he entertains
them.

SINCE the publication of the first edition of the present work, the attention of the world has been re-directed to the United States by the ferment which the operation of the tariff occasioned there; and some politicians foreboded therefrom a dissolution of the Union. We did not anticipate that result; but, even if it had taken place, the propriety of the original federation would have remained unimpugned, and equally so those social institutions upon which the prosperity of the Union has hitherto rested. Nothing, in short, would have been proved, but that an erroneous system of policy must always produce, eventually, discontent somewhere; and that no frame of government can secure permanent tranquillity but by the avoidance of measures of a partial effect, and the observance of those strict principles of justice on which the happiness of States is no less dependent than that of individuals.

September, 1833.

DEDICATORY PREFACE

TO

COUNT THIBEAUDAU.

March 18, 1832.
MY DEAR FRIEND,

It was at your suggestion that I began, about six years ago, to write the following Letters upon the United States, and it was to you that the first four were addressed : it is therefore with peculiar propriety that I dedicate the whole to the friend but for whom my work would never have seen the light. I trust you will receive the last six letters with the same indulgence as you did their precursors. An interval of nearly six years has elapsed between their composition; notwithstanding which, the intention of the work remains equally seasonable, that of making known in Europe, and particularly in France, the institutions of the United States, and the manners of the inhabitants.

Indeed, this task becomes every day more important, for a form of government more or less similar to theirs is the point towards which Europe is gravitating, not only since our time, but since

b

the revival of letters, and the first moment in which
Greek and Roman civilization began to penetrate
the dark clouds of barbarism. The white race, to
which you and I belong, is eminently perfectible ;
that even is its distinction among other sorts of
men. This race had attained, without foreign assistance, to a very high degree of civilization (from
which, even in some respects, we are still very
distant), when the barbarians of the North, who
fell upon it, came to slacken its progress, and throw
it back in its intellectual career. As a frozen
liquid added to a quantity already in a state of
ebullition stops that effect immediately, and is
warmed itself in the same proportion as the boiling
liquor with which it is mixed is cooled; in like
manner the barbarians, at the very time they were
apparently destroying Roman civilization, were
profiting by it, and were themselves gaining in light
what they made the conquered people lose. The
march of the human mind, therefore, did not stop;
neither did it retrograde, but all its vital forces
were employed in counteracting the effects of the
invasion of the barbarians, and in harmonizing and
combining the new materials, which had thrown the
established economy into disorder.

Centuries were necessary to this labour, but it
was at last accomplished. The sciences were immediately carried back, by the study of their
books, to the point at which the ancients had left
them; and the improvements we have made upon
them are too evident to need more than an allusion.

It was not, however, the same with political institutions. They had been completely undermined long since, and the very traditions of liberty were lost under the feudal slavery. The interest of two powerful classes, the nobility and the clergy, resisted every attempt at amelioration. Barbarism was obliged, however, in the end, to yield to the progressive march of light, and to the ardent desire for intellectual emancipation which it created : it was then that governmental matter became divided. The devil's plan was adopted. Mixed systems were introduced. The payment of kings was continued, but on condition that they should do nothing. The barons were even willing to listen to the humble representations of the Commons. The latter, however, became from day to day more powerful, and we are now arrived at the time in which they are every thing, and the barons nothing but fossil remains of past ages, still considered as necessary parts of those worn-out and antiquated pieces of mechanism, called 'constitutional monarchies' by the liberals, and 'state governments' by the kings of the Holy Alliance when they promised them to their subjects.

All these old mechanisms have been acknowledged defective, and an excellent workman is at this moment occupied in patching up the oldest, and that which has served as a model for all the others. They are only good at most as governments of transition, to prepare a future generation for the enjoyment of a system unknown to its ancestors.

But you well know that the best machines are
always the most simple, and of the latest invention. It is to suppress the useless wheel-work
that the greatest improvements in mechanism are
limited. The same thing must take place in the
moral order. But the cogs of the wheels must be
altered, those which are superfluous quietly removed,
and above all, the whole well greased, to prevent it
from creaking, and that it may not break all at
once. This reparation when completed may be
an improvement; it is, however, better to build
after a plan than to replaster an old tenement;
and the general destruction effected in the last forty
years has certainly made us leap far above those
periods of transition which might have absorbed
perhaps many generations.

People desired, and now desire, a rational government. The questions to be asked are, Has it been
obtained? Have they not got into the old track?
Have they not destroyed one species of tyranny
only to establish another? Has liberty gained
by the change? The happiness of the people
as a body (for that is really the vital question)
has it been increased? These questions do not
apply to the revolution of 1830; for the answer
would be too easy, it would be forcing an open
door; but they regard the first great leap of 89,
and all the governments which have ruled us
since that time. I am far from denying that a
great progress has been made; but have not the
people a right, considering the price that has been

paid for it, to ask whether it ought not to have been greater? People have lost themselves in search of a theoretical liberty, while they have altogether neglected that practical liberty which is of main importance. The United States alone have obtained the latter.

You will immediately ask me if I think the constitution of the United States the best possible, and if I think it applicable to France, or any part of Europe? This question has been asked me a thousand times: I do not answer it, at least at present, for it is not that which is of immediate concern. It is not so much the constitution and laws of the United States that I admire and love, as the reason why the United States have this constitution, and these laws. It is the *principle* of the government. You ask me if it is the republic? Not so; the republic is but a consequence more or less necessary of the principle in question.

This principle, from which so much good has emanated, and which is destined to govern the world, is what is called in America "Self-government,"— GOVERNMENT BY THE PEOPLE THEMSELVES. Provided the people govern, I am satisfied. Of little consequence is the form of the machine and who turn the wheels, provided it be so constructed as to receive and obey the least breath of public opinion, that it be then strong and irresistible, but powerless to disobey or resist it.

That is, in my opinion, the great problem which has been resolved in so satisfactory a manner

in America. Do people concern themselves much
about it in Europe? Public opinion, it is true, was
once consulted, and consented to give itself a
master. A second time it pronounced in favour of
the same man; in a non-official manner, truly, but
not on that account the less energetically. But,
with this exception, when has the nation manifested
a will ? There have been twenty changes of government during the last forty years, but (without
speaking of those which have been imposed by the
foreigner) they have always been effected by a minority. For even supposing Paris unanimous, the
provinces have never been consulted.

I think I know my own affairs best; and moreover that, even if I deceive myself, it is my own
affair, and nobody has a right to thwart me. I
think I have a right to prevent any one from
coming to teach me magisterially what is my
best interest, and force me despotically to submit
my judgment to that of another. I think, also,
that the general interest is the result of all the particular interests, and that the government should, in
like manner, be the result of all the individual wills.

But in Europe it is not so. There is too much
desire to govern. Every thing becomes matter of
government, as well as matter of taxation. What
does it signify whether it be the republic or the
Bourbons, who cause me to be watched by the
high police, who open my letters, exercise a censor-
ship over my newspapers, and require me to procure a passport when I desire to avail myself of

my natural right of locomotion? What have I gained by the republic, if it is as tyrannical, as dear, as suspicious, as the monarchy? What imports it whether the nobility be old or new, as long as there is a nobility? What interest have I in personal changes of the government, when my voice will have as little influence with the new comers as with the previous depositories of power; when I shall remain either deprived of my vote, or have it neutralized by other votes bought or intimidated? It was against all these things I wished to see a revolution made. It will be time enough afterwards to trouble one's self about and discuss calmly the form of the government. That is only of secondary importance.

There was a time, immediately after the revolution of July, that I thought the thing was done. Lafayette understands republican institutions, as I do, in the American manner. He had proclaimed their existence; he had announced the commencement of the best of republics. I thought that all political police was going to be destroyed; that all constraint on the liberty of locomotion was going to be suppressed; that the election of their representatives was henceforth to be given to the people themselves, and not to electors comprising the aristocracy of citizens; that an elective senate was about to replace a chamber of peers; that the initiative of the chambers was to become in future the ordinary mode of presenting laws; that the right of petition would cease to be a word without

meaning; that ministerial responsibility was to be
at last established, as well as that of all inferior
persons in office; that all accumulation of places
would be strictly interdicted; that trade would be
rendered free by the abolition of monopolies and
restrictions, which arrest it at every step in passing
from one *commune* to another; that a system of
duties would be adopted, which should protect
industry without forcing it into unnatural channels;
that a budget would be presented defining all the
expenditure in a specific manner; that sinecures
would be abolished, and useless expenses suppressed;
that the discussions of political matters in the tribunals would cease to be subjected to influence;
that grand juries *(jurys d'accusation)* would be
established; that every accused person would be
admitted to bail, except in capital cases; that
means analogous to writs of *habeas corpus*, *mandamus*, and *quo warranto*, would be invented to
protect the liberty of the subject, to insure the
execution of the laws, and to prevent the encroachments of power; that the *communes*, the towns,
and even the departments, would be free from *la
centralization*, would cease to be in tutelage to
the capital; that they would have the election of
their magistrates, the disposal of their revenue, and
the right of assessing themselves, provided that privilege did not cramp the internal trade; that the
will of the people governed would at last be established every where, instead of the good pleasure
of the governors. I thought sincerely that in foreign

affairs a system worthy of France would be adopted; that it would not be mixed up in any confederacy of kings; that it would not tie its hands by any abstract doctrine of intervention or non-intervention, but that in that respect it would follow its interest and its glory. I was deceived, ... all Europe was so too, for it flew to arms.

Full of these soft illusions, burning to see the place of my birth, to embrace old friends and a beloved family, whom I had (in my delirium) invited to meet me in Paris, I leave my plantation and my studies, and set off, believing that the cause of liberty was sure to be attacked, and sure also that a defender more would not be refused, that it would not be against me that the ranks of the French army would be closed. I hasten, but it takes me near three months to come from my home to Europe. . . . . My God! what is my disappointment! . . . . And is it to arrive at such fine results as these, that the whole world has been shaken to its foundations? We have certainly advanced some steps in the career of liberty, but alas, how few! . . . . It would certainly be better to postpone these alterations to the day in which the accounts will be definitively arranged between liberty and despotism, and which cannot be long deferred, than to sacrifice the lives of so many brave patriots for nothing, or next to nothing. . . . In short, the entrance into France continued to be interdicted to me as under the government by divine right. In the meantime war was going to

commence. The French army was in motion, but
its ranks were closed to me. What was to be
done ? A neighbouring nation had conquered its
liberty even more completely than France had
known how to conquer hers. It was to support
its liberty that France was advancing. On the
other hand, the Dutch seemed to rely upon the
assistance of Prussia. Even the position which
the French army took showed that its leader expected a general war, for he manœuvred so as to
take the line of the Meuse against the Prussians,
leaving the Belgians and the Dutch to manage
between them. A general war, a real duel, hand
to hand, between revolution and counter-revolution, was about to ensue, and I should have
taken no part in it! If the French army was
closed against me, that of its allies was not. I
arrived among them, asked and obtained service. A
prince, not one of those who are afraid of their
shadow; a prince who understands liberty better
than any of the journals of the movement at Paris,
or the Tory journals of London who rail against it
every day, held out his hand to the exile, and
received him in such a manner as to command his
gratitude. It is secured to him. The storm passed
off, however, in frowns. I, therefore, gave up the
command I had received, ready to take it again on
the first report of war (for I did not reckon upon
serving during peace), but not without having been
harassed by the representatives of the despotic
powers. This is all right: I do not complain of it;

quite the contrary. Those delicate attentions with which these worthies pursue, with all their power, a young man who has never yet been distinguished for any thing whatever, who has still done nothing for history, show th● opinion they have of him. I am very proud of it. They serve to reveal my resources to me. This persecution extends from great to little things. It forms a part of my existence, so much am I accustomed to it. If, on the one hand, it is attempted (without success, however,) to get me dismissed from the Belgian service, (perfectly right, since I entered it only to fight against them;) on the other, a celebrated ambassadress refuses to endorse a subscription card to a ball (of which she was patroness,) for a lady, declaring it would compromise her very much with her court if she did it! What elevated views!

The only persecution which would be sensibly felt by me would be that of the French government, because it pretends to represent France. In the time of Charles X., I should not have cared, because it had not that pretension. But the thought would be cruel to me, that it was the nation that continued my exile. That would destroy one of the few illusions which yet remain to me.

But let us leave this personal digression, and return to the hopes with which the revolution of July has inspired me. You will consider, no doubt, that it was the republic I desired. Not at all; it was GOVERNMENT BY THE PEOPLE THEMSELVes. The republic is but one of the means of arriving at

that end.   It is liberty I desire: no matter under
what name, provided I have the thing.

But you will say, Do you think it possible to
France or Europe? Let us distinguish. If it were
desired, first of all, to destroy every thing, have
recourse to anarchy, and from these rude materials
construct a republican edifice, preserving and making the best of all the tools and means of the
government of despotism, I do not think that
liberty would ever be attained. That experiment
has already been tried once. But I am firmly convinced that it might be established in a better way.
Let the government once sincerely desire it; let it
cease to encroach continually upon the people, to
desire to fix every thing, settle every thing, foresee
every thing, prevent every thing; let it leave to
each branch of power, to each opinion, to each
party, and to each individual, the degree of power
and moral weight which respectively belongs to
them, and that will approach very near to liberty,
if it be not the thing itself.

I repeat it, all the governments of Europe, to
whatever party they belong, are always too fond of
governing. The executive power, for instance, no
matter what may be its form, ought not to direct
public opinion, but follow it. Its province is not
to make laws, but to execute them. If chambers, so
elected as to be really the representatives of the
nation, and without any ministerial influence, pass
bad laws, that is not the affair of the administration. *Fate voi, gran duca, le gale sone vostre*, it

says to them; I wash my hands of it. It cannot be responsible for that; but the nation will take care to see justice done to itself,—and the representatives, whether ignorant or traitorous, who may have voted for a measure proved bad by experience, will be turned out at the next election, and the measure repealed by a new chamber.

Do you think that an executive power, which should adopt as a maxim, not in anywise to direct legislative opinion, but follow it; which should recommend some laws, but propose none, leaving the chambers to make use of their initiative; which should not offer any opposition to the reductions they might make in the budget, but strictly confine itself within the limits fixed by them; should have no secrets, and be ready to open to them all its portfolios, and to give all the information they might require;—do you think, I say, that an executive power, who should thus act, would not soon establish liberty in the country it governed? This is what Washington did. He was the first president. It was he who created the part. If he had amused himself finessing with congress, wishing to play the master, putting his nose in every thing, directing the state-elections, or dictating decisions to the courts of justice,—liberty, it is true, would have been established, because the people knew it and would have it; but the period would have been retarded, and he would have been overturned, bequeathing, probably, to his country a long career of anarchy. The task of government ought to be

divided among many. Each should be employed in
his department for the general good. They who
pay, they who suffer by your faults and your mistakes, are at hand to reward or punish at the next
election.

This government of upright dealing exists at present in Belgium, therefore perfect liberty is enjoyed
there; and if commercial prosperity is not yet returned, that is owing to the diplomatic position of
the country, and to causes wholly independent of
the government and the people. I do not think the
nation has much to congratulate itself upon in its
representatives: they lose too much time. As to
the Senate, it sleeps tranquilly, nobody troubles
himself about it, and it troubles itself about nobody.
The people will apply a remedy in this quarter at
the next election; but the government keeps itself
strictly within its prerogatives, with a good faith
which does it infinite honour. The courts of justice
are independent, and lately showed it in the affair
of a journalist of the orange party, who was let off,
orangist as he was; for the laws are for all alike.
Such a decision speaks equally in praise of the tribunal and the government, against an agent of
whom it was given; and makes every one feel that
he lives in a country wherein his liberty is protected.
It is objected that the government falls into the
hands of the catholics. I am sorry for it; but what
is to be done, if the majority of the nation belongs
to that faith? The nation must be altered before
a change can take place in its representation, and,

in the meantime, the only alternatives are submission or leaving the country.

I foresee your objections. A government like this, say you, could not be established in France, because Mr. Such-an-one could not remain at the head of the administration. What a capital misfortune! So much the worse for Mr. Such-an-one. But, you rejoin, here is a number of functionaries, full of ability and experience, who have sworn to and faithfully served all the successive governments of the last forty years. The nation would reject them immediately, they have not its confidence. How then shall we do to govern?—Without them. Have I not told you that it is 'GOVERNMENT BY THE PEOPLE THEMSELVES' that I seek? The governors who possess not the confidence of the governed ought, without question, to be shewn the door. The people will find plenty of persons ready to undertake the management of their affairs, nor will they be at a loss how to select them. But, you add, do you think the people are sufficiently enlightened respecting their own interests to make a wise choice?—Not, perhaps, now; and if the present rulers continue, never will be. It is like expecting a person to learn to dance while his feet are tied. But let the system of election be introduced, and in a very short time everybody will become accustomed to think of public matters. Let us suppose, for example, that in one of the least enlightened departments the people have to elect a prefect. I concede to you, that the first year they will make a bad choice. They will be ill governed, and find it out. There will certainly be two or three persons desirous of becoming prefects, and who will be obliged to go and solicit people's votes from door to door, instead of frequenting the anti-chambers at Paris, as is now done. One will say to the electors, " Gentlemen, you are governed in such a way. If I am elected, I will do so and so, and every thing will go on well."—" Every thing would go on ill," says another candidate. " The bad government of the present prefect is not owing to the cause stated, but to this. . . . . . And this is the way in which I would take upon myself to remedy it." In short, there would be as many opinions as candidates, and the people would be called on individually and contradictorily to decide these questions, and would inform themselves about them. Journals would soon be published in each department, as vehicles for local politics, and to support the different candidates. Every question would thus be brought home to each person; public affairs would become the constant topic of conversation; and, at the end of three or four elections, the people would be sure to choose proper persons.

But, perhaps, you will say, and this is the last objection I shall answer, would Europe permit us to adopt a more perfect system of liberty? Have we not been obliged to accept pardon for our revolution, by not following up the consequences? Really, I do not know that the French nation would have needed the ratification of Europe, in

order to make the changes it desired at home. And
if you were afraid of Europe, and were constrained
by fear not to follow up the principle of the revolution after having effected it, why effect it? But by
what right would the foreigner intermeddle with
what you do in France? It certainly is not by the
right of the strongest, for if the counter-revolution
has princes and armies in its favour, the revolution
has the people everywhere. They have made some
progress in 40 years, and France would no longer
find enemies among them. You have seen the sympathy excited in the English nation by the revolution of July. The old prejudices are destroyed;
an alliance founded upon common interests and
upon the force of circumstances, not upon vain
diplomatic oaths, exists between France and England, and ensures the triumph of the cause of liberty
in Europe. France free has no enemies among the
people. But in order to preserve this elevated and
advantageous position at the head of civilization, it
is necessary that it be wise, in other words, that it
be disinterested; that it does not think of making
conquests, but of ensuring the liberty and independence of other nations upon a principle of equality
and reciprocity. It was thought, formerly, that the
prosperity and riches of nations were increased by
the misery of their neighbours; but this notion has
been exploded, and it is now ascertained that there
will be no liberty nor stable prosperity for France
until she shall be surrounded by nations at once
great, powerful, rich, but above all, free. Do not

think, however, that I recommend the principle of non-intervention; I should then be a dupe. As long as kings could interfere in the affairs of nations to prevent them from attaining their liberty, the system of intervention was the political law of Europe; but since 1830, since it has been feared that France assists the revolution party elsewhere, in order to procure herself allies, everybody has adopted the principle of non-intervention. Gentlemen, this is not fair. It is necessary that we try a little, in our turn, your system of intervention, our only object being to remove the evil which it has done to us in your hands.

The fact is, however, that every nation ought to concern itself in its own affairs, and not permit any other to interfere in them; but, above all, they should absolutely refuse to acknowledge the right of an alliance of powers to take upon themselves to preside over the destinies of the world. Let them treat with all the powers individually, well and good; but let them keep aloof from congresses and conferences. Finely have they treated the poor nations whom they have been intrusted to proto-colise? Look rather at Greece, which these ten years has been under the hands of unskilful operators. France has no need of coadjutors. She desires the good of all. Her own first, afterwards that of others. Acting upon these principles, therefore, let her interfere here, refuse to interfere there; permit no further the intervention of a third party; but let her in each particular step be guided by the

nature of the thing, without being tied by any metaphysical principle, which could only render her the
dupe of her enemies, or the Don Quixote of liberty.

Let her renounce then all propagandism; let
her not suffer herself to be dazzled, either by the
tinsel of philanthropy or of Christianity; let her
not revive the times of the Crusades. But, when
her interest guides her thereto, let her assist other
nations in regaining their nationality, their unity,
their natural frontiers, and their liberty. Never
will she be sure of her own while Italy and Ger-
many are not united, free, and flourishing. The
liberty of the civilized world will be then established. The tendency of the age is not only
towards free governments, but towards the establishment of great powers, and the absorption
of small. In our day, great rivers and mountains
have ceased to be boundaries. There are roads to
go everywhere; but even if they could stop armies,
they could not stop books and newspapers. Every
thing tends to government by public opinion, to
which end unity of language is necessary. It is
language, then, which determines the boundaries of
nations. All who speak German are German, all
who speak Italian are Italian, and so of the rest.
The time will come when there will be only a
government, by language; then peace will reign
in Europe: for the great powers who compose
it will know their interests too well to dispute
for nothing, and their boundaries will be settled in
a stable manner by language.

What is to be made then of their armies, of all those turbulent elements which exist in the bosom of European societies, with this addition of population which starves them? Colonies, moral conquests over barbarism. Let the armies of the European powers quit Europe for Asia and Africa. Let there no longer remain an armed man in the mother country, unless it be to recruit continually the conquering and civilizing armies that it would keep up abroad. This was the policy of Rome in the midst of barbarians: let it once more be that of Europe. France has just set a noble example. The conquest of Algiers opens the way, and serves as an example for other conquests. Africa and Asia are large enough to offer a vast field, in which French chivalry may reap glory. As to power, France has enough.

But, I repeat it, this general peace among the *languages* of Europe, cannot take place until the nations have acquired 'GOVERNMENT BY THEMSELVES,' because it is only then that they will be governed according to their real interests, and that the equilibrium of their power will be established upon a firm footing. Once established, nothing can disturb it, and their future peace will be as well secured as that of the internal States of America.

It is there, in a few generations, that it will be necessary to go for models of the arts of peace, for I can foresee nothing to trouble theirs. But, even now, it is the American Union which gives us the best model of government. I have endeavoured

4

to describe it as I have seen it. I must admit, that
nothing in the United States has astonished me.
Everything is reasonable, and became familiar to
me with great facility; what astonishes me is that
every other nation is not governed in the same
manner.

I expect that my letters will draw upon me much
criticism. There will be superficial travellers, who
will find that I have not described faithfully. Let
them remember, that they cannot pretend to know
the country as intimately as I do, who not only
have lived there more than nine years, but who
have engaged in all sorts of business. I married
there, and there I have a family and numerous
friends dear to me, and whose esteem I highly
prize. I have travelled a good deal about the
country; am settled in the woods, where I have
seen a new nation spring up; have seen it pass
through all the possible degrees of civilization. I
am a lawyer, a planter, an officer of militia; I have
filled, according to circumstances, other offices,
either by the appointment of government or the
election of my fellow-citizens. There is not one of
the questions adverted to in these letters that I
have not discussed daily, and often in public. In
short, I am truly become an American in heart and
habits, and certainly I shall always feel myself
honoured by the title of citizen of the United States,
and by the proofs of esteem and attachment which
I have received everywhere from this nation, - a
nation the most reasonable, the most sensible, and

the least easy in the world to be dazzled. And dazzled
by what? . . . . I was poor, alone, exiled . . . .
I found there a country, which Europe refused me.

I am aware, that among the opinions I support in
these letters, many are not 'those of the majority;
but they are mine. As a free citizen of the United
States, I have a right to express my opinion upon
men and things; I have said nothing here which I
have not supported often in Florida by my vote,
and I flatter myself that my friends will recognize
my conversation in my style.

Why cannot I, my dear friend, enable you to
judge of this, and renew with you our Hirtemburg
confabulation in the garden of those good brothers
G——! We were prisoners there; but Austria has
not still found out the art of confining the mind.
It was under the yoke of its despotism that you
communicated to me the results of your long experience, and guided my young reason in the study of
the theory of liberty. I have since observed the
practice of it myself, and it is right that I present
you the fruits of my labour. Accept them, as well
as the assurances of a long friendship, which has
survived ten years of absence.

ACHILLE MURAT.

SKETCH

OF THE

UNITED STATES OF AMERICA.

LETTER FIRST.

GENERAL VIEW OF THE UNION.—*Introduction; Erroneous Notions of Travellers; New England States—Massachusets, Connecticut, New Hampshire, Vermont, Maine, Rhode Island; Central States—New York, Philadelphia, New Jersey, Delaware, Maryland; Southern States—Virginia, North Carolina, South Carolina, Georgia, Alabama, Mississippi, Louisiana, Kentucky; Western States—Old and New Countries, their comparative Advantages for Settlers; concluding Remarks.*

Wascissa, near Tallahassee, (Florida);
June 1826.

You recall to my recollection, my dear friend, the promise I made you on quitting Europe, to sketch you, calmly and on the spot, a picture of my country. Should you still retain the same desire to settle here, nothing would give me more pleasure; I wish more than I dare hope, that it may be so. But this is not to the

B

purpose; since you desire a description from me, it shall be my endeavour to satisfy you. You know my character sufficiently to feel assured, that, although prepossessed in favour of my adopted country, I shall speak of it with candour, and state faithfully its merits and defects; for, knowing that my representations may influence the serious determinations of yourself or some of your friends, I should severely reproach myself if I laid a foundation for future regrets.

If I were addressing a man of business, desirous only of information relative to the investment of his capital and the interest of money, I should say to him—look at our growing prosperity, and you will see in it a guarantee of the eligible employment of your fortune. But this is not your object, at least not your principal one; your life has been devoted chiefly to public affairs, and you would come here to find principles of government more conformed to your own. It is, then, of the moral condition of society that you require information.

Europeans who visit this country, with the exception of a few naturalists, intent only upon pebbles and herbs, confine themselves to a drive or two through our atlantic towns, and return to Europe persuaded that we are a nation of shopkeepers. These are almost all people in business, who see no other society but that of their correspondents; they have no consciousness of the government, and do not trouble themselves about it: I have heard many of them deny even its existence. Few visit the interior, or hear politics spoken; not that, in this free-speaking country, the subject is avoided from any motives of distrust, but because there is a fear of being wearisome in talking upon subjects which might not be interesting to foreigners. The consequence is, that such persons, in general, return to Europe with a favorable impression of our politeness and ability, and a notion that the government still exists because nobody meddles with it, everybody being occupied with his own affairs. There are, however, exceptions; some English travellers have penetrated into the interior, their avowed motive being to study man; but, for the most part, these have been Methodists, or other sectarians, who have viewed everything through the medium of their own ridiculous fancies. Their works, besides, are full of British prejudices, by no means favorable to their conquerors.

But even though England might, by these means, possess a correct idea of the United States, that would be no reason for concluding that

France or the Continent are equally possessed
of it. Indeed, from my own experience, I believe
that in neither are juster ideas entertained of
England itself than there are of America.

The fact is, we are much more an agricultural
than a trading people; but we are, above all, a
thinking and discussing people. Our politics
are so different from those of Europe, that the
few foreigners who do give them any attention,
absolutely comprehend nothing about them.

You have only to cast your eye over a map
of the United States, to be convinced that the
agricultural interest preponderates greatly over
those of the commercial or manufacturing.

The first grand division of the Union is between the States which recognise slavery, and
those which do not.

All the States to the south of the Potomac
and North Maryland, all those called "Slaveholding States," are entirely agricultural. The
little commerce which is carried on there is in
the hands of some inhabitants of the northern
parts; and it is only a few years ago since
Maryland first engaged in manufactures. In
all that extent of country, Baltimore is the
only city in the east, and New Orleans in the
west, which so employ capital. At Charleston,
Savannah, &c. the capital employed belongs to

merchants of New York; and the trade there
is carried on by their agents. To the north-
west of this line, the country is entirely agricultural; and it is the same with Pennsylvania,
except Philadelphia. To the north-east, the
interests are divided at least equally.

This first division involves a delicate point
in our policy. The northern States are jealous
of our slaves and of our prosperity; we envy
them nothing. All that they produce we con-
sume. They have more capital than we, but
less revenue. As long as they confine themselves to preaching against slavery, and to
forming establishments upon the coast of Africa,
&c. we shall not make ourselves uneasy; but
if their spirit of proselytism should lead them
so far as to attempt the emancipation of the
blacks, the State legislatures would put a curb
upon them; and if Congress consented to make
laws upon this matter, as it attempted to do at
the time the State of Missouri was admitted
into the Union, the finest edifice raised by man,
the American Confederation, would be destroyed;
the Southern States would be obliged to separate from those of the North: such an event,
however, is merely imaginary. The hypocriti-
cal sympathy which a certain class of men in
the North affect for our slaves, will not hasten

their emancipation by a single day; and will only render their situation, in particular cases, less supportable. This emancipation, which every enlightened man desires, can only be reasonably expected from time, and the private interest of the proprietors. To precipitate this measure would be to expose the Southern States to internal convulsions, and the Union to disorder, without producing any advantage to the Northern States.

Another great distinction observable in the character of the people, is among the inhabitants of the South, of the North-east, of the West, and of the centre. It is so strong, as to change entirely the aspect of the country.

The six New England states, Massachusets, Connecticut, New Hampshire, Vermont, Maine, and Rhode Island, form of themselves a constellation extremely remarkable among the States of the Union. Their interests, their prejudices, their laws, even their follies and their very accent are the same. They are what in the rest of the Union we call *Yankees*; a name which the English have very erroneously extended to all the nation. These six republics are one fraternity. Their industry and their capital are immense; they cover the ocean with our flag, and furnish our navy and merchant-

ships with seamen; they have also given birth
to many of our greatest men. Their character
is very remarkable, and admits of comparison
with no other people on the earth. The most
gigantic enterprises do not frighten them, nor
are they above engaging in those of small detail;
all which they conduct with a spirit of order
and minuteness quite peculiar to themselves.
These men seem born to calculate shillings and
pence, but they raise themselves thereby to
count by millions, without losing anything of
their exactness, or of the littleness of their
ordinary views. They betray a shameless
avidity after profit, and, like Petit-Jean, can-
didly tell you

"Que sans argent honneur n'est qu'une maladie.*"

This spirit of calculation and avarice is strange-
ly blended with the strict observance of the
Sunday, which they call Sabbath, and of all the
puritanical practices of the Presbyterian religion, which they have generally adopted. They
are in this respect so scrupulous, that a brewer
was reproved in church for having brewed on
the Saturday, by which the beer had been exposed to work on the Sabbath. They call this
morality, which, according to them, consists
much more in not swearing, singing, dancing, or

* Without money honour is but a disease.

walking, on Sunday, than in not making a frau-
dulent bankruptcy. This species of religious
hypocrisy is so natural to them that the greater
number practise it as a thing of course. They
glory in calling themselves "the country of
steady habits," not because they are more virtuous than other people, but because they assume a contrite air once a week, and eat nothing
on Saturdays but cod-fish and apple pies.
Boston, their capital, abounds, however, in men
of literary eminence: it is the Athens of the
Union; it was the cradle of liberty, and produced many of its most zealous champions in
the council as well as in the field. Instruction
is much more generally diffused there than in
any other part of the world. They possess, in
fact, all the elements of greatness, and evince
enlarged views, without foregoing anything of
that petty spirit of detail which mixes itself
with all their proceedings. Everywhere a
Yankee may be recognized by his adroitness in
asking questions about what he already knows,
by the evasive manner in which he answers
questions addressed to himself without ever
affirming anything, and particularly by the address with which he manages to eclipse himself
when there is something for him to pay. In
politics these six States are united, they vote as

one man. Here is the seat of the commercial
interest, although since some years, they turn
their attention to manufactures also, with the
success which accompanies all that they undertake. The country is very populous, very well
cultivated, and even in it the capital employed
in agriculture is as considerable as that absorbed
in commerce.

The central States are very far from being so
united in interest, or having so marked a physiognomy. The State of New York forms a
nation of more than a million of souls. The
city of New York contains a hundred and
twenty thousand inhabitants;* the houses built
there during the last year are not less than fifteen hundred, and it is expected that three
times that number will be built during the present. Nothing can exceed the spirit of enterprise, activity, and industry of the people. Here
are no straitened views; people speak of but millions of dollars; business is done with unequalled rapidity, and yet in general so as to escape any severe shocks: everything advances
with giant, but at the same time regular, steps.
This state of things has received a fresh impulse
from the genius of the present governor, M. de

* Now more than a hundred and fifty thousand.—
(*October* 1, 1831.)

Witt Clinton, who originated the idea of the great canal which unites Lake Erie to the sea. The internal activity of this State is so great, and so entirely absorbed within itself, as to leave none for its affairs with the Union. Accordingly, its influence is hardly felt there, for having everything within itself, it unites in its own deputation the interests of agriculture, commerce, and manufactures: the commercial interest, however, predominates. It is worthy of remark that this State has sent to the national councils very few men of superior mind. The people are absorbed and annihilated in their internal politics, which are extremely complicated, and are said to be full of very silly intrigues. A stranger can comprehend nothing of all this, but may perceive that parties are bitter and personal, two very bad signs.

Pennsylvania, New Jersey, and Delaware, form a group more resembling each other. The people are distinguished by their goodnature, tranquillity, and industry. Except in Philadelphia, the manufacturing and agricultural interests prevail. These States are in great part peopled with peaceable Quakers and Germans. Everything goes on quietly, without shock or anything to excite observation. If Boston is the abode of literature, Philadelphia

is that of science; which gives, perhaps, to its
society a tinge of pedantry.

A year or two ago, New Jersey attempted to
leap forward in the perilous career of great enterprises, and to imitate its northern neighbour,
but after committing some errors, it has now
returned to wiser principles. The legislature
this year peremptorily refuses to incorporate
new banks, and has even withdrawn the charters
of some of the old ones.

Maryland is also divided in interest, like these
other States; for while Baltimore is one of the
most trading cities of the Union, the rest of the
country is agricultural and manufacturing. The
character of the people is a singular mixture of
the simplicity and good nature of the Pennsylva-
nian Quakers, and the pride of the Virginian
planters. It is the only State in which religious
intolerance exists, rather through ancient habit
than actual prejudice; the Jews cannot vote
there. This State finds itself, with respect to
its Negroes, and perhaps in a higher degree,
in the same difficulty as Virginia.

This latter State has, during a long period,
played the chief part in the Union, by means of
its politics and its great men: it is the birth-
place of four of our presidents. But Virginia
is much fallen in splendor, for which, indeed,

it was principally indebted to party irritation. Its interests are wholly agricultural and manufacturing. The people are noble, generous, and hospitable, but coarse, vain, and haughty. They pride themselves, above everything, on their frank honesty; and their laws, usages, and politics, partake of this laudable ostentation. They are very united as a people; and never is the opinion of the State given unsupported by the suffrage of *all Virginia.* Their politics, however, are apt to be personal, factious, turbulent, and noisy. It is, beyond comparison, the State most abundant in lawyers, or at least in persons studying the law; and who, although they boast much of democracy, are the only real aristocrats of the Union: witness the right of suffrage from which the populace is excluded in this State.

Tobacco and corn are the staple cultivation of Virginia and Maryland; the first of these articles requires slave labour, the other is more profitably cultivated by free hands. Tobacco exhausts the land very rapidly, and only thrives in new and very fertile soils; hence it follows that, these lands being now nearly exhausted, at least comparatively, and the price of tobacco being diminished, owing to the quantity grown in the west, the planters are reduced to cultivate corn, and are obliged to rid themselves of their

slaves, who are no longer profitable. The day,
therefore, is not distant when we shall see these
two States unite themselves with those of the
North against the slaveholding States. However,
since a year or two, they, particularly Virginia,
have successfully undertaken the culture of
short cotton, which has given fresh value to
their negroes, and may perhaps restore Virginia
to its former splendor. But since then, short
cotton, in common with all other cottons, has
undergone a great reduction in price, in consequence of which all the southern States are
in a declining condition.

North Carolina is a bad imitation of Virginia;
its interests and politics are the same, and it
navigates in its own waters. Notwithstanding
its gold mines, it is the poorest State of the
Union, and the one which supplies most emigrants to the new lands.

South Carolina, Georgia, Alabama, Mississippi,
and Louisiana, constitute what is properly called
the South. Their interest is purely agricultural;
their productions are cotton, long and short,
sugar, rice, and maize, all which require slave-
labour, and yield a sufficiently good profit to
deter them from any other employment of their
funds. The excellence of the land, together
with the luxurious climate, so well second the

labour of the cultivator, that it is much more advantageous to employ the negroes in the field than in the factory.*   Although character necessarily varies considerably over so large an extent of country, the features of a common race are discernible.   Their frankness, generosity, hospitality, and liberality of opinion, have become proverbial, and form a perfect contrast to the Yankee character, much to the disadvantage of the latter.   In the midst of this group stands South Carolina, conspicuous for a combination of talents unequalled throughout the Union. The society of Charleston is the best I have met with in my travels, whether on this or on your side of the Atlantic.   In respect to finish, and elegance of manners, it leaves nothing to be desired, and, what is of more value with people who, like you and me, attach little importance to mere politeness, it swarms with real talent, and that without the alloy of pedantry.   In all questions of a common interest, this State always leads.   The politics of the other States, except Georgia, are not yet sufficiently of a decided character to justify me in speaking of them. As to Georgia, with pain I must declare to you, that nothing can equal the fury of its factions, unless it be those of Kentucky; in the latter,

---

* I have now some doubts of this.

however, the contention is for principles; whilst
the disputes of Georgia are merely about men.
The present governor has pushed matters so far
that the evil is in a fair way of being cured by
its very excess.

The other States form the west; incomparably
the largest and richest part of the Union, it
will be ere long, if it be not already, the most
populous; power will follow shortly, as well as
luxury, instruction, and the arts, which are its
consequences. Their interests are manufacturing
and agricultural; the former bearing the chief
sway. The character of the people is strongly
marked by a rude instinct of robust liberty, de-
generating often into licentiousness, a simplicity
of morals, and an uncouthness of manners, ap-
proaching occasionally to coarseness and cyni-
cal independence. These States are too imma-
ture to enable me to say much of their politics,
which are, for the most part, sour and ignorant.
Universities, established everywhere with luxury,
afford promise of a generation of better informed
politicians, who will have their fathers' faults
under their eyes to assist in their own enlightenment.

Our country is so happily constituted, that
we may, without great danger, make trial of a
law or a constitution. The States, like good

swimmers, support one another, and are always ·
ready to keep above water the adventurer that
may be near sinking. The Federal Constitution,
besides, is at hand, to prevent too dangerous
experiments. Its limits arrest speculation at a
safe point, and this is the prime consideration:
each citizen, to whatever state he may belong,
is obliged to consider the Federal Constitution
as the safeguard and source of that greatness
to which our Republics will be elevated.

I have spoken to you of the manufacturing,
commercial, and agricultural interests, without
defining in what they consist. You will con-
jecture, I have no doubt, that the western States
are full of manufactures, but you will be mistaken. Their interest is not constituted by the
manufactures which they actually have, but by
those which they reckon upon having. It
is two years ago since a reform of the tariff
duties was submitted to Congress. This proposition put everything in motion; the old
parties were roused, but in vain; the interest
of the people was too manifest, and they saw it
too clearly to admit of this being made a party
question. The inland towns, part of the central
States, and almost all the west, voted in support
of a measure which favored their manufactures,
present or future. The maritime towns, and

some places upon the eastern canals, composing the commercial interest, were opposed to whatever might diminish, even temporarily, the activity of commerce. All the south, uniting its interests to those of the commercial, expressed themselves strongly against the tariff. What will seem to you singular, I was, I remember, among the very few who combated this blindness. The tariff passed, but amended in such a way as to deprive it of much of its force, although enough remained to do a great deal of good, as our planters begin to find out, since an internal market for their cottons opens upon them in the north and the west, instead of their being left dependent upon foreigners. In this case, I beg you will observe, that the east and the south were united against the west: in the event of an European war, the contrary would take place, the west and the south would unite.

Independently of the two divisions I have indicated, there exists a third: the old and the new lands or countries. This division, which is explained by its name, cannot be denoted upon the map, because there are many of the new country districts inclosed within the old; however, it may be stated in general terms that the 'territories,' and all the west of the Alleghany mountains, are new. This division is the most

c

interesting to you. It is the point which you
must especially examine. Will you fix yourself
in a part of the country newly, or anciently
peopled? Both have their disagreeables and
their advantages; if you dislike trouble, are
satisfied with your position in the scale of beings,
and do not care about advancing yourself therein,
your income being sufficient to live upon,—reside
in the old countries; you will find in them the
arts of Europe, its luxury, its politeness, and a
little more hospitality, but you will be a foreigner
there for the first five years; and then all the
oversights you may have committed during that
time will be reckoned with you. Another inquiry to be made is, what profession will you
adopt? for you must not think of living here
without occupation, you would wither with
ennui, and lose all consideration. If you intend
to devote yourself to commerce, or if your early
homage has been paid to Esculapius, the old
countries offer you most resources. It is only
there that business, commercially speaking, is
carried on upon a large scale, and your licensed
murders will be lost in the crowd, whilst the
touching recital of a miraculous cure, ingeniously
inserted in the daily papers, will put into your
hands the lives and the purses of a new volley
of patients. Agriculture will bring you nothing,

and will employ all your time. It is only profitable to the small proprietors, to those who are
accustomed themselves to work at the plough.
The bar opens to you a wide field; but you will
have to contend against the first men in the
nation as your rivals, and you will infallibly be
crushed. Nevertheless, for an European, this
division of the country may be preferable: it
more resembles Europe; but if he is not very
much persecuted in his own country, or if his
love for our institutions is not extreme, I advise
him to remain at home. But, instead of that,
what if he come into our new countries; and
muster courage to plunge suddenly into our
habits, our laws, and our forests? Leaving
behind him for some years the remembrance of
partaken delicacies, let him harden himself
against privations, by a passing effort. If he
destine himself to trade, let him establish a
market where none are in existence; if to the
bar, let him be the first pleader in the first
cause, in the first term, in a new court; if he
be a physician, let him establish his reputation
where he will have nobody, not even the dead,
to contradict him; if he would be an agricul-
turalist, let him grub about new soils alone,
without a neighbour, depending only upon himself; and he will be very liberally recompensed

for his pains. He will find himself in fact, if
not in law, naturalized from the day of his
arrival, for nobody will interfere with him. If
you come from Europe or from a remote state,
you have not to struggle against established
prejudices, acquired reputations.   There all
depends on individual effort; every one must
depend upon himself. No government, in reality,
makes itself felt; no social grimace shackles
the march of the mind.   This condition of
things does not last long; four or five years, at
most, and you see start up villages, towns, universities, &c.; then you will find yourself interested in all these, and may say with pride

"Quorum pars magna fui."

And if, as many do, you retain a taste for
rural life in the woods, set out, emigrate for two
or three years towards the west, carrying with
you your light baggage, until the Pacific Ocean
stops your progress. This, however, would not
be according to my taste: I should prefer the
city of which I had seen the first stone laid, for
which I had helped to clear the ground; to
watch its rising in the magically short space of
three or six years, until it became a new sovereign State; to see new laws, a new social edifice elevate itself on a spot, from whence the
barbarous cries of the Indian had been wont to

terrify his timid prey; to hear our interests discussed, or our sinners frightened by the not less barbarous accents of a Methodist preacher. This is the step I have myself taken, feeling myself disgusted with public affairs and society, and being of too active a temperament to remain idle. For a foreigner, this step has another advantage; he almost unconsciously leaps over those five years of probation in which he is not yet a citizen, although he has ceased to be, in point of fact, a foreigner; an awkward situation, which he escapes in the wilderness.

I do not shut my eyes to the difficulties and privations with which such a resolution is attended, particularly to foreigners. The greatest inconvenience is the multitude of rogues and intriguers, who, from all parts of the United States, take up their abode in a new country, and who are sometimes so numerous as to possess themselves of the government. This, however, is but a momentary evil; the honest people, sooner or later, regain the ascendancy, which cannot be other than a very agreeable occupation. I know nothing so amusing as to be employed in shewing these gentry to the door. It is the image of a revolution, as hunting is the image of war. Besides this principal objection, there is a sort of courage necessary to sever

one's self for some years from all society suited
to the education and habits of an accomplished
man, to give up theatres, the comforts of life,
a good house, the newspaper every evening, and
one's letters every morning.

"Ici point de bon vin qui nous grise et nous damne."

We have nothing to produce the same effects
but whiskey, known to you under the name of
schnaps. We live very simply, without ostentation. All this changes in two or three years;
and, indeed, he who is so effeminate as to regard
these temporary privations as too high a price to
pay for that manly independence which I have
described, may remain at home, we do not
desire his company.

On looking over my letter, I see that it will
not be intelligible if I let it go alone. Be it so.
I regard this beginning as a sort of engagement
to furnish you with information about my country until you tell me you have had enough, or
until you come here yourself to prove to me that
I have satisfied you of the numberless advantages which our government, and ours alone,
possesses over those of Europe. I have unfolded
to you some views new to France, where nothing
is known of us but as the United States. The
twenty-four independent republics which compose them which have their constitution, their

laws, their politics, their parties; which move in sublime order, without hitherto jostling in the respective orbits traced out for them by the federal government, nobody speaks of these, nobody concerns himself about them. It is to their internal politics and their mutual relations that I propose to direct your attention.

You must contemplate the tranquil and majestic march of this republic. You can form no idea of it; you, who have only known liberty but in the midst of tempests, (in which, indeed, it has also its charms,) and attacked by parties equally subversive of its principles. Here principles are irremovably established in minds and hearts. The people are unanimous respecting the government. There are no differences of opinion but about persons and secondary measures. Shall a bank be established? shall a canal be made here or there? shall a law be made against usury? shall we send such or such an one to Congress? These are the objects which occupy not a bustling minority, but all the nation. There is a stir until the law is made, or the election over; afterwards, there is no further question about it: nobody thinks of protesting. I propose, then, to draw your attention to the internal politics of these republics, and to the relations which subsist among themselves.

LETTER SECOND.

GENERAL VIEW—ORIGIN AND HISTORY OF PAR-
TIES: *Fundamental Principles of the Government; Federalist and Democrat; Form of the
Government; First Congress; Senate and House
of Representatives, the President, their respective powers; Presidents—Washington, Adams,
Jefferson, Madison; their Characters; Election
for President; Characters of the Candidates,
Adams, Jackson, Crawford, and Clay.*

Wascissa, near Tallahassee, (Florida);
July 1826.

I HAVE said nothing in my last Letter of the
parties¹ which divide the republic. It is, however, necessary that I should do so, to complete
the general picture. If all men had the same
tastes, and all equally well understood their
proper interests, there would be no parties, no
clashing, no divisions; but neither would there
be any more alterations, diversities, or novelties;
man transformed into a mere machine at his
ease, would vegetate all the same, like wheat in
the midst of a field. Would he be more happy?
Mr. Robert Owen thinks he would; and upon
that principle establishes his new societies. For

my part, I think differently: pleasure consists only in the accomplishment of our desires, as happiness does in that of our passions; but in order that desires may become passions, there must be opposition; without opposition, then, there is no happiness, no collision of opinions out of which the truth is elicited. The powers of the mind are as different as those of the body. Hence it is that men vary not only in their desires, but in the means of satisfying them.

Herein is the distinction between a party and a political interest; the one is a matter of fact, acknowledged by every body, the other a difference of opinion respecting the means of attaining it; in the meantime, the blindness of passion is sometimes so great as to affect our real interest, and even ignorance makes us deceive ourselves. The inhabitants of the South, for instance, are in this predicament with respect to the tariff of duties: they mistake their own interest, not through the blindness of passion, but through ignorance of the true principles of political economy. In Spain, on the contrary, the miserable rabble who bawl "*Viva el rey absoluto! muera la nacion!*" must be in nothing short of a paroxysm of madness, on such a point, to mistake their true interests.

With us there is nothing of this species of
party; the fundamental principles of government are fixed. By the law, the sovereignty
is in the people; this is no more matter of speculation; whatever abstract opinion may be
with regard to this subject, here it is a matter of
fact, acknowledged by the written law of the
country. The nation is free to declare its will,
either individually, through the press, &c., or
collectively, by means of conventions and meetings, which every citizen has the right to convoke, and which take an official character when
they are composed of a majority. The constitution recognises the right of resistance to oppression. It is not, then, upon the form or the
principles of government that parties turn; it
is principally upon the measures of administration, and upon public men. Parties emanating
from such differences of opinion are favorable
to the public object; they are the winds which
make the vessel proceed, and to which it can
always adjust itself; other parties are currents
which run it aground, and hurry it away inevi-
tably to its destruction. For the rest, whatever
party fury may occasionally exist, is rendered
harmless by the habitual attachment to government, which is common to everybody. At the
last election for President, all the Union was

split into very violent parties; the day on which he was elected all these parties disappeared, or rather adjourned until the next election; but it never occurred to any body to resist the forms of the constitution, although the successful candidate had decidedly a majority against him. I have seen in the country places very tumultuous elections, drunken people, boxing, &c.; but I have never seen the least attempt to violate the suffrage-box, or the freedom of the voters.

A party does not consist only in a difference of opinion upon an isolated measure; it is a body of men having one political code, according to which they judge of men and measures, and having leaders from whom they receive their impulse more or less blindly. According to this definition, there exist only two parties in the United States; both of which, under changes of name, are likely to be perpetuated as long as the government: these are the Federalists and the Democrats. To comprehend their history, it is necessary to revert to their origin; and to explain their principles, a brief sketch of the complicated plan of our constitution will be an assistance.

When the English colonies, which had made so many sacrifices during the war with France,

and shown so lively an attachment to the mother country, were forced to have recourse to
arms to resist the tyranny of George the Third
and his venal Parliament, nobody entertained a
thought of independence; very few men fore-
saw it, and the mass of the people were opposed to it: Washington himself, at the beginning, had no idea of such a thing. The colonies
at that time formed thirteen governments, perfectly unconnected with each other, having all
a representative constitution, and receiving governors from England. A common interest induced them to form a Congress, composed of
plenipotentiaries of sovereign States. When
this Congress proclaimed the independence of
the colonies, there was still no question of any
compact among them: it was simply an alliance
against a common enemy. In 1778 these States
formed a Confederation, which was far from
being as close as the Germanic Confederation.
A Congress, composed of delegates, elected in
each State, in a different manner, voting by
States, represented during the recess by a committee of the States, had the power to make
peace or declare war, to assess among the States
the contingents of men and money, to contract
debts, to settle a federal coinage, to establish
the post, to create courts of Admiralty, and, in

fine, to decide differences among the States. The States, on their side, renounced, in time of peace, the privilege of raising land and sea forces for their own account, but nominated officers for their own contingent; they renounced treating among themselves except through Congress; the citizens of one State became entitled to enjoy in all the others the same rights as the citizens of the particular State in which they might originate; the States retained the power of regulating internal commerce; and, in general, all other sovereign rights not expressly delegated to Congress. These articles were not ratified until 1781, and in full rigour until 1787. It is easy to perceive the weakness of this compact, and that anarchy and probably war between the States would be very possible consequences. A new constitution was proposed, and, after much opposition, was at last adopted and ratified by the States; and, with some slight amendments, it continues still to govern us. The history of every federative government has demonstrated the feebleness of the authority which is compelled to have recourse to other governments. To remedy this inconvenience, it was determined to invest the federal government with power to address itself directly to individuals, and to

compel their obedience. To that end, matters
of government were divided into two classes:
objects of general and objects of private interest.
War and peace, the army and navy, foreign
commerce, the post and the mint, belong exclusively to the federal government. The civil
and criminal laws, as well as the internal administration, were preserved to the States. The
army was rendered independent of them; they
had no longer a contingent to furnish; but the
federal government might raise troops at will.
It was rendered equally independent of the
States for its expenses by the creation of a national treasury, and the power to raise contributions. A judicial federal power was insti-
tuted to take cognizance of cases between foreigners and citizens, between citizens of different States, between States, and of cases in which
the United States are party. The Admiralty
jurisdiction was given to it.*

This reform in the powers of Congress rendered necessary another in its form. Whilst it
had no authority but over the governments of

* The State of New York has always contested the exclusive admiralty jurisdiction of the courts of the United
States; but it seems that the constitution is clear upon that
point. For the rest, this difference of opinion has not yet
been decided.

the States, it might be composed only of plenipotentiaries; but when its power extended to
individuals, it was necessary that they should
be represented there. Hence the institution of
two Chambers, the Senate and the House of
Representatives. The former is composed of
two members from each State, whatever may be
its population. They are appointed for six years
by the State-legislature, and receive instructions.
The latter is composed of deputies of the people
of the United States, divided into electioneering
districts, each comprising a population of forty
thousand souls; they are not subject to any
instructions, and their functions last two years.
In both Chambers the votes are individual.
The concurrence of both is necessary to the
passing of a law.

The executive power resides in the President,
who is elected for four years, and in the Senate,
which ratifies treaties, consents to and advises
peace and war, and the nomination to the various
government offices.

The judicial power is confided to a supreme
court, to circuit courts, and to district courts.

You see from this relation that every citizen
exerts an influence on three perfectly distinct
powers, and is represented three times, or in
three ways: as a citizen of the United States in

the House of Representatives, as a citizen of
his particular State in its own legislature, as a
member of the Confederation and part of a
sovereign State in the federal Senate. The
Congress, then, is composed of two elements,
the one repulsive, the other attractive. The
Senate represents the individual interests of the
separate States, the House of Representatives
the interests of the people in general, or of the
citizens of the Union. From this order of
things, extremely complicated, but entirely new,
is produced a system of balance and counter-
poise infinitely superior to anything which
before existed. The strength of this government is incalculable. It is so constructed as to
be sensible to the least breath of public opinion,
and is powerless in opposition to it.

  This government was very imperfectly understood at the time of its introduction, and its
enemies were numerous until experience had
confirmed its solidity. Those who were in favor
of the constitution took the name of Federalists,
their opponents that of Democrats. The Federalists of that time consisted, 1stly, of people of
enlarged views, (when Washington was their
chief,) desirous of rendering the Union of the
States perpetual; 2dly, of people who found the
small States too circumscribed a theatre for

their ambition; 3dly, of a remnant of the tory
or aristocratic party, who saw in the adoption
of this constitution a great step gained towards
a monarchy, or a re-union with England. This
last division of the Federalist party was, for a
long time, at the head of it, but it has now completely disappeared. The Democratic party
was composed, 1stly, of genuine republicans,
intoxicated with the momentary triumph which
the peace had just given them over England,
and much too confident in the strength of the
separate States; 2dly, of some ambitious men
who, having figured in their own State, antici-
pated that they should be eclipsed on a new
theatre in which they did not feel themselves
sufficiently powerful to appear; 3dly, of some
sensible people upon whom the fear of a monarchy was stronger than that of a division of
the Union.

At that time the French revolution was extending its benefits and its ravages over all
continental Europe. England, unable to sub-
due it, calumniated it in its newspapers, which
where the only ones read here, owing to the
identity of the language. The Federalists
compared the Democrats to the Jacobins, and
prognosticated the same anarchy if they
triumphed; whilst the Democrats called the

D

Federalists agents of England, enemies of national independence, aristocrats, &c. This first division continued and created a French and an English party, which lasted during the government of Bonaparte. At this time, these parties (who were only Federalists and Democrats disguised under other names) played a part more decidedly national, by means of the continental system, the effects of which were felt even by us. The inhabitants of the sea-ports, and all that I have described to you as constituting the commercial interest, here, as was the case in Europe, became anti-French, and, consequently, English and Federalists. Those, on the contrary, who thought like Jefferson and Patrick Henry, considering the great towns as the ulcers of the republics, were confirmed in their principles.

The restrictions on commerce caused a general irritation, which was increased by the arbitrary measures of England; people began to foresee a war. The Federalists feared it, and opposed themselves to it, whether because they thought that it would enfeeble the federal government, or because they did not like the idea of uniting with France against England, or, in short, because it appeared to them that commerce would suffer still more by a war, even of short

duration, than by the shackles imposed on it
by the belligerent powers of Europe. The
Democrats, on the other hand, saw in the war
a fair chance of the States regaining their primitive independence, and of humbling England.
Full of a noble national spirit, they dared to
flatter themselves with success in so unequal a
struggle. Events thus gave birth to two new
parties, those of war and peace, which were
still but the old parties considered under a
different point of view.

Washington was elected president at the
time of the acceptance of the constitution.
He was one of the first to recommend an union
as close as possible among the States; and
although he was too wise and too firm to
become either the chief or the tool of a party, he
was generally thought to favor the principles of
the Federalists. His firmness towards the
ambassador of the French republic confirmed
this opinion. To his administration succeeded
that of Mr. Adams, who was all English, all
tory; and became so unpopular, that he could
not get re-elected. The excess of his Federalism
turned the scale in favor of the Democrats, who
elected Mr. Jefferson. Without possessing, to
speak fairly, talents so superior as have been

represented, he was a philosopher, a scholar, and an amiable man.

Never did anybody render himself so popular, and understand so well how to organize a party. He was so much master of his own, that, whatever measure the administration proposed, took immediately the name of Democrat, and was carried by that party. We had, during his presidency, an opposition party, who, as in England, blindly opposed the administration, and called itself Federalist.

Mr. James Madison, who had commenced his career with the Federalists, but who afterwards occupied a distinguished. rank in the other party, succeeded Jefferson in the presidency and in his influence over his party. He declared war. This measure occasioned a schism in the Federalist party, and soon after its apparent destruction, and the abandonment of the name. I have stated that some of the Federalists were republicans and patriots, whilst others were aristocrats and English. The former. resided principally in the south, the latter in the north and east. Both opposed going to war as strongly as they could; but no sooner was it declared, than the former joined the army, and shed their blood for the common cause, whilst the others opposed themselves to every defensive measure.

Parties, at this epoch, were to be found acting in perfect opposition to their principles. But for the idolatry of the Democrats to Jefferson, and the excitement of passion, the constitution would probably have suffered by war; but this was, in point of fact, what consolidated it for ever. The Democrats, in spite of their mistrust of the Federal government, voted an army of one hundred thousand men, and some direct contributions, (which they considered as unconstitutional and impolitic in the general government;) they restored the navy, which Mr. Jefferson had annihilated, and by their confidence in the administration, increased its energy tenfold, by putting the militia in motion, in all the States in which they were masters. The Federalists, on the contrary, threw every obstacle in the way of government. The governor of Connecticut refused to call out the militia upon the demand of the President. In short, after two unfortunate campaigns, chiefly through the fault of those in the north, deputies from the different States of New England assembled at Hartford, to consult on the means of putting an end to this unnatural war, (as the partisans of England called it.) This convention was secret; it sent a deputa-

tion to Washington; but it arrived just at the moment of peace, and therefore made no communication.   This convention has been accused of
desiring to separate the New England States
from the Union; but, as its deliberations were
secret, nothing certain can be affirmed on that
point; and I wish, for the credit of those gentlemen, that it may not have been so, although
I havesome doubt on the subject.

If the war had not always been very successful, nothing could be more glorious than the
peace by which it was followed.   It sealed the
triumph of the Democratical party.   That party
had succeeded beyond its most sanguine hopes,
and made the most of victory.   The Federalists
who took part in the war, renounced a name
now become odious, and it ceased to be applied
except to the members of the convention at
Hartford and their partisans, by way of reproach.
All the newspapers, all the speeches, &c. proclaimed the cessation, the triumph, or the
reconciliation of parties, each according to his
colour; but it was well understood that party
existed no longer.   All irritation disappeared,
and the very names were forgotten except in
election disputes.

You will not fail to see, however, that these
two parties, (in the primitive sense of their ap-

plications, divested of all accidental circumstances,) are the essence of government, and
under different names ought to be perpetuated.
They serve as counterpoises to each other, and
preserve the government in a right medium. A
single observation will suffice to dissipate any
fears that may be entertained of their future
influence; it is that neither of them desire to
alter the constitution, but both have a whole-
some fear of its destruction; the one through
the encroachments of the Federal government,
the other through those of the governments of
the States. They are two vigilant centinels,
whose object is negative and preventive.

It seems that at the present session of Congress
these two parties are to appear divested of all
external ornament. The treaty of Georgia, with
the Creeks, and the internal improvements-
question, will probably give rise to a division. I
shall apprise you of what passes.

You have no doubt seen that the newspapers
make a great deal of noise about the last election
for President, and I have no doubt that many
persons in Europe have expected that a civil
war was on the point of breaking out. Nothing
could be more ridiculous than such a notion;
the parties of whom I am about to speak were
nothing of importance; all the irritation arose

out of the personal opinions which each person entertained of the candidates. It is true that a remnant of the Federal party bestirred themselves in favour of Mr. Adams, whilst the opposite opinion, the Democratic, was divided between his three rivals. The local, or sectional feelings, entered greatly into this Election. All the east voted for Mr. Adams, whilst the west was divided between Jackson and Clay: Georgia was for Crawford. If you would know the history of it, here it is. First of all you should know that the manner of electing the President differs in the different States. Each State sends a number of electors equal to its delegation to Congress; they vote individually; but in some states the people vote for all their electors together, which is called election by General Ticket; in others, the people are divided into districts, each of which nominates an elector, this is called voting by District; in others, the electors are nominated by the legislature. If none of the candidates have one more than half of the votes, the election devolves upon the House of Representatives, who are obliged to choose out of three candidates who have the most voices in voting by State.

Four candidates offered themselves, all men of considerable talent, but whose merit was differently estimated by every one: some exalting them to the skies, others calumniating them without measure. Here are their names and their titles to recommendation:

1st, John Quincy Adams, of Massachusets, son of the former President. The greater part of his life has been passed in public employments, but always out of the United States. He has been professor of Belles Letters, and is altogether a literary man. He was always of the Federal party, until lately that he has been endeavouring to depreciate it. He is remarkable for his style, and his reserved and diplomatic manners; and is of the school that believes it is necessary to deceive the people, in order to govern them. At the time of the election he was Secretary of State.

2d, Andrew Jackson, of Tennessee; educated for the bar, where he distinguished himself: at the commencement of the last war, he headed some militia, and displayed great military talents against the Indians. Appointed to the command of the army, he gained the famous victory of New Orleans, and saved, by his civil no less than his military talents, all the west from invasion. He has always been a Democrat; he is distinguished by his austere Republicanism, his courage, the clearness of his views, his uprightness, probity, and purity, above all suspicion. At the time of the election, he was member of Congress for the State of Tennessee.

3d, W. H. Crawford, of Georgia; his career has been chiefly legislative and diplomatic; he has been ambassador to France. He too has always been a democrat; if he is remarkable for anything, it is for a turbulent spirit of intrigue and corruption. He was Secretary of the Treasury at the time of the election, and he is reported to have made the influence which that office gave him subservient to his private views.

4th, Henry Clay, of Kentucky; his career has been legislative; he was one of the plenipotentiaries to Ghent. He is distinguished by his eloquence, his address, his talents as a lawyer, and his personal amiability. He was Speaker of the House of Representatives, and possessed great influence among them.

Jackson lost the election by very few votes; Adams followed him at a distance; and Crawford followed close upon Adams. The House had then to choose out of these three Candidates. Their respective strength in the House, where the vote is taken by States, was found pretty nearly equal, and the election depended upon the part which the friends of Clay would take. They sided with Adams. Public opinion loudly denounced this election, for Jackson had un-

questionably a very considerable majority over
either of his competitors. The nation thought
that its will should have been law to its representatives. The clamour redoubled when, as
the first act of his administration, the new
President appointed Mr. Clay Secretary of
State. From one end of the Union to the
other were to be heard cries of scandal, corruption, and venality. These reports were perhaps
exaggerated, but the proofs of an odious bargain
seem to me too clear to be rejected.

In Europe, what would have been the consequences of such an election, in which the
choice of the people had been defeated by intrigue and the most shameful corruption? A
civil war would have taken place, and during
some years there would have been two Presidents.
Here there was nothing of the sort. Everybody
submitted to the law, promising himself to take
care not to be duped at the next election. There
cannot be a more majestic spectacle than that
of a nation submitting with dignified silence
under the yoke of laws of its own ordaining.
Although the present President is, in my opinion,
the worst choice which the representatives
could have made, and although I do not expect
anything great from the present administration,
I think, however, that this example of submission

to the law, will have the happiest effect on the
future. Public opinion, moreover, is so strong
here, that, whatever may be the administration,
it is carried along with it; and if it does not do
good, it cannot do any harm. Would not such
a state of things be desirable everywhere?*

I forgot to tell you that on the 18th of January
we laid, at Tallahassee, the first stone of the
future capital. A year ago, this was but a
forest; now there are more than a hundred
houses, two hundred inhabitants, and a newspaper. On this occasion an excellent oration
was delivered, and there was a dinner of fifty
persons. Is not this magic?

---

* The parties adjourned after the election of Mr. Adams
by the House of Representatives, and at the next election
Andrew Jackson was elected by an immense majority. He
is the actual President, and although his administration has
not come up to the idea his friends had formed of it, it is
probable that he will be reelected for another term of four
years.

LETTER THIRD.

DESCRIPTION OF THE NEW SETTLEMENTS.—*What is meant by a Territory; Indian Traders, (white men); Indians; Squatters, their habits and characters; Nature of the Country; Formation of the Territorial Government; Sales of Public Lands, preparatory proceedings, general bustle, the auction-day a day of great interest, results of the sale; New Residents; a Post-office established; increased Facilities and Comforts; New Plantation; First Court of Justice, singular arrangements; Office of Delegate; A Country Election, mode of conducting it, its humours and oddities; Situation of the New Planter; Supplies from the North; Lawyers, Pettifoggers, Jobbers, their manœuvres; Celebration of Holidays, a Barbecue, a Ball, the band; Session of the Legislature; The Territory becomes a State; concluding Remarks.*

Lipona; July, 1826.

You ask me what is meant by a territory? a question, though not very easy, I will however attempt to answer.

The picture I am about to bring before you will remind you of those heterogeneous beings

spoken of in the Greek fables; you will behold
a new Proteus continually changing form under
my pencil.   May the copy possess in some degree the interest of the original.

It is nothing less than the birth of a nation,
and the history of its progress to maturity, that
I am going to sketch to you.   Do not smile,—
you will see it in a dozen years raise itself
gradually from barbarism and ignorance, to
the summit of civilization.   This is a miracle,
of which twelve States present the confirmation;
and, at this moment, three infant States, which
are yet as it were upon the stocks, afford us the
opportunity of observing the process of this
transformation, and of taking nature in the act.
Here we see pass under our eyes, and may
study, what historians represent to us as the
labour of ages.   These countries resemble the
enchanted gardens of Armida;—people and
nations multiply in an eternal spring:

E mentre spunta l'un, l'altro matura.

TASSO.

You have no doubt been struck, on looking
over a map of the United States, with the small
proportion which the States occupy.   Did you
ever ask yourself by what process these immense
countries, which belong to the Confederation,

are peopled and governed? I will endeavour to
tell you. Without entering into a history of
any particular territory, my relation may serve
as generally applicable to them all.

The Indians occupy the space beyond the
limits of the States, and even within many
lands, which, either willingly or otherwise, the
Confederation give up to them by little and
little. When I speak of Indians, I must not be
understood precisely to mean savages. It is
here indeed that the wonderful process of
civilization commences: many nations or tribes
to the west of the Missouri, who have never
seen a white man, nor had direct intercourse
with him, are, without doubt, savages; but the
Creek, or the *Cherokee*, enclosed in the midst
of civilization, cultivating his lands, having
organised a representative government, and
established schools, is more civilized than the
Irish or Austrian peasant.

A white man arrives among a nation, still
entirely savage, and living in all the barbarism
and pride of ignorance and anarchy; this man
is in general what is called an Indian trader. An
intrepid hunter, a shameless cheat, he undertakes the perilous trade of going across countries, and through unknown dangers, to sell to
the Indians, powder, arms, coarse stuffs, but

particularly whiskey, in exchange for skins.
They in general settle upon some navigable
river, at the extreme circumference of civilization.   These white men usually live with
Indian women, who serve them as interpreters.
Every year they come into some large town to
supply themselves with provisions, and are for
a long time the sole medium of communication
between the man of their colour, and the red
man.   Very soon the Indians not only accus-
tom themselves to the conveniences of life, but
can no longer do without them; and, instead of
hunting, as formerly, for their means of subsistence, they now do so chiefly with a view to profitable traffic.   Thus is the first degree of civilization established.

On the other hand, the American hunter forms
a class as enterprising as intrepid.   The return
of an Indian trader, with a rich booty, brought
from a yet unexplored region, in which he has
found the chase abundant, the earth fertile, the
water salubrious, very soon causes an emigration
of men of a like sort.   How shall I describe
them to you, after COOPER, in his *Pioneers,*
and the *Last of the Mohicans*?   They are
inimitable.   I refer you to those two romances:
there you will see that they adopt the life of
the savage more from inclination than necessity,

and that they unite to his address, his patience, and his daring courage, the softness and humanity of the white man. It is by them the knowledge of the new countries is first gained ; they explore every part of them, and spread reports more or less exaggerated.

The Indian, meanwhile, does not remain stationary. He can no longer do without a gun, some powder, liquors, and blankets; he settles himself near some dealer, and begins to buy horses and cattle. The introduction of tools offers him the facility of building excellent huts; the women (squaws) begin to clear all the ground adjacent, and to plant a little maize and tobacco; in short, Indian villages spring up in the desert. The Indian trader does good business; other dealers follow him; the country becomes inundated with hunters; they mix with the Indians, and are not long without having some dispute with them. It is generally on occasion of one of these disputes, which almost always terminate in war, that the government of the Union interferes for the first time. The Indians kill the whites whom they meet, and sometimes even advance into the midst of the settlements, and massacre women and children. The hunters, on their side, continue the war with no less ardour, and are not long before they receive the assistance of some troops of the line, or of the militia of a neighbouring State. The Indians are defeated, their huts burnt, their cattle destroyed, and hostilities terminate with a treaty of peace, after they have been taught to appreciate the power of the United States.

The Indians select chiefs, who assemble upon some central spot, where they find prepared to meet them, commissioners from the United States. There they have a *talk*, or conference. The articles of the treaty are in general the following: 1st, the Indians renounce the greater and more fertile part of their lands, and the government, under the name of *reserve*, guarantees to them such part of it as it thinks proper. 2d, the United States pay to them an annuity, part in cattle, tools, agricultural implements, and provisions, and part in money. 3d, the United States establish near the nation an agent, without whose permission no white can trade, nor even pass the frontier. 4th, the Indians also are not to pass their limits without a passport from the agent. 5th, it is to him that both the Indians and the whites must carry any complaints they may have to make against each other, and he is to see justice done between them. 6thly, the United States establish an

agency house, a blacksmith, a carpenter, and
a schoolmaster, for the use of the nation. 7thly,
if the crops have been destroyed, the United
States allow rations until the next season.
Some of these reserves are still found in the old
States, and even in New England. Thus packed
in, the Indians apply themselves to agriculture.
In some instances in the south they have pros-
pered, and are become civilized; but, in general,
they have fallen into idleness and misery, and
diminished in number to a frightful extent:
some tribes, once powerful, are now utterly
extinguished.

But let us leave the Indians and turn to the
white population now extended around them.
The war which has taken place has made the
country of which it has been the theatre better
known; the government begins to take an
interest in it, and establishes there, within
reach of the agency house, a military post composed of forty men, troops of the line.

The first species of settlers, or cultivators,
is what we call Squatters. These are poor
citizens, generally not very industrious, who,
not possessing the means of buying land, live
upon those of others, and work them until they
are expelled by the proprietors. Their poverty
is entirely the fruit of their idle and drunken

habits, for those among them who are industrious never fail to make a fortune. There are,
however, many of them who,. although industrious, and with the means of rapidly augmenting their substance, pursue this sort of life
from choice, from taste, and, perhaps, even from
habit. For the most part, they have a wife
and children, some negroes, and, sometimes,
very numerous flocks. They rarely raise two
crops from the same land; on the contrary,
they quit a district as soon as it becomes
peopled. Under their hands the country soon
assumes a new aspect: every seven or eight
miles rise up huts, formed from the trunks of
trees. Iron is too dear for them to permit
themselves the use of it; wood, therefore, supplies its place, even for hinges and locks. One
of these huts may easily be constructed in two
or three days; one may see them spring up like
mushrooms. More than once when on horseback in the woods, in search of my horses or
strayed oxen, I have met in the very midst of
the forest, a cart loaded with household furniture and children, and one or two men escorting
about thirty cows and hogs. After the questions, Where do you come from? Where are you
going? which are always cordially answered,
the head of the family has asked me some

details relative to the country, and requested me to direct him to the creek, or the nearest spring. A week after I have been astonished to see a good hut there, a field of cattle, and some poultry; the wife spinning cotton, the husband destroying trees by making a circular incision in them, called a girdle, —in short, settling their household gods without making any inquiry as to whom the land belonged. Frequently, also, I have seen them, after a few days' sojourn, abandon their dwelling for the slightest cause, and transport themselves—God knows where. This population of Squatters is sometimes very numerous; it attracts the speculator in cattle and the pedlars, a sort of travelling packs, who do not differ from those of Europe, except that their shop is in a cart.

Among these first settlers, of whom some are destined to make large fortunes, whilst others continue always wandering, there exists no form of government; every dispute is amicably terminated by the fist. As they live out of the United States, they have neither election nor politics; the land or the houses have, in their eyes, but a secondary value; they attach the idea of property only to the cattle; each of these has its mark; and if any are stolen, he assembles his neighbours, and, the proofs in hand,

they go together to the thief, and administer to
him a punishment more or less severe.   According to their morality, cow stealing is the greatest
crime; no laws yet exist; and, in the meantime,
the population increases in a way to make Mr.
Malthus and his friends tremble for the consequences; religion is limited to the observance
of Sunday, and to going to hear some wild
Methodist, wandered into a country which he
soon abandons, as too poor and too laborious
to work upon.

Around the huts which I have described, the
eye opens upon irregular fields; the trees are
still standing, but dead; props of cleft wood
surround them.   Numerous pathways, well
beaten and indicated upon the barks of the
trees, lead from one hut to another, and some
cart-roads wind across the forest in the shade of
the old trees.

In the meantime the eyes of the enterprising
citizens of the neighbouring States are opened
upon this rich booty; some of them go to look
at it; it is mentioned at Congress.   Government
proposes to form into a territory the space
between such and such limits; a bill defines the
form of the territorial government; in this first
stage it is as follows: 1stly, the executive
power is vested in a governor, appointed by

the President of the United States for a fixed number of years. He appoints to the territorial offices, and has the power of pardoning offences against the territory, and of delay when the offence is against the United States: he is assisted by a Secretary of State, who is also Treasurer. 2dly, the legislative power is in a council, composed of twelve members appointed every year by the President of the United States. They have a general power of making laws, which must, however, be sanctioned by the Governor, and may be rejected by Congress. 3dly, the judicial power consists of a judge for every district into which a territory may be divided; he unites the jurisdiction of the United States and of the territory. 4thly, a delegate is every two years elected by the nation to represent it at Congress, where, however, he has no vote. Thus is completed this very simple government, which I must now show in action.

The second step, which generally follows very closely the creation of a territorial government, is the establishment of a land district. I have already said that all the vacant lands belong to the United States; the question is how to sell them. In all the States which have been admitted into the Union, this rule does not hold good; at Kentucky there existed land warrants from the State of Virginia, to which the country originally belonged. In Louisiana and in Florida, concessions of land made by the old governments, and the rights acquired by the old inhabitants, from real or pretended purchases from the Indians, occasionally produce a perplexity as to titles, which it is sometimes found impossible to adjust. For this purpose, recourse is generally had to an administrative commission, who, without deciding upon the conflicting claims of individuals, confines itself to separating the alienated lands from those remaining in the power of the United States: it is only of those of this latter species that I now propose to speak.

There exists at Washington a department for the public lands, in correspondence with the different districts into which the country is divided. When it is proposed to create a new district, this department assigns the external limits, and, in general, a central spot destined for the building of a city, probably the future capital of the State. A Surveyor-General is appointed; he removes with his family and assistants to the starting place; from this point, with the assistance of the compass, the surveyors begin by sketching the base and meridian, going north and south, east and west, in a direct

line, across woods, marshes, rivers, &c.; the
line is marked upon the trees, on each side of
the chain, in such a way as to make it easy to
follow. Every six miles the surveyors fix a
post; from these posts other lines are drawn
parallel to the base and meridian, which divide
the country into squares of six miles. Each of
these squares is called a township, and is numbered according to its position; each township
is afterwards divided into squares of one mile,
by lines traced upon the trees, in the same
manner but with different marks; these second
divisions, called sections, contain six hundred'
and forty acres, and are divided by imaginary
lines into eighths, of eighty acres each. The
sections and eighths are numbered in each township, and these numbers are indicated upon the
posts found at the corners, so that on meeting
with a line in the midst of the woods, and following it to the corner, one knows where one
is.* One provision is very important; the section No. 16 of each township is appropriated
to defray public education, and cannot be sold.
This operation gives employment to many
people, the Surveyor-general usually making

* For instance, the house from which I write is situated,
eastern half of the S. E. quarter of section 8, township 1,
range 3, S. E. from Tallahassee.

advantageous contracts with the surveyors, for
so much work as he may think proper. The
maximum price fixed by the law is four dollars
per ordinary mile, which is not too much, if one
considers that each surveyor must have six or
seven men with him to assist him.

While these geodætical operations are taking
place, the government gets organised; the
governor, generally a distinguished man, and
intending to settle in the territory, arrives with
his family and negroes. The judges arrive in
their turn; the lawyers follow them, with what
*Figaro calls "all the ravenous law-shops of the
country."* All these official persons have families and friends who come to settle. The legislature assembles in the middle of a wood; a
log-hut is erected, a little larger, but as rudely
constructed as usual; and there the rustic
assembly sits with as much dignity, and often
with as much talent, as it could do in the capital. What can be the subjects of legislation, it
will be inquired, in a society so new, and of
which, so to speak, there exists but the frame-
work; they are these: to determine a spot for
the capital and other towns, if deemed expe-
dient; divide the territory into counties; organize
the justices of peace and the superior courts;

* "Toute l'enragée boutique à procès du pays."

make civil and criminal laws (for this assembly,
though held in tutelage to Congress, is already
sovereign); in short, to petition Congress upon
all subjects that it may deem proper.

This first session of the council gives an
immense advance to the territory; but that
which gives it body is the sale of the public
lands. The President, when he thinks proper,
issues a proclamation, announcing, that at such
a time and place, certain public lands will be
sold. A register and a receiver are appointed
by the President, and the great auction day at
length arrives, a day of the highest importance
to the little growing society. Immediately on
the issuing of the proclamation, the country
begins filling with strangers; some seeking for
lands to settle in as soon as possible; others for
a son or a son-in-law; others merely speculators,
who buy only to sell again. These all spread
themselves over the country with their com-
passes in hand, according to the marked lines,
examining the lands, taking notes, keeping profound silence, and avoiding one another. Perhaps some of them have bought from a surveyor
the supposed secret of an excellent and unknown
section: little portable plans, mysteriously figured,
circulate privately. Nothing is talked of but
lands, their qualities, probable prices, &c. In-

trigues and knavery the most unblushing display themselves in all their lustre.

The rising capital in which this sale takes
place has, however, assumed a form since the
session of the council. A plan has been adopted;
the streets have been cleaned; the lots sold on
credit; a capitol or court-house has been decided
on. A crowd of people are waiting at the sales,
at the courts, at the assemblies of the legislatures. Taverns rise up, empty the greater
part of the year, their open walls are filled on
these memorable occasions beforehand. The
cloth is laid for thirty persons. Two or three
large rooms, which you would not deign to call
barns, receive, in a dozen beds, twice that number of occupants; those who cannot find better
room extend themselves in their bed-clothes on
the floor. No places reserved for dining or sleep-
ing; we are too much of republicans for that.
Every one pays his dollar, and has a right to
eat and sleep where he pleases, provided he
does not disturb a former occupant. It is
understood that a bed contains two individuals,.
and nobody is so ridiculous as to trouble himself
about who is next to him, any more than in the
pit of a theatre.

The great day at last arrives. The crowd of
busy and curious people is augmented; the

speculator, the jobber, are in motion and con-
sultation. The farmer, whose object is to settle,
is calm: he has limited his views, and fixed his
price. The hour approaches: the poor squatter
runs about the town; he has been labouring all
the year that he may buy the land upon which
his house is situated; perhaps, for want of a
dollar or two, it will be taken from him by
greedy speculators. Anxiety and trouble are
depicted upon his honest and wild countenance.
A jobber accosts him, pities him, and offers to
withdraw his pretensions for the sum of three
dollars; the poor simpleton gives them to him,
not doubting that the jobber cannot now bid
against him. This is what is called hush-
money. The crier puts up the lands by eighths,
beginning by a section and township in regular
order; the prices are different, but the sale
always opens at one dollar twenty-five cents per
acre;*. this is the lowest price at which the
United States sell. An old Indian village, a
situation for a mill, the plantation of a squatter,
a place to which a road or a river leads, or
which seems likely to become the seat of a city
or entrepôt, are so many circumstances which
augment the value of lands tenfold or more;
all the sales, too, being made according to lines

* Lately reduced to 75 cents.—*Translator.*

real or imaginary, it often happens that the field
or dwelling of a squatter is found cut in two.
The sale, and the bustle which it occasions, continue until all the lands contained in the proclamation have been offered; those which remain
after that in the possession of the United States
may be entered for 100 dollars per eighth.
Those, then, who are acquainted with the good
lands, and know that they are the only ones, do
better to wait till this time; for there being no
competitors, they obtain them at a low price.

And now, the sale being over, the speculators,
their titles in their pockets, have returned home
to see what will come of them; the planter is
gone to seek his negroes and his family; the
poor Squatter is returned to his home with a full
heart, not having been able to realise his hopes,
and being obliged to go still once more in search
of a spot on which to settle; it may be also,
that he is hired, as manager, to the planter who
has bought his house and lands. For the rest,
it must be observed, that it is the planter's
interest to leave the squatter upon the land until
he has need of it himself, for his presence
doubles the value.

Meanwhile the inhabitants of the townships,
particularly the innkeepers, have made a good
deal of money. Instead of their log-houses, ele-

gant houses of timber-work and planks, painted
all sorts of colours, have risen, as if by enchant-
ment, in the midst of the woods, now called a town.
Trees are felled on all sides; the burnt stumps
indicate the streets and public places. The
importance of the place is soon augmented by a
post-office (there was none before,) and the residence of a post-master, an important personage;
for, in the present state of things, the accession
of a family, or even of an individual, is not a
matter of indifference. By this time newspapers are abundant; every one, besides a paper
from Washington, or from some Atlantic town,
receives that of the village from which he has
emigrated; for every village has its own, and
we shall soon have ours. Reviews and magazines, literary journals, novelties of every sort,
come to us from New York, Philadelphia, and
England, at a moderate price, and a month or
two after their publication over the Atlantic.
I had read, I have no doubt, the last romance
of Sir Walter Scott before it had reached Vienna.
But let us leave the city at this point, and see
if the country places have made progress in
proportion.

The planter having returned home, sold his
lands and house, and added to the number of
his negroes, has set out with all belonging to

him; his goods and provisions in carts, his negroes on foot, himself and his family in a wheeled carriage, or on horseback, according to his circumstances. They encamp every evening, traverse the deserts, open ways, make bridges, and arrive at last upon the new property. The first thing to be done is to build huts, from the trunks of trees, for the negroes and the family; this takes two or three weeks: during which time they bivouac. A field is soon opened and planted; but the great difficulty is to subsist the first year. Maize is scarce, always dear, and carriage very expensive. Happy is the squatter who has made a good crop and can dispense with it, if he is near a planter. He gets his own price, he "enters" his lands, becomes a planter himself, and lays the foundation of an independent fortune. And now, instead of little irregular clearings, for small huts scattered among trees, we have great ones of fifty to a hundred acres, for the first year, surrounded with good fences or hedges; villages, with regularly-built huts for the negroes, and a large log-house, containing three or four very convenient rooms, with kitchen, stable, &c. for the family. These buildings, it must be admitted, look very miserable outside; but go in! This country is

the country of contrasts: within this almost
savage habitation you will find a family as well
brought up, and as intelligent, as you do in
Boston or New York. Its manners are not
rustic; it has left the world for a time, and is
engaged in creating a new one around it. It
receives its letters, its newspapers, and is
acquainted with the politics of the day. In
one of these establishments you will often meet
with some one whose name you have been
accustomed to read with respect in the newspapers, figuring with eclat at Congress or in
the State legislatures. This is some citizen
come to lay the foundation of a new country.
The women, in particular, support their privations with a patience truly angelic, soften by
their presence the excessive wildness of the
scene, and produce a most singular contrast.
A planter never comes alone; he persuades some
relations and friends to emigrate with him, or
at least to come and see the country; the
greater part of these visitors settle there. In
the midst of this infant plantation, and of this
circle of old acquaintances, he lives happy and
tranquil at home, and it is but seldom that
business calls him out.

He is, however, obliged to serve upon the
jury, for the first court is about to sit, and the

F

sheriff is come to summon him, and to dine with
him. A judge arrives, generally a man of
merit, but not unfrequently, in this state of
society, the refuse of the other tribunals. No
court-house is yet in existence; the judge therefore selects the largest room of a tavern or a
spacious loft. I have seen the court sitting in
a warehouse, in which planks laid upon barrels
of pork or meal formed the seats of the audience. A court-week is of course an occasion of
excitement and profit for the inn-keepers. The
people come in crowds from fifty miles round,
either on business or out of curiosity. The
epoch of this concourse is turned to account by
all those who have any thing to gain by the
public; one offers his negro for sale; another
exhibits the graces of his stallion, that he may
attract customers; the lawyers look out for
clients; the doctor for patients. The sheriff
opens the court and calls the causes, the noise
ceases. Upon a couple of planks are ranged
twenty-four freemen, heads of families, house-
keepers, forming the grand jury. What an
assemblage! from the hunter in breeches and
skin shirt, whose beard and razor have not met
for a month—the squatter in straw hat, and
dressed in stuffs manufactured at home by his
wife—the small dealer, in all the exaggerated

graces of the counter, sitting beside the blacksmith;—up to the rich planter recently arrived:
all ranks, all professions, are here confounded.
Silence is commanded. The lawyers begin their
pleadings with more or less talent. The judge
makes his charge with as much dignity as if
he sat at Westminster, and the verdicts savour
nothing of the whimsical appearance of the
court and the jury. In the evening the court
adjourns till the next day, when the same scene
takes place. It must be added, that the pleaders
harangue the people in the taverns upon the
justice of their cause, &c. This is also the
moment selected by candidates for the office of
delegate to present themselves to the people;
they and their friends are busy in gaining the
suffrages of the multitude by every possible
means of persuasion, and sometimes of deception. Stories of the candidates are, by turns,
related and denied; each harangues, or gets his
friends to harangue, the people in his behalf.
Disputes ensue and finish, in general, by boxing,
particularly towards evening, when temperance
is not the order of the day; for each candidate
has treated his friends.

It is, however, in the country places that an
election should be seen. The day arrives. For
some months previous the candidates and their

friends have been in motion, making their calls
from habitation to habitation, trying to persuade,
accuse, explain, &c. In general, the friends
take more trouble than the candidates themselves. The governor, by proclamation, fixes
the day, and divides the country into precincts,
in each of which he chooses a central house,
and appoints three election-judges. These
three dignitaries of a day, meet on the morning, and swear, kissing the Bible, to conduct
themselves with integrity, &c. They seat themselves round a table at a window. An old cigar
box, duly patched up, with a hole in the lid,
a sheet of paper, and a writing-desk, form the
materials of the establishment. Every one
presents himself outside of the window, gives
his name, which is registered upon the paper,
deposits his ballot in a box presented to him,
and withdraws; if the judges doubt his quali-
fication as to residence or age, they administer
an oath to him. Within the room every thing
passes in an orderly manner; but it is not the
same outside. The wood is soon filled with
horses and carts. The electors arrive in troops,
laughing and singing, often half tipsy since the
morning, and exciting one another to support
their favourite candidate. They or their friends
present themselves to the electors as they

arrive with ballots ready prepared, often printed, and expose themselves to their jokes and coarseness. Every new comer is questioned about his vote, and is received with applause or hisses. An influential man presents himself to vote, declares his opinion and his reasons in a short speech; the tumult ceases for a moment, and he draws away many people after him; nobody offers to molest him. In the meantime the whiskey circulates; towards evening every body is more or less tipsy; and it is not often that the sovereign people abdicate their power without a general battle, in which nobody knows what he is about, and in which all those who have managed to retain their carriage take good care not to embroil themselves. Every one goes home to sleep. The judges scrutinize the suffrages, and send the result to the capital. The next day beater and beat are, as good friends as if nothing had happened, for every one has learned, from his childhood, to submit to a majority. *Vox populi, vox Dei*, is here an absolute axiom. It should be observed, that the public interest does not suffer from these tumults, because, generally, every one has made up his mind long before voting, and holds to it, drunk or sober. The excitement of an election is very soon over. Before it takes place nothing else is talked of; the next day there is no more question about it than about the great Mogul.

The post of delegate is the most sought after of any in the territory; for, besides the advantage of being a member of Congress, of passing the winter in the midst of feasts and the best company, of being personally known to the most distinguished persons in the Union, his influence over the destinies of the territory is immense. He is consulted, ex-officio, upon all that regards it, and it is generally upon his presentation that the offices are filled. He has been making promises to the people which he will try to fulfil. These will probably be roads, canals, post-offices, to change the districts of the courts, to augment or diminish their number, to obtain gratis public lands for the purpose of building towns, to erect bridges, to increase the number of members of the legislature, to have such a law confirmed or rejected, &c. He will succeed in some of these objects, and fail in others; his party will endeavour to justify him, the other will find everything wrong he may do; and amidst this conflict of opinions, it is an even bet whether he will be re-elected, the more so, as, during his two years of office, the interests of the population will have changed, and even the population itself.

The first year the planter is provided by what
he has brought with him; provisions, tools, and
everything he requires to clothe his negroes,
but it is otherwise afterwards. Assorted cargoes
are sent from the Atlantic towns by our immense
rivers or canals; warehouses are established in
the rising towns; they yield large profits, for
in them everything fetches two or three times
its value. The first things sent are provisions,
such as beef, pork, and salt fish, ham, butter,
bacon, spirits, different sorts of meal, and stuffs
for the family and the negroes, cast-iron, earth-
enware, saddlery, ironmongery, medecine, &c.
Everything is sold pell-mell in the same shop
by the same person. The dealer, who, in general
is only the co-interested clerk of some great
northern house, usually brings with him his
family, and also the graces and fashions of the
great town from whence he comes; he dresses
himself in a most incredible style, and forms a
perfect contrast to the rest of the population.
He does in general very good business, although
he is often obliged to give credit to the planter
until the next harvest. He engages almost
always the productions of the country from
whence he sets off to the north, when the first
cargo is exhausted, and to which he returns
with a new assortment.

The lawyers of every description, from the
juris-consult to the notary, also arrive. Our
country abounds in poor devils, without any
pecuniary means, who, however, have received
a sort of education. They study the law without
external assistance, engaged at the same time
in some trade, or in the army, a counting-house,
or a tavern: and as soon as they can sustain an
examination, get themselves admitted, and live
by it. I need not tell you how many of them
spring from nothing. Being generally pettifoggers, the greater part seek to sow dissentions
among the poor ignorant people, and involve
them in law proceedings, during five or six
sessions, solely to extract a few dollars. Nothing
can be more respectable than the bar at the old
States, but nothing more miserable than the
assemblage, who, in a new country, multiply
round a court. Many of these gentry, however,
become, through practice, very skilful in their
profession, make money, and acquire principles
and consideration. Some lawyer regularly educated for his profession, however, very soon
comes to establish himself in the country: he
monopolizes the practice, and the fees; and the
pettifoggers, thus eclipsed and annihilated, are
obliged to quit or to seek their fortune in some
other way.

It is at this period that the territory becomes
the prey of vagabonds, bankrupts, jobbers of
every sort, who appear to meet here from every
part of the Union.   Before, the country was
too poor, and did not offer any prey of sufficient
importance; and, at a more advanced period,
their tricks and pretensions are seen through.
There is, however, a species of sharpers who are
worth a separate notice.   I have mentioned that
up to this period our territorial proprietors had
a great part of their lands conceded to them by
the former government.   Jobbers buy for a
mere nothing the doubtful titles from the poor
original grantees; frequently they make false
titles, or buy lands from the Indians, which is
contrary to the law, and therefore nul.   They
get drawn out some fine well-coloured plans of
their possessions; and if the titles are doubtful,
they have lawyers ready, who, after due consul-
tation, pronounce all clear.   Provided with these
instruments of deception, they go into a country
in which emigration is commencing, and exchange their imaginary lands against any sort
of real property.   You can have no idea of the
address and talent which some of them have
displayed, and of the extent of their plans.
They sometimes become powerful enough to
shackle the march of civilization.   They gain

much influence by their impostures, and are
sometimes able to control the elections.

But this state of corruption is never of long
duration: the population increases every day,
society becomes formed, and these vampires
are obliged to withdraw. The first indication
of regular society is generally public holidays.
The 4th of July, the day of independence; the
22d of February, the birthday of Washington;
the 3d of January, the battle of New Orleans;
are so many occasions. Sometime, before a public meeting is convened at a tavern, and a chairman and secretary (for everything is done in
form,) are appointed by acclamation. An orator
proposes to celebrate the day, and gives his
reasons; afterwards another moves that there
be a dinner; the proposition is discussed, and
is opposed for want of a room large enough to
contain those who would desire to partake of it.
Another proposes a barbecue,—dining in the
open air: this is supported, and carried; another,
that a speech be delivered: carried also.

Somebody proposes a ball; but there are only
three ladies in the town who dance. Had there
been four, assuredly the motion would have
passed. The meeting appoints a chairman, and
a managing committee, and separates. The
resolutions, duly signed, are inserted in the

newspaper, (for already there is a weekly one,)
to the great satisfaction of the editor-printer,
who is short of matter.   On the day appointed,
the citizens form themselves into a procession,
and proceed to the church, or the tavern, to the
court-house, or to a granary, according to circumstances, and hear a speech, which is in
general sensible and eloquent; for I must always
remind you of the contrast which is found here
between the man and what surrounds him.

From thence the meeting repairs under the
trees, where an ox and some pigs roasted, await
them.   The expense is defrayed by subscription,
and toasts are given expressive of the political
opinions of the people.   The following year
there are another barbecue, speech, and ball.
The ball is also by subscription.   This time the
court-house has been prepared for the purpose;
the judge's bench is occupied by an old negro
scraping the violin, accompanied by two little
negroes playing the tambourine and triangle;
tallow-candles illuminate the scene; but the
women are as pretty and as smart as at New
York.   The planter has doffed his coarse hunt-
ing-jacket, and drawn from his trunk the blue
frock of former times and of another country,
and his manners are those of the best society.

The defects of the music do but augment the mirth of the dancers.

In the mean time the sessions of the legislature have been held, and every year has witnessed an accession to its numbers. The government has taken its seat; courts of justice, respectable for the talents of the judge and of the bar, have been established in each county; every year the number of these has been doubled. Taxes upon negroes, cattle, &c. have been imposed; charters of incorporation have been granted to different towns: the time has arrived to pass to the second degree of territorial government. This consists in giving to the people the election of the Council, and other privileges in the judicial organization, on which I cannot enlarge without entering into too many details of a technical nature. The people are not long before they experience the benefits of this self-government. Public opinion takes a decided character; the intriguers and sharpers reform or quit the country; in short, the last steps are made with the greatest rapidity. Emigration continues in geometrical progression; capital accumulates; a public bank is established. From year to year a census is ordained.

At last the desired period arrives, in which

the territory counts forty thousand souls, and
it is admitted to the rank of a State. A convention is assembled to organize its constitution,
which consists always of an elective governor,
and two legislative chambers. The legislature
sends two senators, and the people a representative, to Washington; and the new State begins
to revolve in its orbit, augmenting its strength
by such or such an interest, and affecting the
equilibrium and political balance in the senate.

In this rapid sketch I have not spoken of
religion, because, usually in this state of society,
it is a disgusting imposture under the name of
methodism, or baptism, and I care not to speak
of it. In proportion as the people become enlightened, religion, however, becomes more pure,
and one may judge of the progress of civilization
by the establishment of a presbyterian church,
but particularly by that of an episcopal one,
which is best of all. In the state of society
which I have endeavoured to describe, education
and religion are conjoined, and go hand in hand.
Preparatory schools, in the hands or under the
influence of the ministers, and academies in the
hands of some Yankees, are all which exist.
But as soon as the territory becomes a State,
and often even sooner, the sixteenth section
becomes its property, and is available to the

establishment of a permanent fund for public education, employed either in detail in each town, or centralized in universities, colleges, &c. This subject is, however, of sufficient importance to be treated of separately.

I have only spoken of the south. I have never travelled in the north-east parts of the United States. I imagine, however, that my description in great part applies to them also, if you suppress the negroes, and suppose the squatters more active and industrious: religion also enjoys there a more considerable share of attention; the land speculations in the north, have also, I believe, been made in a more liberal spirit. The speculator is not contented to wait the result, but improves the lands by making roads, establishing factories, and farming them out to others. These variations are decisive, but I cannot follow them into their details.

I shall conclude this sketch with one important reflection. We have bought Louisiana of France, and Florida of Spain. These countries were peopled, and had laws in general so opposed to the spirit of our government, that when even they shall have attained the necessary population to become States, a territorial government will be immediately required to amalgamate them,

and break their ancient habits. It would not
be the same with the British possessions upon
the Continent, and in the West Indies; they
are organized in provinces which have their
legislatures and their laws. To unite them to
the Union, nothing is to do but to admit and
receive their senators and representatives at
Congress. But God preserve us from them!
The augmentation of influence which the
southern interest would receive, would be far
from equalling the proportion which would
accrue to the north. In the present state of the
Union, it is the only chance of dissolution which
menaces it. In twenty years, when the south
shall have gained an ascendancy sufficient to
secure its interests from danger, this accession
of territory will be desirable; but much more
for the subjects of his Britannic Majesty than
for us.

LETTER FOURTH.

On Slavery.—*Erroneous Notions on the Subject;
the Question argued on the principle of Natural
Right; Purchasers at Guinea; Necessity of
having Slaves in New Countries; Political Advantages; Advantages to the Slave; Character
and Treatment of the Negroes; Description of a
Plantation; Treatment different in different
places; Laws concerning Slavery; Free Negroes;
Difficulty of the Question respecting them;
Societies in Favour of Emancipation, &c.; the
Colonization Society; Conclusion.*

Lipona; February 1827.

I am sorry to see that you partake of the prejudice, too general in Europe, against our
southern States. Like many other things,
slavery seen from a distance has quite another
physiognomy than when seen near. The
severity of the law is softened by its exercise;
abuses destroy each other, and thus the horrible
and monstrous in theory become frequently
perfectly tolerable in practice. It is, then, to
correct your notions, and to give you a just
idea of the condition of our negroes, that I

devote the present Letter. Upon our continent
and islands there is no subject more important;
and I often ask myself, how does it happen
that out of so many writers of travels in America,
not one has given to it the attention it merits?
You may find, indeed, in some English travellers, disgusting and exaggerated pictures of
the filth of the negroes, and the cruelty of the
masters, but I defy you to show me a page of
common sense on the subject of slavery.

Without changing the condition of the working classes and, consequently, all the social
relations; without creating entirely different
manners, and exercising the greatest influence
over religion and education; slavery is and will
be the grand pivot on which our internal politics
must turn. Its influence is felt in all our parties, even in those which seem to have the least
connexion with it.

I shall not refute the gross and ridiculous
calumnies against the slave owners; they are
not worth the trouble. It is not sentimental
pathos that must be opposed to the general
practice of all ages, but sound arguments, well
founded in morality and, above all, in political
economy. Why have not the friends of the
blacks had recourse to this mode? Calumnies
and prejudices owe their existence in Europe

G

chiefly to British jealousy. The English ministry, desirous of preventing emigration to the
United States, have condescended to employ
mercenary authors to write travels full of lies
against the people and the government. In all
these books, which have been very popular with
John Bull, slavery is always made a very pro-
minent feature.

Another cause of error is the growth in
England, and, as a consequence, the establishment here, of certain religious sects, having a
theocratic tendency, and of which I shall speak
to you another time. They seem to imagine
that they ought to save our souls at the expense
of our lives and properties; and the English
ministry, to avail itself of their influence, has
been obliged to second them. It is to these
sects we owe the suppression of the slave-trade,
and the laws to protect the liberty of horses;
and to them also England will, ere long, owe
the loss of her West India colonies; for the
proceedings of its government are diametrically
opposite to reason.

The motives which a man may have for not
becoming an owner of slaves, can be but of
two classes: they must be founded either on
right or on calculation. I shall endeavour to
destroy them; and, first of all, justify the right

of the master, in order to show you afterwards
that, at certain periods of society, this order of
things is equally advantageous to the slave and
to the master. There can exist no doubt upon
the question of right, where there is a desire to
be explicit and to be understood. Error has
arisen from considering the right as an absolute
thing, whilst it is always relative in respect to
custom and to the person. According to individual right, which everybody improperly terms
natural right, the individual has a right to
appropriate to his use any external object, and
to destroy every obstacle which may oppose his
wishes. Whether the subject of his desire be
a stone, a plant, or an animal, does not at all
affect its subjective quality as an external object
or an obstacle. But the individual can only
judge subjectively. It must be borne in mind,
however, that this right of the individual is
relative but as it respects himself, for the
obstacle has an equal right to appropriate the
individual to its use, or to destroy him; in this
case he changes place and name. A man meets
a lion : he has incontestibly the right to appropriate to himself the lion's skin, but the lion
has a right equally incontestible over the flesh
of the man. But, as the one defends his skin,
and the other his flesh, it happens that the

spontaneity objective of each of them becomes
an obstacle to the other which he has a right
to destroy. Here, then, are two unquestionable
rights placed before us: there does not, nor
cannot, exist between them any arbiter but the
great general laws of nature. The man does
not pretend to make the lion acknowledge his
right to skin him, or to punish him if he do not
submit; he pretends to force him, to constrain
him.

The social state brings about great changes
in the rights of individuals; however, the three
following rules may be regarded as indisputable.
1stly, Societies act among themselves as individuals act between one another, without being
regulated otherwise than by individual (natural)
right. 2dly, Societies act according to the
same right towards individuals who, in respect
to them, are foreigners. 3dly, The members of
a society recover their individual independence
towards objects foreign to the laws of that
society.

A man catches a horse and tames him. Has
he acquired any right over that horse in respect
to that horse? No: he has the right to appropriate the horse to his use; the horse has the
right to throw him to the earth, and to gallop
away. The laws of nature, which secure

victory to the strongest, but above all to the
most skilful, decides this conflict of individual
right. The horseman has, however, acquired a
social right over this horse, not towards it, but
towards society; society is engaged to protect
his industry and his labour, and to secure to
him the use of their fruits. It will interfere to
prevent this horse from being killed or stolen;
if it escape, society will assist the horseman in
re-catching it, will permit him to exchange the
advantage he may have acquired by its labour
against any other advantage acquired by another, and to substitute that other in his rights.

Without doubt, a man has no right over
another man in respect of that other; nevertheless he may have a right over him in respect
to society. Firstly, if, both being members of
society, they are bound by any contract whatever, the violator of the contract commits a
moral offence, for which he merits a punishment from society proportionate to his offence.
Secondly, if one only of the two be a member
of society, and if it guarantee to that one any
rights whatever over the other, in such a case
there being no contract, there can be no moral
offence, nor no punishment; but in case of
resistance, a combat, which each has a right to
push to the utmost, and in which the member of

society has a right to demand its assistance. In fine, the slave has as much right to resist his master, and to make his escape, as the master has the right to appropriate him to his use, and to constrain him to obedience. There exists no contract between them, consequently no reciprocal right: for one social right can only be founded upon another. Error has arisen from wishing to attach to the slave a moral duty of passive obedience, which is absurd; for that would suppose a contract, in which all the advantages would be on one side, and all the disadvantages on the other, a contract which is nul *ipso facto.* The master has, meanwhile, as much right to be supported in his authority over his slave as over his horse.

But let us leave these abstract considerations and come to particular cases. At the time of the colonization of America, there certainly did not exist any contract between the Indians and the whites; they had then, reciprocally, the right to appropriate each other to their respective uses, and to destroy one another whenever they might think proper. According to the eternal laws of nature, the weakest in physical power, but the most skilful, triumphed, and the natives were reduced to slavery in all the Spanish possessions in America, which were then inha-

bited by a soft and effeminate people. It was
not the same in the United States; warlike
nations resisted the attacks of the whites, and
often exercised their right of destroying them,
and appropriating their spoils to themselves.
The whites treated with them, and concluded
by making, with most of them, conventions,
more or less advantageous.

All labour deserves its price. Merchants
went to the coast of Guinea, and there purchased slaves from nations who had no compact
with theirs; these slaves were sold either in virtue of the laws of their society, which considered slavery as a legal punishment, or because
they had been taken in war, and appropriated
to the use of the conqueror. But the merchants
might have taken them for nothing, as that
would not affect their right. If I catch a wild
horse in the plains of Missouri, the trouble of
taking him and taming him, the risk that I run
of his escaping, are all considerations which
constitute the price I pay. The intervention of
society is limited to satisfying itself that none
of its members had an anterior right to my booty.
Every society has, without doubt, the right of
regulating the labour of its members, and of
interdicting such and such species of industry;
but, in the present case, quite the contrary hap-

pened. All the nations of Europe, more or less, encouraged the slave trade. Many colonies attempted to resist the introduction of slaves into them, but were forced, by the metropolitan towns, to open their ports to this traffic; thus were the masters supported, not only by abstract right, but by the express and positive legislation of the society of which they were members.

The revolution on our continent, although almost simultaneous, was, nevertheless, partial; each colony preserved its independence through-out the struggle, and when the Thirteen United Republics were acknowledged, though a central government was established, they remained not the less sovereign States, perfectly independent of each other in everything concerning their internal legislation. At the time of the revo-lution, a portion of the United States had already got rid of their slaves; since then, their example has been imitated by others; and, at a future time, more will probably imitate it, but some of them are so situated as to make it absolutely impossible for them to do without slaves, and these States will probably continue to have them for a long time to come. No authority has the right, or has ever pretended to have it, to regulate their domestic affairs; yet questions, relative to slavery, are every day submitted to Congress. The United States, who possess the exclusive right of regulating commerce, have prohibited the slave-trade since 1808. Nobody complains of this measure, which was announced long before; but I do not hesitate to say, that any attempt to make laws respecting our slaves would compel the southern States to separate themselves from the Union. This is an obligation founded upon the right which every man has to defend his life and property. Would you believe that there are people so foolish as not to be sensible of this, and so short-sighted as to be willing to run the risk?

The general opinion in the southern States is, I believe, that slavery is necessary, but that it is an evil. I am far from considering the matter in that light; on the contrary, I am tempted to consider it, in certain periods of a nation's existence, as a good. How, for instance, can great capitals be employed in agriculture in a new country, without slaves? To this resource we owe the rapid population of our deserts. Just as the marble formed into a statue is first dug from the quarry with the pickaxe, then cut by the chisel, and afterwards polished by the file, so is it necessary that a savage land, before it becomes capable of receiving an eminently civilized people, should

previously possess different classes of population.
There must be a succession of tools to cultivate
the soil, no less than a succession of books to
educate a man, and a succession of institutions
to educate a people. In countries cut off from
the north, where all the land is fertile, where
numerous rivers render communication easy,
where the heat of summer is tempered by sea-
breezes and the elevation of the soil, a population of small proprietors may establish themselves, and enjoy, in a few years, all the conveniences of life. But in the immense southern
plains which are watered by great rivers, only
at considerable distances; where the good lands
are in an infinitely small proportion with the
eternal heaths, where the heat of the climate
renders labour in the open air fatal to any white
man; large capitals, and a black population, are
necessary to put the earth into cultivation. If
small proprietors alone attempted similar settlements, they would become entirely cut off from
civilization, and exhaust their resources in
carriage and stores. Labour would be too dear
for them, for it would be necessary to pay for
the risks that every one run for his life. Great
capitalists, on the contrary, discover the oasis
of the desert, transport all at once, an entire
population, open roads, make bridges, drain

marshes, and after some years of expense, realize immense profits. Under the protection of these great proprietors, the country soon abounds in people of moderate fortune. Ere long the great fortunes are divided, by the death of the possessors; small proprietors subsequently take their places; the number of these latter increase; they become naturalized to the climate, and from that time partake the labour with the negroes, to whom the climate is extremely salubrious, for it is never of heat that they complain. Lands, which are now considered of no value, are thus brought into cultivation, as soon as all the good lands are taken, and the pasture-system begins to be adopted.

If slavery, in political economy, facilitates the population of our southern States, its effect on society is not less advantageous. The planter, released from all manual labour, has much more time to cultivate his mind. The habit of considering himself as morally responsible for the condition of a great number of individuals, gives to his character a sort of austere dignity favourable to virtue, and which, tempered by arts, sciences, and literature, contribute to make the southern planter one of the most perfect models of the human race: his house is open to every comer with a generous hospitality; his purse is too often equally so, even to profusion; the habit of being obeyed gives him a noble pride in his intercourse with his equals, that is to say, with any white man, and an independence of views in politics and religion, which form a perfect contrast with the reserve and hypocrisy to be met with but too often in the north. To his slaves he is a father rather than a master, for he is too strong to be cruel.

In politics the effect is not less favourable. Our country is still young, the population is thinly sown, every one has his business; here are no idle people, no cockneys, no populace; but it will not be always so. Already, in the great northern towns, on many occasions, tumults have arisen among the working classes and the sailors. Are we destined to see renewed among us the scenes of the Roman forum? To protect us against such scenes, shall we have recourse, as in England, to the cavalry? The remedy would be worse than the evil. An insular State has nothing to fear from similar commotions, for the other States would come to support it; but what would become of the Union, if Congress were to be dissolved by, or be subjected to, the populace of Washington? To deny citizens the right of voting, because they have not a certain fortune, as Virginia has done, is, no doubt, one way; but that is contrary to the spirit of our institutions, and the fixing of this sort of regulation is always arbitrary; besides, that would never prevent the people from conspiring. Compare the elections in the great cities of the south, and of the north; what tumult in the one, what tranquillity in the other. In the north the inferior classes of society tumultuously invade the election places, and drive away, so to speak, by their indecent conduct, every intelligent and enlightened man. In the south, on the contrary, all the inferior classes are blacks, slaves, mutes; enlightened people conduct the elections quietly and reasonably; and it is perhaps to that alone that may be attributed the superiority of talent which may be remarked in the Congress of the United States in favour of the south.

Hitherto I have only spoken of the comparative advantages of slavery, as it respects the masters; but the slaves are the first who profit by this state of things. In all countries, and in all times, a great majority of the human race is condemned to subsist by manual labour; and I do not doubt that this portion of society is more happy in a state of slavery than otherwise. Compare the condition of our negroes,

well clothed, well fed, and having no care for
tomorrow, no trouble with regard to their family;
compare it, I do not say, with the degraded
race of free negroes and mulattoes, having all
the burden of liberty, without any of its advantages, but with the white labourers of
Europe, working two or three times as much,
and always, in old age, dying of hunger, they
and their families. I do not scruple to say that
our negroes are more happy, not only than the
labourers in the English manufacturing towns,
but even than the peasants are generally in any
part of Europe. You will tell me that the
mere idea of liberty counterbalances the privations and disquietudes to which this same
liberty gives rise. I will answer that is true,
as it respects you and me, but that there
must be a certain degree of instruction, a certain moral energy, to relish the noble idea of
liberty. Take an Austrian, Hungarian, or Bo-
hemian peasant, transport him into America,
and tell him that he is free: the first Sunday
he will find nobody to waltz with him; he will
curse the country, its liberty, and its elections,
and prefer returning to his *Schatz*, to his *Ver-
walter*, to his *Wirths-Haus*, and to his *Roberth*.
On the other hand, if you transported one of our
Squatters into Europe, making him partake of

all imaginable advantages, the idea of being
obliged to acknowledge a superior would render
him miserable. Those who, in destroying the
feudal system in Austria, imagine that they will
ameliorate the condition of the peasant, deceive
themselves grossly, unless they commence by
enlightening him; this change in his mental
condition ought to precede, for he will not live
happy while he feels his moral degradation.
This is nearly the case with the free negroes and
mulattoes in some parts of the Union; but
our slaves are happy, and do not desire any
change.   Although the contrary has been
asserted, the negro is incontestably an inferior
race of man to the white, and does not seem
capable of the same intellectual enjoyments.
Why have they remained savage from the commencement of the world until the present day?
Why do they become savage as soon as they
are left to themselves, as is the case at this
moment at Hayti.   Their felicity is limited to
animal felicity, and that they enjoy more liberally
in the state of slaves than they could do either
free or savage. This picture does not accord,
no doubt, with that of Mr. Wilberforce and his
saints. But you will ask me, how can a negro be
happy under the whip of an overseer, continually exposed to see himself separated from

his family, or to see it dishonoured by the libertinism of a master or a manager? All this is pathos misapplied. I hire a white labourer; he forces the door of my warehouse, robs me, is discovered, and condemned to the public works, dishonoured for life, and loses the little morality and honesty he had; his evils are perhaps aggravated by those of his family, to the support of whom his labour was necessary. Let one of my negroes do as much, he is whipped and corrected. The bodily pain once undergone, he feels no bad consequence from it, and innocent children do not suffer for the fault of their father. Whatever may be said on the subject, cruel punishments do not take place, for they would be contrary to the master's interest. If a hired labourer do not work, I send him away; but I cannot thus get rid of my negroes, and I am obliged to force them to work by corporal punishment. In large plantations, in which some hundreds of negroes are united, a discipline and rules of police, more or less rigorous, are necessary, without which every thing would soon be destroyed or stolen. As to seeing themselves separated from their family, it is necessary, first of all, that they have one; generally they attach themselves to a woman and keep to her; but they are often

inclined to change. Those among them who
are religious marry, it is true, at the church, but
every time they have a change of wife, they do
the same; and I know some of them who have
been married a dozen times, and have as many
wives living, each of whom has as many husbands. As to dishonouring the young negresses, that would indeed be curious. It is in
vain that their modest blush is hidden by the
colour of their skin. How many times have I
learned, with affright, that my young friends had
quitted the bed which my hospitality had prepared for them to slip into the cotton-house!
I dreaded seeing, the next day, my negro Vir-
ginius immolate his daughter Dolly; but not
at all; the good father was too sure of her
virtue. I have seen him smile at the tempter,
and politely ask him for a quid of tobacco, as if
in mockery of the inutility of his efforts. As
to the virtue of the old negresses, mothers of
families, who would have the courage to meddle
with it? Far from this state of things being
an aggravation of the condition of the slaves,
I consider the perfect liberty they enjoy in this
respect as a sort of compensation for their ser-
vitude. Although the masters try to encourage
marriage, by throwing in the way of the con-
tracting parties a number of little advantages,

H

it is not often that a negro marries upon the
plantation where he lives; he likes better to go
to his neighbour's.

A well-regulated plantation is, in truth, a
very interesting spectacle: every thing prospers
and goes forward there in a perfectly orderly
manner. Each negro has a hut; in general
they are disposed in regular order; he has some
poultry and pigs to himself, grows his own veget-
ables, and sells them at market. At sunrise
the sound of a horn calls him to labour; every
one has a task proportioned to his strength and
abilities; in general, this task is concluded
by three or four o'clock in the afternoon; at
noon the labour is interrupted by dinner. The
task done, no more work is required of him; he
cultivates his garden or hires himself to his
master for some extra labour, or rather, goes to
see his wife or mistress upon the neighbouring
plantations. On the Sunday morning he puts
on his fine clothes and goes to the habitation
to receive his weekly ration: he employs the
rest of the day as he pleases, very often in
dancing. The overseer has only to give out
the tasks in the morning, and to see, in the
evening, that they are all well performed. The
master takes a turn on horseback over the
fields, and gives general orders; all this goes

on by rule, like a regiment; and I have known
six months slide away without having even to
scold. Nevertheless, there are, from time to
time, quarrels and thefts to punish. At Christ-
mas, the negroes have three days' rest; twice a
year the stuff necessary for their clothing is
given to them, which they make up themselves,
according to their taste.

Those who live in the house are treated
exactly like the white servants in Europe;
they are, in general, born and brought up in
the family, of which they consider themselves
as forming part; there they become very much
attached and very faithful; every time the
master has a child, he gives him immediately
a little slave of its own sex and age, who is
brought up with it, and becomes its confi-
dential servant. The little negresses, or mulatto girls, thus brought up in the house, are, in
general, excellent sempstresses, and often very
pretty; the mistresses pay great attention to their
morals, particularly if they live with ladies of the
family; if they conduct themselves amiss, the
punishment they most fear is that of being sold.

Besides these two classes of negroes, there
are many labourers, such as carpenters, black-
smiths, tailors, &c.; in general, the proprietors
let them on hire, and treat them like white

labourers.   Very often the masters content
themselves with requiring an annual compensation for their skill, and allow them to let themselves out as they please.

Does this picture, which is a true one,
resemble the absurdities printed by the missionaries? It is easy to take a particular case,
to exaggerate it, to generalize it, and afterwards
to compose declamations.   There does not
exist, it is true, any law to protect the slave
from the ill-treatment of the master; but he
has, in public opinion, a stronger protection than
all laws; the man who would let himself be
carried away by his passions, in the way
described by some English writers, would lose
for ever the character of a gentleman.

The negro husbandman is not treated everywhere in the same manner. In Virginia and
Maryland, for instance, the farmers do not give
them task-work; they lodge them in large brick-
houses, have their provisions cooked for them, in
short treat them like the farm-servants in Europe.
The consequence is, that the slave, losing sight
of the distance which separates him from the
freeman, is discontented at not being quite his
equal, and at not receiving wages; he becomes
insolent, is punished, deserts, is retaken, and
finishes, probably, by being sold to an emigrant

in some new country, who soon brings him to
submission. In these new countries the proprietors, in general, besides the old family
negroes, carry away all that their means permit
them to buy. A certain degree of severity,
therefore, becomes necessary, at first, to restore
order to this heterogeneous mass; the more so,
as the labour, being irregular, cannot be divided
into tasks, and that the new slaves try the character of their master; a little energy on his part,
however, soon terminates this time of trial and
disorder.

It would be impossible to give you a digest
of the laws concerning slavery, for they vary in
different States. The constitution of the
United States secures to the master the right
of pursuing his run-away slave into the States
in which slavery is not recognised; the particular laws of the different States afford every
facility to the master in the like case. To steal
a slave, or to aid in his escape, is almost
everywhere a capital offence. A negro, free or
slave, cannot travel without a passport; and
every white has, in that case, a right to arrest
him, and to deposit him in the nearest gaol,
where he is detained, if he cannot prove his
freedom. The children follow always the condition of the mother. The penalty of death is

inflicted on the slave who attacks a white, or
resists him violently. The testimony of a slave
·is not received in a court of justice against a
white. In fine, almost everywhere the penalty
of death incurred by a slave, may be commuted
in his sale, on condition of his exportation from
the State.

The laws concerning free negroes are much
more complicated, and have given rise to much
discussion both in and out of Congress. The
equivocal situation of this population renders it
very dangerous to our Southern States; it is
they, and not our slaves, who are discontented;
it is of them, and not of us, that these latter are
jealous. All the Southern States have laws to
regulate emancipation, which, in general, cannot
be granted, but on conditon that the emancipated slaves quit the State within a certain time.
They are submitted to a very severe police, and
in some places, to particular taxes. In some
States they are obliged to have guardians of
their property; in most they may be sold to pay
the debts contracted by their former masters
before their emancipation, or even to pay their
prison fees, if they are stopt travelling without a
passport, or a certificate of their liberty. It
seems, in short, that the main object of legislation in the Southern States is to diminish this

unfortunate, but dangerous, class, or at least to promote their emigration to the north; but they cling to the southern climate. And, besides, it is a gross mistake to suppose they are better treated in the north, or in New England. In thirteen of the twenty-four States they are not admitted to vote by the constitution; and in almost all the others there are particular laws which prevent them; it is only in Pennsylvania and New York that they possess that right.

By very severe laws, some of the southern States have prohibited the importation of free slaves, and have subjected them to severe penalties if they willingly violate those laws. The constitutionality of this measure has given rise to a question which is not yet decided, and which will not be, probably, for a long time; it is a delicate one, and nobody likes to grapple with it. The constitution of the United States (art. 1, sect. 2, §1ᵉᵣ) declares that every citizen of a State shall enjoy, in all the other States, the rights which their citizens respectively enjoy. But a free negro of New York is a citizen of that State, and, consequently, of the United States; but a free negro of South Carolina is neither a citizen of that State nor of the United States; the free negroes of New York pretend to enjoy at Charleston the rights

of citizens. In the south, it is objected to
them, that they ought to be assimilated to the
free negroes, and not to the citizens of the
States in which they may happen to be. When
I say that they pretend, it is not them,—they do
not care about voting,—but it is their white
friends who raise this pretension for them.
The question has not yet been decided, and
everybody holds by his own explanation.

At the time of the admission of the State of
Missouri into the Union, in 1820-21, an article
of the constitution of the new State, which prohibited the admission of free persons of colour
within its limits, gave place, in Congress, to a
long and dangerous debate; the article was,
however, approved, with the condition, that it
should not be applicable to any citizen of another State; which is only embroiling the matter
more and more, instead of elucidating it. The
discussion upon the admission of this State,
commonly called "the Missouri question," violently agitated the Union, and, at a certain
period, threatened its dissolution. To avoid
grappling with similar questions, some States
have imposed a poll-tax upon every free individual of colour, and even authorize his sale, if
he cannot pay it otherwise. Is not this measure
as unconstitutional as the other?

This class of free men of colour is very embarrassing, for if, on the one side, common sense says, that once free, they ought to be entirely assimilated to the white citizens; on the other side, a prejudice, stronger than any reason, retains them in a state of moral degradation, and excludes them from any honourable occupation. This prejudice is even stronger in the east, where they are treated with much more contempt than in the south. They are very dangerous to our slaves, who envy their idleness; they have among them preachers who are connected with the religious societies of the north, of whom I shall speak presently, and who do not cease to work upon our slaves, in order to make them discontented. If you reflect, that the life and property of every inhabitant of a southern State are concerned in these measures, you will not fail to see that, constitutionally or not, we cannot give up on that subject; and that a separation from the Union would take place, if the attempt were made to constrain us. However disastrous this step might be, it would be better to hazard it, than to be annihilated. With us these questions are not speculative, they affect the private interest of every one; it is then ridiculous to seek to persuade us to the contrary. You would much de-

ceive yourself, however, if you thought we run
any danger. The Union is as safe on this side
as on any other; the division of interests and of
opinion only serve to produce an agitation and
often tempests, which prevent the political ocean
from stagnating. In fact, who are they who desire the sudden emancipation of our slaves?
Enthusiasts or religious hypocrites. It is true,
that these noble Don Quixotes have a mighty
support in public opinion in the north; but can
that be compared with the unanimity of the
south, founded upon the mainspring of politics,
private interest? Besides, the southern States
are stronger and richer; a separation would be a
much heavier blow to the north than to us.
Their vessels would continue to export our tobacco, our cottons, and our sugars; but they
would pay duties, and they could not sustain
the competition of English manufactures. We
should continue to supply ourselves with provisions from the best market. The religious enthusiasm of a Yankee does not carry him so far
as to save his soul at the expense of his manufactures and commerce. They have therefore
taken much less part in the societies for emancipation, abolition, manumission, transportation,
colonization, &c., than the honest Quakers of
Pennsylvania and Maryland.

It would require a hundred mouths, each with a hundred tongues, and lungs of brass, to recite to you the different charters of these societies; besides, it is necessary to know them. Some try, it is said, to make our slaves revolt, thinking, thereby, to save our souls; but I can hardly credit so great a degree of absurdity. The most part try to get emancipation for the slaves, take under their protection those who have already been emancipated, and prevent the laws, which are already so severe, from becoming still more so. Their object is good, but they conduct themselves so imprudently, that they become dangerous to the masters, while they do as much good to their *protégés* as Don Quixote used to do to his. The Colonization Society, however, deserves to be particularly distinguished. It has bought or taken, I do not know which, but at last it has got a place in Africa, called Liberia, where it sends the free negroes who consent to emigrate; they there become savages as fast as they can; but that is all the same to us, provided we get rid of them. The great difficulty is the slowness of the society's operations; it transports, per annum, two or three dozen penitent street-porters and loose girls from the great Atlantic towns, and in 1820 we had 233,527 free persons of colour.

Two or three years ago, an envoy from St. Domingo, a very respectable man, Mr. Grainville, came to visit the northern States, and persuaded a great number of persons to emigrate to Hayti; but they almost all came back again, preferring the idleness and corruption of our great towns to honest industry in a free country.

In concluding this picture of slavery and its consequences, allow me to make another observation against the ridiculous projects of our Quixotic emancipators. What is the use of hurrying time? The total abolition of slavery will take place in the United States whenever free labour becomes cheaper than that of slaves. Is it Christianity which has abolished slavery in Europe? Is it Islamism which perpetuates it in Asia? Neither the one nor the other have produced these results; it is only to the calculations of private interest that we must attribute these contradictory effects. Formerly slavery was general in the United States; but in proportion as free labour has become cheaper, the legislatures have abolished it. The same thing is taking place under our eyes just now in Virginia and Maryland: the population having increased, the price of labour and that of slaves have fallen. The proprietors rid them-

selves of them as fast as they can; these slaves
are bought to be sent into the New States,
where manual labour is dear. In a few years,
there will remain hardly any slaves in these
two States, and then the legislature will do well,
for form's sake, to abolish slavery. The same
thing will eventually take place in all the present and future States, and the Union will
finally get rid of this domestic plague.

It is more difficult to know how we shall
manage with the free negroes; it is, meanwhile,
very clear, that they would cease to be dangerous, if they were not supported by those whose
chief business it is to meddle with what does
not concern them. General and universal philanthropy is, doubtless, a very fine thing; but
it is not to it that we owe our liberty and our
prosperity; it has never, that I know, made
anybody the richer; it is our duty to apply
ourselves assiduously to our own affairs, without
regarding those of our neighbours. This is a
political maxim which Washington has be-
queathed to us, and which might be very use-
fully adopted by the various religious sects with
which we are variegated.

LETTER FIFTH.

ON RELIGION.—*Tranquillity of America contrasted with the general Agitation in Europe; Variety and number of Religious Sects in America, their Harmony; Rigid Practices of the First Settlers in New England; Unlimited Toleration first established by Penn; Arrangements respecting Church and Chapel Property, and the Payment of Ministers; Episcopalians; Presbyterians; Tenets of the Methodists and Baptists; Description of a Methodist Camp Meeting; Equivocal Tendency of these Meetings; Unitarianism extending in the United States; Dr. Channing; Presbyterians; their character, tenets, zeal, and activity; Education for the Pulpit, mode of providing for numerous Preachers; Foreign Missions; Itineracy within the Union; Effects produced by the Preachers in the first instance, and subsequent reaction; Societies, a Female one to provide Wives for the Missionaries; names of others; Great Expense of the American Clergy, voluntary on the part of the People; Splendour of their Buildings for Religious Societies; Religion, though diffused, on the decline in the United States; Unitarianism on the increase; Mr. R.*

Owen, the Harmonists, Miss Wright, their exertions, and opinions; Mr. Owen's incomplete success in America; his Public Discussion with Mr. Campbell; his Visit constitutes an Epoch; Silent spread of Scepticism.

London; March, 1831.

WHILE a death-struggle is waging in Europe between those who would maintain institutions, the offspring of ages of barbarism, and those who would raise them to a level with modern enlightenment; while in every civilized part of the globe, a more or less considerable portion of every nation is agitated with a desire for a state of liberty, which they do not know, and which they seek more from instinct than calculation, marching towards that great end by fallacious paths, which only lead them further from it; it is curious to observe the tranquillity which prevails in the United States, the only country in the world in which the principles of liberty are established without mixture or opposition. It is a government something similar to this which is now called for by the wishes of all the nations of Europe; but owing to their ignorance of the object of their desires, their efforts are almost always ill directed. These reflections are sug-

gested to me by the popular tumults which have
lately taken place in France, during which the
people amused themselves by pulling down
crosses from churches; and by the law which
assimilates the rabbins to the catholic priests
and protestant ministers, in making them pen-
sioners of the State. It is not for me to criticise
or to approve what has been done in France; I
shall content myself with giving you a sketch of
the state of religion in the United States, where
it exists free and independent of the government
without being at all in each other's way. You
will easily gather, from what I am about to tell
you, my own opinions on this subject.

Do not suppose however that I am going to
undertake an exposition of all the dogmas of the
thousand and one sects which divide the people
of the United States. Merely to enumerate
them would be impossible, for they change
every day, appear, disappear, unite, separate,
and evince nothing stable but their instability.
From the pure doctrines of Unitarianism to the
gross absurdities of Methodism, all shades may
be found here, and every opinion has its partisans, who live in perfect harmony together.
Among this variety of religions, everybody
may indulge his inclination, change it whenever he pleases, or remain neuter, and follow

none. Yet, with all this liberty, there is no country in which the people are so religious as in the United States; to the eyes of a foreigner they even appear to be too much so; but that is only apparent, as I shall explain to you.

When the States of New England were first peopled by persons banished from the mother-country on account of religion, they established among themselves a species of theocratic government. Although the persecutions they had suffered ought to have taught them tolerance, they began to persecute with all their might Quakers, Catholics, and witches. They had digested a code of laws called, I know not why, "blue laws," which established a variety of ridiculous practices as an integral part of good morals. The Sunday was to be observed in the most rigorous manner; on that day people were not permitted either to travel or to walk in the streets, (except to and from church,) nor to cook, nor even to kiss their wives. A particular cut was prescribed for the hair, and certain dishes allowed only at particular times of the year. A thirty-sixth of the public lands were set apart in each town to endow a school and a church, of any denomination whatever, provided it were Protestant. In the States colonized by government, such as Virginia

I

and South Carolina, the Church of England
was established as in the mother-country,
and so it remained until the revolution. The
Catholics, banished from England, founded
Maryland, and then introduced intolerance.
Louisiana and the Floridas, settled by French
and Spaniards, had churches and convents
richly endowed. It was reserved to the great
Penn to be the first to establish unlimited
toleration in the colony of Pennsylvania. This
system was gradually followed by the other
colonies, and is now the law in all the States. On
the adoption of the constitution of the United
States, the principle of general toleration was
not only adopted as part of the federal compact, but Congress was even interdicted from
legislating upon religion. In all the States,
the churches and their property, if they have
any, belongs not to the ministers, but to
the congregations. Thus, when a new city is
founded, a lot is put aside for the first congregation which may demand it; trustees are appointed, to whom and to their successors in office
the lands are given or sold for the use of such or
such congregation. From that moment the corporation is formed, and becomes a person empowered to *bargain and sell, to sue and be sued,*
according to the conditions prescribed by the

charter of incorporation. This body corporate col-
lects gifts, borrows money, builds a church, sells
part of the pews, lets others, sells or lets choice
places in the churchyard, &c.; and when all this
is done, elects a pastor, pays him, keeps him,
dismisses him, changes him, as it pleases. Sometimes a minister has a fixed salary only, sometimes only fees, besides the use of a house
or the rent of the pews. In short, each congregation makes its agreement with its pastor,
as it chooses. Many of these congregations
are very rich, many are poor, or, wasting their
means, become bankrupt, in which case,
their church is sold by auction, like any other
property. It often happens that a preacher is
thought to preach some doctrine ill-sounding to
pious ears. The bishop or the consistory ex-
communicate him; in which case, the congregation either changes its religion and keeps its pastor, or changes its pastor and keeps its religion.
It generally happens, that the excommunicated
pastor, with a minority of the congregation,
form a new sect; then a new corporation is
formed, and a new church built or bought.
The sect takes, and other churches of the same
denomination are established; or it dies with
its founder, and the congregation either again
changes its religion, or is divided, or remains

without a pastor; which last, however, is not very common.

The sects most spread in the United States are the Episcopalians, or Church of England, and the Presbyterians. In fact, almost all the rest may be reduced to these. Each State forms a diocese. In some, there is a fund belonging in common to all the episcopal congregations, to provide for the expenses of a bishop, a cathedral, and a seminary; in others, each congregation contributes a certain portion of its revenue for those purposes. An episcopal convention composed of a certain number of lay deputies from each congregation, and a certain number of the clergy, elects the bishop, pays him, and directs, in concert with him, all the spiritual concerns of the church in the State. Deputies from the State conventions unite, from time to time, in a general convention of the Protestant episcopal church in America.

The Presbyterians do the same thing, except that not having bishops, it is in the conventions that their supreme spiritual power resides. The same is the case with all the other sects who are numerous enough to follow the example. In short it is the doctrine of the sovereignty of the people which governs the Church as well as the State. Each congregation says to his pastor, we will give you so much to preach such doctrines.   When a congregation differs in doctrine with the convention, it must either give in, or make a schism, and that, as you may easily suppose, happens every day.

For the rest, all these congregations, conventions, &c. are only recognized by the law as corporations, having the faculty of buying, selling, sueing and being sued at law, in the same manner as other corporations whose object is charity, public works, or commercial speculations.   Masonic lodges and chapters are incorporated in the same manner, as well as museums, picture galleries, and learned societies. · The privileges of the clergy are limited to being exempt from militia duty, and from serving on the jury, the same as postmasters, schoolmasters. doctors, &c.   In some States also they are exempt from paying tolls at bridges and gates, when travelling for religious purposes; in some others, they are ineligible to all public employments. But these privileges and these disqualifications apply equally to the ministers of all religions, provided they are recognized as such by a congregation, and do not continue if they quit the church. Everybody, indeed, who has the desire, may preach if he can find auditors, (a matter of no difficulty;) and from that moment he becomes

a clergyman. This takes place particularly
with the Methodists and Baptists, the two most
numerous sects in the United States, particularly
in the south. They believe in predestination and
efficient grace; they think that, as soon as a
man has felt the grace, has been converted,
and has been assured by the inward possession
of the Holy Ghost of his election, that from
that moment he can sin no more, but that it is
the devil who sins in him. The Methodists are
certainly the most extraordinary as well as the
most characteristic, and the most spread of all
the sects in the United States. They have
bishops, congregations, churches, like other
sects; but besides these they have meetings of
those who are converted, or, to use their own
expressions, 'of the saints,' at which everybody
preaches, speaks, and sings. Where they have
not regular churches, they have elders who
exhort, and all the country is divided into
circuits, each of which has a circuit-rider, whose
business it is to visit all the churches, congregations, meetings, and families, in his district
or circuit, and to cherish fanaticism everywhere.

Once or twice a year, in each district, is
held what is called a camp meeting; for this
purpose, a suitable place is selected in the
woods, generally near a brook or a spring; a

large circular space is there cleared out, under
the old shade of the giant trees of the forest;
split logs serve for seats; a sort of rostrum or
pulpit is erected, capable of containing a dozen
preachers together. The most remarkable place,
however, is the "pen," the *sanctum sanctorum.*
It is a place of about twelve yards square, enclosed like a sheep-pen, and filled, to the height
of about a foot, with clean straw.   All the
religious families of the neighbourhood come
or send, beforehand, to build themselves a tent
outside the cleared place; so that towards the
appointed time of meeting, the forest assumes
the appearance of a little village of rural huts,
and greatly resembles the cantonment of a regiment of cavalry, except that it is not so regular.
On the day appointed, generally a Sunday,
families arrive in crowds, on horseback, in
coaches, and in carts, bringing with them beds,
furniture, and kitchen utensils; each family
installs itself in its hut, as if for a stay of some
months. All the methodist preachers, exhorters,
elders, circuit-riders, &c. take care to be present, from a hundred miles round.   The bishop,
or the local preacher, or the circuit-rider, according to circumstances, commences the ceremony,
by giving out a psalm, which is sung by the
people; afterwards comes a prayer, then a ser-

mon, or two, or three, according to the inspiration of the preachers who fill the pulpit. The
service continues in this manner almost without
any interruption, for five or six days. I do not
mean to say that everybody remains to listen or
to preach all that time; on the contrary, everybody
does as he pleases. The rich provide very good
dinners in their cabins, and invite the preachers
and the poor. This is a place chosen by the
young people of both sexes to court and arrange
marriages. Indeed, nothing can be more poetical than to wander in the shade of the forest,
by moonlight, hearing from afar the singing of
hymns, or the fervid eloquence of the inspired,
with a young girl, all whose senses are agitated
and the reason staggered, by this clutter, whilst
her mother believes her to be engaged in prayer.
Piety in the heart of women has a soft influence
which disposes them to love, and it cannot be a
matter of surprise if, in these nocturnal walks,
prayers are directed to others than the Lord, and
other rewards obtained than those of the Spirit.

Indeed, a camp meeting is an excellent place
for all sorts of business. It is a point of union
for all the loungers and young people; for those
who have bargains to make or to conclude, and
for the candidates who mean to "electioneer,"
(a word which you have not in French,

but which you will be obliged to adopt whenever you have a government really free:)
every one minds his business, sleeps, eats,
makes love, cheapens a horse, depreciates or
exalts a candidate. The holy place is deserted;
silence for the first time reigns around the
pulpit; the full moon, though in her mid career,
is veiled by a passing cloud, and everything
seems to invite to repose and to a suspension of
the labours of the day; when—a preacher who
has remained alone kneeling within the pulpit,
rises up slowly; inspiration begins to visit him;
he begins a hymn, at first with a very feeble
voice, but which, *crescendo* by degrees, soon
attains the melody of Stentor. Some pious
souls retake their places upon the seats, other
preachers join him, and curiosity soon repro-
duces an auditory. An enthusiastic and pa-
thetic prayer follows: he engages the saints to
pray for the conversion of the poor sinners who
are in the midst of them; he represents to them
the greatness of God's mercy, and the pains
of hell; he exhorts them to lay aside false
shame, and make a clear breast before their
brethren. Five or six persons rise up, and
advance slowly towards the *sanctum sanctorum.* At the sight of so many converts, the
possessed saint becomes doubly heated: he

deputes two saints to pray with each of them.
The new convert, kneeling upon the straw,
sighs, accuses himself, sobs, and cries; whilst
on each side a saint, kneeling beside him,
vociferates in his ear a description, after his
manner, of the glory of God, and the wickedness of Satan.   These eighteen or twenty
persons, men and women, in the pen, make a
clutter that may be heard for some miles;
everybody bawls, sings, prays, cries, preaches,
together....... The owls, attracted by the
odour of the kitchens, answer them from the
tops of the trees, and fly away from this
noise, which they cannot emulate.   A young
girl in the meantime has wandered in the woods
with her lover longer than she supposed; time
passes swiftly in the company of a beloved
object, perhaps for the first time, and in the
spring of life, dreaming of ages of happiness in a cherished union, tasting perhaps its
reality in passionate declarations; .... suddenly
she is recalled to her senses by this clutter, her
spirits still agitated, her soul in a strange state
of emotion, her nerves stunned and shaken.   She
approaches, is troubled, fright seizes her; at first
she believes herself damned—then converted—
she enters within the sacred inclosure, there she
is soon stunned and seized with hysteric con-

vulsions; she cries out, weeps, sobs, rolls herself
on the straw in a frightful delirium.   The
assistants, the preachers and the saints, redouble
their vociferations, the people cry Amen!   The
clutter and tumult increase: a conversion so
sincere, so exemplary, must not be hidden by
the shades of night; torches of pitch-pine,
gathered from the neighbourhood, are soon
brought, and cast a vivid light upon this scene
of horror. The mother, the sisters, of the young
girl run thither on hearing the noise, but instead
of helping her, admire the mercy of God, who
is pleased to call her among his saints.   They
join their voices to those of the people, and do
not convey her into their cabin until she has
become quite insensible. The following day
she believes herself to be a saint, and no more
subject to sin, whatever she may do.   Further,
she will give her experience, as it is called, for
the edification of the community, and relates
in public by what winding paths the Lord has
been pleased to conduct her to himself, and
exhorts others to follow her example.   And
such is the power of imitation on the nerves,
that it rarely happens that a conversion of this
sort takes place without some other persons
falling into hysterics also.   Frequently, twenty
persons, of every age, sex, and colour, roll them-

selves together pell-mell upon the straw, with
haggard eyes and foaming mouths, in the midst of
the saints, who pray, sing, sob, and cry with joy,
to see so signal a triumph obtained over Satan.
Methodism equalizes everything, so that you
may see an old negress preaching to her master,
a negro praying by his young mistress. You
think I am joking, that I am speaking to you
of the farces of Saint Medard, which made so
much noise in the time of Voltaire; but what
will you say when you know that, among a
people eminently reasonable, this sect is the
most diffused, and reckons three times as many
members as any other? It augments every
day, and will, probably, in a few years, be the
only religion among the ignorant classes of the
people.

Unitarianism, on the other hand, is likely to
become the predominant sect among enlightened
persons. Although its followers are not yet
very numerous, it, nevertheless, makes rapid
progress. Nothing can be more simple than
their doctrines. They do not believe in the
Holy Spirit, nor consider Jesus Christ but as
an inspired man, created to serve as a model to
the world. They do not believe in the eternity of
future punishments, and they deny the inspiration of the Old Testament. Their worship is pure,

elegant, and free from every species of ceremony or superstition; they address themselves solely to the reason, both in the judiciously selected hymns they sing, and in their sermons, which latter are in general moral discourses of considerable literary merit. They have at their head, at the present time, a man of the rarest merit, and of exemplary virtue, a genuine Plato—Dr. Channing: nothing can surpass his eloquence, or the purity of morals and doctrine which distinguish his preaching. The liberality of this sect draws upon them the enmity of all the rest, but particularly of the Presbyterians, who reproach them with being nothing but ill-disguised Deists, and with blaspheming the name of Christ every time they invoke it. Others deem the first reproach well-founded, and that they do not go far enough.

Of all the sects in the United States the most formidable is that of the Presbyterians. Its bilious children, austere disciples of the gloomy Calvin, have inherited all his gall and venom, and do not scruple to invest the Divinity with their spirit of vengeance and Satanic wickedness. According to their doctrine, all men, without distinction, have been created to be damned, and deserve it richly for having committed the crime of being born. God,

however, by a return of clemency, sent his
Son to suffer for a part of the future race, and
allows his merits to be applied to a small number
of predestinated beings. Those, then, who are
comprised in that number will be saved; the
others, whatever may be their merits, will be
damned, for good works cannot of themselves
cancel original sin, and Jesus Christ does not
apply the merits of his atonement but to whom-
soever he pleases. Some of them go so far as
to preach that good works are opposed to salva-
tion, because they inspire a false confidence!
Pretty religion, indeed! as well worship the devil
at once, as a god of their fashion. This sect,
which was and is still the predominant religion of
Scotland, where the inimitable Sir Walter Scott
has shewn it under its true colours and in his most
forcible manner, is very numerous in the United
States. Whether it be real belief, or whether it
be hypocrisy, this sect shows more zeal for conversion than all the others put together. If it
had been let alone, it would soon have brought
us back to the time of the "blue laws." They are,
it is true, divided into a thousand different sects
in respect to doctrine, for few of their preachers
go so far as I have just said; but in spite of
that, they are all united by their discipline, and
present a solid phalanx to those without, what-

ever disunion there may be among themselves.
It is principally they who send out missionaries
to preach everywhere, who publish tracts, and
who found societies of a thousand different
sorts.

In the United States, competition is the
grand maxim of the public mind, and this
distinctive feature is perceptible in everything,
—in the government, in private enterprises, and
in the church. Many young people receive an
entirely literary education in the thousand and
one colleges of the Union; those who have
wherewith to live independent, or sufficient
means to enter into a profession without depending absolutely upon it, can do very well;
but there are many of them, the sons of poor
husbandmen or mechanics, who have nothing,
and yet cannot quit the Muses for the plough or
the plane. This is particularly the case in
New England, where everybody is well-educated.
The most enterprising become lawyers or doctors, and, finding the ground near them pre-
occupied, go and establish themselves on the
frontiers. Many become schoolmasters; and,
indeed, in all the Union, there is not a schoolmaster who does not come from these States.
The more idle become preachers. This road
never leads to equal emolument with the two

first, but it is more sure, and produces something
from the first, whilst in them some reputation
must be obtained before a man can make
wherewith to live.   If the young preacher
possesses talent, he enters into disputes with
the elders upon some obscure point of doctrine;
he is excommunicated, raises a cry of persecution
of the saints, founds a new sect, and his fortune
is made.   He may, however, fail in this attempt,
and the surest step is to enrol himself quietly
among the Presbyterian clergy.   But how,
with a limited number of good congregations
which pay well, and which the old naturally
desire to keep to themselves, how provide for
this innumerable quantity of juvenile preachers?
Herein priestly ingenuity displays itself.

First of all, missions must be sent to all the
heathen nations.   There are some of them in
the two Indies, but particularly in the islands
of the Pacific, in which the American priests
have created for themselves a little Paraguay
in the Sandwich Islands, where too they have
done much harm by stopping the only trade for
which the inhabitants of the country felt an inclination.   Some of them may be found also
among our Indians, whom they pretend to civilize, and to whom they do great injury, by encouraging them to oppose government, for fear

of losing their stations, which are excellent and
very productive farms. Moreover, some of them
are sent wherever, throughout the United States,
there may not be a church of their denomination
regularly established. They travel on horseback, stopping at the houses of the devout,
where they and their horses are well taken care
of, for which they make payment in prayers
and sermons. They correspond with directing
committees, raise subscriptions for building
chapels, which perhaps will never exist, preach
everywhere, convert, intrigue, sow dissension in
families, and when they have made some impression upon a few dozen persons in a village,
celebrate what they call a "revival of faith."
To this end, five or six preachers at least unite
and pray, sing and preach all day long for
many following days. Enthusiasm seizes the
minds of the people, particularly of the women;
they fast, they make collections for building or
repairing the church, or for some other pious
object. They distribute bibles, tracts, and religious periodicals, organize some religious
society, appoint a lay-committee to go from door
to door to gather information as to the spiritual
condition of families, and exhort them to go to
church, and avail themselves of the present
moment, while the door of mercy is open to re-

K

ceive them into the communion of saints. These gentlemen are indifferently received by people of a decided opinion; but timid people, who at first keep out of sight, are afterwards not proof against their persuasions, and thus swell the list of conversions despatched to head-quarters. The apparent effect of these "revivals" is to place a handsome new Bible in every house in the district, to displace a certain sum of money from the pockets of the citizens, in order to put it you may easily imagine where, to put a stop to enjoyment, break the violins and flutes, cause the dancing-master to emigrate, lengthen by a foot the faces of the inhabitants, and turn their complexions yellow. These effects, however, do not last long, for the ladies soon discover that metamorphoses of this sort do not improve their chances of getting husbands; and when the young preachers so holy and so eloquent, who displayed such fine teeth and a frill so well plaited, are gone away without making choice of any of the belles of the place, and are more-over replaced by a brigade of topographical engineers, come to make the plan of a canal, men who wear smart uniforms, swear, drink mint-julap, do not go to church, but love to dance,—gaity returns, and, to ensure their being captivated, faith disappears, faces become round

again, and the complexions of the fair recover
the roses which belong to them.

Marriage is indeed a profitable speculation for
young preachers; if they are handsome young
men, dress well, have in however small a degree
the gift of speaking, they appear with much
advantage from the pulpit; and if the father of
some rich young person is ever so little devoutly
disposed, it depends upon him to secure to himself the benefit of spiritual advice, on the same
conditions as the *malade imaginaire*, in Moliere,
wishes to secure that of medicine.   In general,
however, if he is young, the preacher who
marries a rich person throws off the gown and
becomes a farmer or a merchant.

Pious souls have so much care for the comforts of the preachers, that there really exists
in New England (at Newhaven, I believe,) a
society of ladies whose object it is to provide
wives for the missionaries destined to remote
countries.   If they have cast their eyes on some
one, they take upon themselves the negociation;
but, independently of that, they have always
ready a store of disposable beauties, pious girls,
receiving a salary from the society on condition
of being always ready to wed the first comer,
and follow and assist him everywhere in his
apostolic duty.   Whenever the Foreign and

Home Missionary Society has determined to establish a new station, whether in Cochin China, the Islands of the Pacific, or in the western deserts, it fixes a salary for that duty, and makes choice of a young man to fill the post. He forthwith gives official information to the female society who find him a wife; they are married frequently without having seen each other before, and pass from the altar to the ship, which may be going half round the globe, before they have recovered from their astonishment at finding themselves together.

The great number of religious societies existing in the United States is truly surprising: there are some of them for every thing; for instance, societies to distribute the Bible, to distribute tracts, to encourage religious journals, to convert, civilize, educate the savages; to marry the preachers, to take care of their widows and orphans; to preach, extend, purify, preserve, reform the faith; to build chapels, endow congregations, support seminaries, catechise and convert sailors, negroes, and loose women; to secure the observance of Sunday, and prevent blasphemy, by prosecuting the violators; to establish Sunday schools, where young ladies teach reading and the catechism to little rogues, male and female; to prevent drunkenness, &c.

This last society in particular is very singular, and very much extended. The members
engage never to drink any distilled liquor, nor
to permit its use in their families; but nothing
hinders them from drinking wine. In that
they mistake the Creator for a bad chemist.
The number of these societies is always increasing by hundreds, because there is forthwith one at least of each sort in each State, and
for each sect or denomination. Thus there are
Protestant-episcopal, Methodist-episcopal, Methodist, Presbyterian, Baptist, Evangelical, &c.,
Tract Societies for the State of New York, New
Jersey, Pennsylvania, &c. &c. There is no end
to them. Of course, whatever may be the object
of the society, there must be at least a secretary
and a treasurer, an office, office charges, print-
ing, postage, clerks, and all the appointments of
a public office, all which are filled by preachers,
and more or less remunerated. This explains a
little how it is that the vineyard of the Lord
is so flourishing; it is by these means that
immense sums are extracted from the pockets
of the people. There is certainly no clergy so
costly to the people as the American clergy;
but it is only fair to add that these contributions
are strictly voluntary, and I, for instance, have

no right to complain, for no preacher ever received a cent from me.

But that you may see their proceedings in all their lustre, transport yourself to the end of Nassau Street, in New York; there you will see a magnificent building, with white marble steps and front: it belongs to a Bible Society, as the gold letters above indicate. Go in: a long corridor gives access to numerous rooms with mahogany doors; read the inscriptions on these doors: "office of such or such society;" "office of the Reverend Mr. Such-a-one, treasurer or secretary of such or such society."   Proceed further, you will find a great bloated reverend gentleman perched upon a three-foot stool before a desk, busy in posting his ledger; around him some junior reverends assist him in his labour. You are, to all intents and purposes, in a counting-house. I know it, because I have had drafts upon these gentlemen; and all the difference I have found between them and a banker has been, that they always invited me to give up the change to them, for the purposes of the society.

A young man, therefore, who enters into the church, always finds his place, and the means of making, if not a fortune, at least of drawing from thence a pleasant existence amidst abun-

dance. If he be good-looking, he marries; if
a man of talent, he preaches, becomes the head
of a sect, and writes; if he have an aptitude
for business, he invents some new society, takes
upon himself the direction of its affairs, and
look about you as sharply as you please, you
will be cheated.

You will ask me, probably, after reading this,
if religion, supported by such means, and disposing of such capitals, does not make great
progress, and if it does not bid fair soon to penetrate everything? On the contrary; with difficulty does it keep its footing: it is like a ship
sailing against the tide, which seems to make
much way if we look at the water, and remains
stationary in respect to the shore; in the same
way is the church carried away by the great
current of opinions, literature, and modern phi-
losophy, which nothing can resist. This, above
all, is the great opposing power, and which will
certainly end by overthrowing the Christian
religion; perhaps even this overthrow, considered as that of a complete system, is more
advanced in the United States than is generally
believed. But, besides that, other causes con-
spire to the same effect; the rising influence of
the Unitarian sect is, perhaps, one of the most
powerful. Pure theists, enlightened and virtuous

philosophers, they do not, it is true, openly attack superstition, but they take away the support of their names, which is much. Boston, for instance, was the centre of bigotry; it is become that of this philosophic sect, and the chief seat of letters. Every distinguished man in that city, whether in politics or literature, is an Unitarian. The University of Cambridge, which is near by, is the head quarters of the sect, and it spreads from one end of the Union to the other. But, in addition to this, there are other philosophic sects which make a direct war on religion.

In this free country every one may entertain what opinion he pleases, publish it, and even live according to it, provided he does not offend against the civil law of the country. Accordingly, the United States have been the refuge of almost every visionary. It is from this cause that the Moravian brethren, the shaking Quakers, the Harmonists, Mr. R. Owen, and Miss Wright, have transplanted themselves here, and made it their home. I shall pass over the three first species of monomaniacs who have neither increased nor decreased since their foundation, about whom nobody troubles himself, and who exercise no influence upon the spirit of the age; but the two last merit more attention. Mr. Owen, you are aware, was the pro-

prietor of New Lanark, in Scotland, where he
established a community of cotton-spinners:
these people lived in common, their children
were educated and well clothed, and, in the
intervals of their labour, which, though shorter
than in other factories, was more productive,
they were occupied with literature and the arts:
so judicious were the arrangements.   Hence the
idea struck him, that the existing state of society
might be improved, so as to destroy entirely all
the causes of moral, and even of physical evil.
To this end nothing was necessary but to live
in common, according to the plan which he
proposed.   Possessed of an immense fortune,
followed by some ardent disciples, himself
extremely enthusiastic and very sincere, endowed with considerable aptitude for business,
the art of persuasion, and invincible patience,
he came to the United States to try to establish
there his co-operative towns.   His doctrine is
undisguised materialism and atheism: he denies
the existence of all morality, acknowledges no
other object of existence than happiness, and
regards everything a good which conduces to
that end: he refers to physical order all the
phenomena of moral order: he does not deny
the existence of crime, but attributes it to the
obstacles which existing society opposes to the

happiness of the majority, and thinks, by over-
turning these obstacles, to destroy them entirely.
There can be no doubt that, if everybody was
happy, there would be no crimes; but happiness is not equally distributed, a position on the
truth of which Mr. Owen, in great part, rests
his system. He pretends that every one has
talents for a particular thing, of which he
ought not to be vain, since it is the result of his
organization; that all arts, trades, professions,
are therefore equal in dignity; that all labour,
therefore, should be equally remunerated; that
if, in his co-operative towns, every one worked
six or eight hours a day, according as each
was disposed, the result would be abundance,
all the enjoyments of luxury and the arts, and
even an increase of capital, to be employed in
the education of the next generation, who, born
in the midst of abundance and happiness, educated without any of our prejudices, far removed
from vice and want, ignorant even of their
names, cannot fail to make immense strides in
the sciences and arts conducive to happiness.
But keep in mind, that there exists no curb to
the unlimited liberty which this system allows.
Marriage does not exist; everybody enters
into and dissolves connexions at pleasure; the
children are brought up at the common expense.

It is true, that far from encouraging libertinism, Mr. Owen pretends that man, being naturally inclined to monogamy, will choose for himself a companion, and hold to his choice more faithfully than if he was constrained by laws. This is very probable. Dreaming, then, of the transformation of the earth into an universal Arcadia, of men and women into innocent beings, enjoying uninterrupted happiness superior to any thing we can conceive of in our present corrupt state,—announcing the destruction of the institutions of the country before the term of two years, and preaching Atheism, this honest enthusiast traversed the country, and finally bought very considerable property in the west. He previously lectured everywhere, even before Congress, and gained many partisans among the literary class, or rather, some young naturalists and medical students declared themselves his disciples. He set off with them to the back woods, there established a community, expended a great deal of money, and, after a time, returned. But Philadelphia was not yet deserted, the institutions of old society still remained; in a word, he had entirely missed his aim. He then returned to England, where he now is, declaring that America is, of all countries, the most corrupted and the least capa-

ble of receiving his doctrines. The society
he founded exists, however, and even publishes a newspaper. His disciples, in adopting his theory up to a certain point, have
abandoned the idea of his co-operative towns;
the truth is, it was easier to find artists, doctors, and naturalists, than labourers, cooks,
and sentimental shoe-blacks, well educated
young men, who felt a natural taste for brushing
clothes or mixing up in a mortar during part of
the day, in order to pass the remainder in literary and philosophical conversations, devoting
themselves, at the same time, to the pure and
refined pleasures of sentimental love.

Owen then missed his aim; but he certainly
constituted an epoch. His frank and polished,
but irrevocable, manner of attacking revelation,
produced a very great effect. He never takes
offence, regarding a man who gives him a box
on the ear in the same light as a tree which
might fall upon his head: he tries to prevent it,
but he does not vex himself about it. The
clergy were all fairly stunned by his arrival,
and dared not persecute him, for fear of increasing his influence. After some time, even
a preacher, the Rev. Mr. Campbell, consented
to enter into a public discussion with him in a
church; it lasted several days, before a very

numerous auditory, and, on taking the show of hands, the minister had an immense majority. Notwithstanding this, the people are now accustomed to hear and read free discussion upon the foundations of their faith, and to reflect, without prejudice, upon these subjects. Thirty years ago, Thomas Paine was all but stoned for advocating doctrines which are now propagated by five or six papers in the United States. There is certainly an improvement.

These improvements would have been still much greater, if Mr. Owen's disciples had limited themselves to attacking old errors, without trying to engraft new ones, and without attempting to reform society. Miss Wright, a person of considerable mental power, has taken in hand the cause of women, so cruelly oppressed by the tyrannical masculine sex, and also those of the negroes and Indians. She adds, from time to time, some little diatribes against every species of social order, and runs about the Union preaching materialism and anarchy in the name of virtue and liberty.

Many other disciples of the same sect are established in the great towns, and try to produce a political convulsion by operating on the minds of the poor and working classes, and directing them against the rich and all social order whatever. They preach Agrarian laws, the equal division of property, the universality of gratuitous classical education, and try by these means to increase their influence. They have already succeeded, even in the city of New York, to control one or two elections; but this infatuation can only be temporary. The people of the United States are too happy and too reasonable to let themselves be led away by a jugglery like this, a true atheistic St. Simonism. After all, these sects do much more good than harm, for, if they mislead some maniacs, they promote a collision of opinions, and thereby elicit truth and counterbalance the exertions of the clergy. The mass of the Athenian people were neither cynics, epicureans, nor peripatetics. These sects existed, and disputed among themselves; the people became enlightened, weighed their arguments, and— doubted. It is to this point the people of the United States are tending. In another generation the nation will be no longer Christian, but it will not be Owenite. It will be wise, happy, and delivered from the yoke of priests, which now weighs upon it.

It must be admitted, that looking at the phisiognomy of the United States, its religion is the only feature which disgusts a foreigner. A Sunday, particularly in the north and east, is a

day of gloom, and calculated to make one
regret any other sojourn, even exile in Vienna.
The Israelites in the desert longed for the flesh-
pots of Egypt. On that day there is no theatre, no
visiting; the shops are shut, the streets deserted,
the communications interrupted. The post
office of the United States is barely permitted
to send despatches, and this, thanks to the
southern representatives. People go out only
to go to church. Every body wears a sullen
and taciturn air. Families have no cooking on
that day; they live on the leavings of the day
before. The women assemble in a circle, each
with a Bible in hand, which she makes believe
to read while yawning. The men do the like,
or under that pretext shut themselves up in
their closet and look into their private business,
sure of not being interrupted on the sabbath,
as it is called. But, who do they mean to deceive? I often said to myself, when looking
on similar scenes, and knowing the individual opinions of the different members. The
fact is that nobody is deceived, although there
is a desire to deceive every body. Every body
knows very well the degree of sincerity there is
in the religion of his neighbour, but nobody
likes to be the first to take off the mask. The
master is there, every body is a candidate

for his favour in a country in which public opinion reigns without mixture. He must be flattered, and the flatterers deceive themselves as to his opinions. The notion generally entertained of the strength of religious prejudices is much exaggerated, and the time is not far distant which will terminate the influence of the clergy and the forced hypocrisy which it produces, and show that those who willingly submit to it, constitute a very feeble minority. The sceptical party has only to know its strength, to shake off entirely the yoke of superstition, and for some time it has been making immense progress towards that object. The influence of the clergy, moreover, is merely apparent; it is absolute, certainly, upon matters of form, but at bottom nobody cares for it. Even formerly it was not strong enough to hinder the election of Mr. Jefferson, who denied publicly all belief in the Bible. Now it could do still less: in fifty years it will be able to do nothing.

Note.—We suspect considerable exaggeration and some mistakes in the statements of the author throughout this chapter, particularly in regard to the Presbyterians and Mr. Owen's disciples.—Tr.

LETTER SIXTH.

On the Administration of Justice. *The au-thor's entrance into the profession of the Law, its agreeableness; general view of American law, its origin; the sovereignty of the people; constitu-tion of the United States,—of the separate States; treaties with foreign powers; statute law; com-mon law; different sorts of tribunals; the supreme court of the United States; inferior courts; jurisdictions of the several courts; different modes of proceeding; Chancery and Admiralty jurisdictions; district courts; Circuit courts; Writs, habeas corpus, mandamus, quo warranto; officers of the courts; the Judge, the Clerk, the Sheriff; Grand jury; Petty jury; witnesses; pro-ceedings in court in criminal cases; in civil cases; in equity cases; conclusion.*

Brussels; January 1832.

My life has been one of agitation. Placed by fate in many singular and contradictory posi-tions, I have always been submissive to its de-crees and curious to observe where the current on which I have been borne would carry me; and truly I have never had much cause to com-

I.

plain : on shores to which I have been carried, I
hardly know how I have gathered many flowers,
and, often, the region I have expected to find
most barren has turned out the most fertile in
agreeable sensations.   I will give you an instance.   Settled in a new country like that
which I have described to you, some reverses of
fortune rendered my financial position embarrassing.   At the age of twenty-six I became a lawyer.
One of my neighbours quitting practice, I purchased of him his professional library for a couple
of oxen and a bill at long date; and thus provided I sat down to study law, during the dead
season of winter, at the same time giving due
attention to my plantation.   I extricated myself
from my difficulties. Moreover, where I looked for
nothing but disagreeable and unprofitable toil,
an employment directly opposite to my tastes,
habits, and previous notions, I found a very engaging profession, one which I have since pursued
with enthusiasm and never speak of but with de-
light.   With us the lawyer is the first man in the
State, the true aristocracy of the country; and
besides the moral and political influence he enjoys, his life is a continual succession of interesting occupations in which he is at once an actor
and a spectator.   To me, indeed, nothing is comparable to the interior of a law-court.   I could·

pass my life in one with pleasure, even if doomed
to be silent.   Talk of the theatre! it is but a very
feeble and awkward imitation of a court of justice.   There, we have the thing itself. Tragedy,
farce, melodrama, comedy, all are there, with the
advantage too of much better actors, because
they represent passions they really feel: I
speak of interested parties and witnesses.   It is
necessary to have practised, to know the pleasure
there is in pursuing an idea, in dislodging a law
which seems to avoid you through twenty
volumes; forcing it from one intrenchment to
another.   And when at last you hold it, after
having verified a thousand citations, what a
triumph! Is not this a much better thing than
entrapping a red fox after a chase of twenty
miles? You proceed to the hearing: how keenly
you enjoy the surprise your discovery produces in
the adverse party.   He wishes to postpone the
cause.   You do not permit him, he must plead
instanter.   The examination of witnesses begins. All are for him,—until you cross-examine
them.   I know nothing more amusing than to
examine, before a good jury, a witness, half fool,
half knave, and well tutored by the opposite
party.   What skill is necessary to make him
contradict himself, and with what facility afterwards, do you demolish the edifice which your

adversary's reasoning has been building. The pleadings follow: the counsel is then an actor, and in his finest part; and if he acquit himself handsomely, whether he lose or gain the cause, he feels conscious of having done everything possible to do, and even his client, though a loser, concurs in the unanimous approbation of the assembly and the court. So that whatever may be the fate of the cause, it is always a means of triumph for the lawyer.

I can speak of this profession in no other manner than *con amore*, for the happiest hours of my life have been those which I have devoted to it, and I am now going to try, well or ill, to give you a sketch an imperfect one, no doubt, of the administration of justice in the United States. I shall endeavour to observe the best possible order, but I must apprise you beforehand that I have no books with me, and consequently cannot cite my authorities in due form. I shall also be obliged to make use of many technical words, because, owing to the difference of the laws, there are no corresponding terms in French, or I am unacquainted with them. I shall abstain from making any comparison between the American and French systems, because the latter is not so familiar to me, and because every one may do so.

Our government and institutions are an experiment. It is true that nearly two generations have passed away since the revolution to which the United States owe their existence, and that so far, if the progress we have in every way made be considered, it must be admitted that our attempt has not turned out amiss. But, as I have already had occasion to say, the principle of our government is wholly new, and very little known out of the country. It consists in the sovereignty of the law, and in the supremacy accorded to its ministers and interpreters: it becomes important, therefore, to examine into the origin of the law and its various kinds.

The people of the United States being sovereign, not only in theory and right, as elsewhere, but in practice, and by the written law of the country, have been pleased to give themselves a constitution and to confide to certain hands the exercise of its supreme power. As long then as the constitution exists, it is the law *paramount,* a supremacy to which everything must yield. The people have made it, the people alone can unmake or amend it; so far it is executive in all the courts of justice, and no law contrary to it can exist. Observe the great difference between England and the United States. In

England, according to the law of the country,
the Parliament, composed of King, Lords, and
Commons, is absolute, and knows no check to
its authority. It can even reconstruct itself,
as it has already done many times in history,
and as it is now employed in doing. In the
United States this power resides only in the
people assembled in convention, or expressing
their will in any other manner equally explicit.

All American law then is derived from the
solemn declaration of independence made on
the 4th of July, 1776, by the American congress. The nation then recognised itself free,
independent, and sovereign, and until, by a new
and equally solemn declaration, it gives itself a
master, it is so in fact and in law.

As I have already stated, the present constitution of the United States was adopted by a
convention in 1788; it has been already amended
many times since, and, until it be changed, it
remains our government. May it long continue
to be so, and to protect our advancement! It is
the sacred ark,—and woe to whoever touches it.

But besides the constitution of the United
States, each State has its own; some older,
some newer, than that of the United States.
There are one or two of them even anterior to
the revolution, and still bear the name of " char-

ters," being considered as granted by the proprietors or by the crown.   When a territory
attains a population of forty thousand souls, it
is authorized by an Act of Congress to convoke
a convention and to give itself a constitution;
which constitution must be approved by Congress before the new State is admitted into the
Union. I may add, that to make a constitution
in the United States, where there are so many
models before it, is not difficult.   When the
people of a State think they discover defects in
the constitution, they do not revolt; there is no
commotion; they simply try to get such persons
elected members of the legislature as consent
to summon a convention. The State of Virginia
presents a remarkable instance.   For a long
time there were two parties opposed, one of
which desired the overthrow of the constitution.
What they found fault with was the fixing of an
electoral rent-qualification, and the distribution
of the representation, a measure which gave all
the power and influence to the longest inhabited part of the State, whilst the more recent,
although now the richest, was entirely sacrificed.
Those who profited by the old constitution defended it; the others attacked it.   Parties were
nearly equal, and for many years all the elections
turned upon this question. The legislature at last,

unwilling to pronounce on the question, ordained
by a law, that at the next election every one should
add to his vote the words "convention," or "no
convention," and that the majority should decide. The innovators succeeded by a small majority. The convention was convoked and never,
perhaps, sat an assembly so remarkable for its
ability, virtue, and experience. All the distinguished men of the State were elected to be
there, for every body is eligible to a convention,
whatever office he may fill besides. Thus the
members of Congress, the old presidents, the
judges, as well of the United States as of the
States, the officers of the federal army and
navy,—all persons generally ineligible by their
offices were there found together. After a very
long and stormy session, they adopted a constitution which was submitted to the suffrage of
the people, and passed also by a feeble majority; and it has now become the fundamental
law of the State. This constitution extends the
electoral right to every white man paying taxes,
equalizes the representation and changes completely the organization of the tribunals. Was
not this a better way of undertaking the reform
of institutions than by cutting one another's
throats for some years, to obtain after all only
anarchy or despotism ?

The constitution of the United States is above those of the States, so that if any one of these contained provisions contrary to that, it would be absolutely null. If, for example, a State convention adopted hereditary magistrates, or titles of nobility, such an article would be considered as of no force, and the courts of justice would refuse to act upon it. The constitution therefore, both as respects the United States and each State, is the highest law, and that contrary to which no power can legislate.

Treaties with foreign powers are the second species of law in point of dignity. According to the constitution, they are the supreme law of the country, so that any law may be abrogated or amended by a treaty. This provision is very remarkable, for as treaties are negociated by the executive power exclusively, and are ratified only by the president and senate, the constitution seems to give to these two powers the faculty of destroying of themselves Acts in which the house of representatives has also concurred. This provision is, however, a wise one; for if it become necessary, in order to make a treaty, that a law be modified, it is desirable to simplify as much as possible the means of doing so. Besides, as every financial measure must first be brought

before the house of representatives, it follows
that any treaty which might have an influence
upon the finances of the State, or might neces-
sitate an expense in order to carry it into execution, could have no effect in this respect, but
by an Act of the three powers, originating in the
house of representatives. A compromise is thus
, effected between the two houses, as the senate
does not ratify without being sure that the representatives will vote the supplies.   Moreover,
this question is still a little obscure, and, like
many others, cannot be made clear but by
judicial decisions.

   The third species of law which prevails in
the United States are the statutes, or written
laws.   These are Acts passed by the senate
and house of representatives, and approved
by the president.   They are published as they
are passed, and also at the end of each session.
Of these laws there exist already many editions,
with notes and references to the decisions of the
courts, shewing their application.   But this is
only a small portion of the written law.   In
political or criminal matters, the laws of the
United States in general suffice in the federal
courts, (unless they decide by the *lex loci*, as I
shall explain by and bye,) but in civil matters,
and in the States, it is very different.   First

of all, there is all the English written law, from
the commencement, until the 4th of July, 1776;
then the laws promulgated by the State from
its commencement; in some States, such
as Louisiana, Missouri, and Mississippi, the
French and Spanish ordonnances have also their
share of power.   By the constitution of the
United States, their laws are superior to those
of the States in the very rare cases in which
these two powers may have happened to legislate upon the same matter.   But what compli-
cates the matter more is that a statute must
never be taken singly, but must be accounted as
part, and being the complement of all the statutes
in pare materia.   A law, therefore, passed yes-
terday, repealing a law passed twenty years
ago, revives, without intending it, a law of a
century old, which latter may have been repealed
merely by a clause in the law of twenty years
ago.   Between contradictory enactments, the
last law has always the advantage, provided
that the meaning be not obscure, in which case
it must be interpreted by all which has been
enacted upon the matter before, and above all
by the decision of the courts.   However, there
are some general rules of explanation: for
instance, every penal statute must be construed
in favor of the accused; all fiscal statutes in

favor of the revenue; all civil statutes in the
most equitable manner; but wherever the sense
is clear, the statute must be construed literally:
the maxim being *sic lex scripta est.*

We come at last to the fourth species of law;
that truly which binds, enlivens, and harmonizes
all the rest: I mean the common law, or law
of custom.   How shall I define it?—a gigantic
incubus, extending from the remotest times
down to our own days; an invisible being,
which envelopes us like the air we breathe; it
is the same, and yet constantly changing : it is a
mysterious sybil, who has always a satisfactory
answer for those who consult her; but an easy
divinity, who allows its high priests to recon-
cile as they can its contradictory oracles, and
changes its will according to their last decision.
Its power covers, explains, modifies, everything;
from the constitution to the gospel, everything
submits to it: people, kings, and priests, nobles
or plebeians, slaves or masters, all are equal
before it.   But if its might is irresistible, it is
not tyrannical.   It is always ready to listen to
good advice, to profit by it, and to settle everything for the best.

How otherwise can I explain to you the existence of this law, which originated, if we are
to believe legal writers, in the customs of the

ancient Britons; was modified by the laws and usages of the Anglo-Saxons; under the Normans, became mixed with the feudal doctrine; followed, step by step, the progress of enlightenment; and always exactly expressed the wants of the nation. Where shall I find it, that I may show it to you? It changes every day in every state. Sir William Blackstone, in his learned Commentaries, has taken it, as it were, on the wing, and made a portrait of it, which was no doubt very like it at the time; and in England people recognise it there still, although since his time it has been much altered and improved: meanwhile Blackstone continues an authority. This law consists in general and often contradictory maxims, overloaded with divisions, distinctions, decisions, which are still explained for fear they should be understood. On one side, for instance, my Lord Coke tells you, very gravely, that common sense is part and parcel of the law of England:—why have I not his book to quote to you?—but a little farther on he adds, that the Christian religion, as understood by the English church of his time, is also a portion of the same common law. Afterwards he tells you that the common law existed from time immemorial. He explains, finally, that the common sense of which he speaks is not that of all the world, but a legal common sense,—moulded, probably, in the interior of the judges' wigs of his time.

But to what purpose do I hold up to you the apparent absurdities of the common law? I could heap up volumes of them. They would form but a very small spot on the beauty of the institutions which it has created. And, another thing, do these absurdities exist now? In England, perhaps, if I may believe Lord Brougham and Jeremy Bentham (a man of system, and too full of prepossessions to be lightly taken for a guide); but in America I can affirm that they have almost all disappeared. In England there exists a party who cling to the errors of times past; it is possible that, with the court, wigs, and gowns, it has preserved physical tortures, the "jury *de ventre inspiciendo*," the "wager of battle," and " the wager of law." I do not, however, believe it; but in America, where the past has no party, where all the nation presses forward into a glorious future of light and prosperity, they have all disappeared in practice; and it may be said emphatically, that common sense forms the chief part of the American common law.

The common law is of prior authority to any constitution, any written law, and even any tribunal, for it is that which regulates the mode of proceeding in the legislative chambers, and even in conventions ; which indicates the manner of forming the statutes; and, as soon as a tribunal is created, invests it instantly with all the powers necessary to its protection, regulates the forms of proceeding there, determines the extent of its jurisdiction, and the respective functions of its different officers. It is true that, from time to time, a statute comes blunderingly across its path; but the great all absorbs it, harmonizes it, amalgamates it with the mass of legislation, comments on it, explains it, until the ground is forgotten, and nothing is known but the decisions to which it has given place. Is there one among a hundred English lawyers, or a thousand Americans, who have read the famous statutes of *Donis,* which regulate the possession of goods by mortmain and feudal tenures; or the statute of frauds, which regulates reciprocal guarantees in personal matters! every day, however, somebody cites them, or rather the incrustation of juridical decisions which cover them.

But you ask me, where then do you find, and where do you study your common law? First of all in elementary books: that is to say, in the numerous treatises published upon the

whole law or its various parts, by eminent magistrates, who take care to cite the decisions of
the courts, on which they rely. Every day there
are new editions with explanatory notes, and
such alterations as the law may have undergone
since the previous edition. The last edition is,
of course, the best. Secondly, in the reports of
decisions in the superior courts; for each supreme court pays a reporter, whose duty it is
to publish the decisions of the court, with the
reasons which have guided it, and a succinct
account of the cause. The infinite multiplica-
tion of these books of reports, both in England
and the United States, have suggested the convenience of digests, setting forth, in alphabeti-
cal order, the subjects of all the decisions: they
refer you to the most important or explicit cause
of the sort, and abridge much labour and research.

When a doubtful question of law comes before an inferior court, it decides it by the decisions of the court of appeal to which it is
subject, provided that court has already decided. In the contrary case, the court is guided
by the decisions of the English courts, by those
of the United States, or of the other States, and
by the opinions of eminent jurisconsults, as
documentary information only, attaching to them

more or less weight according to the reputation of the judges who have put them forth. The court then decides, the judge, intrusted to deliver its opinion, doing so at length in writing, and answering the arguments adduced by counsel. This opinion, which remains on the rolls of the court, becomes the law of that tribunal until it is reversed by a superior court. Any party thinking himself aggrieved by the opinion delivered may appeal from it to the proper quarter, and it is only when the supreme court of the United States, or of the State, has decided, that the law becomes fixed upon the matter. And, after all, as there are never two cases exactly alike it is always easy for the superior court to discover some circumstance, sufficient to destroy the apparent analogy, and permit it to reform the first decision. This is what we of the trade call splitting a hair in four; which is not one of the least agreeable employments of the profession.

It is then chiefly in the courts that the law is to be acquired; the judges are its professors, their opinions the real lessons, as the pleadings of the counsel are the real theses. This is so true, that in England there exists no chair, no professorship for common law * ; those who are

* It is true that, in 1758, Sir William Blackstone was appointed professor of a class of common law founded at the

M

intended for the bar being admitted into the
studies of the practitioners, whom they attend
to the courts, residing in their houses; submitting to an university discipline in buildings con-
tiguous to the court of justice, called the inns
of court, and receiving no other instruction than
from the mouths of the judges, the real source
and fountain of common law.

To understand perfectly the different sorts of
courts which exist in the United States; it is
necessary to consider them under different
points of view, and first of all as to their origin.
Now all the courts were created either by the
constitution, or by a law of the constituted power,
or they existed previously to any constitution
and all laws, from time immemorial.

The first sort of courts are the key of the
social arch; their duration is coeval with the constitution; they are one of the co-ordinate poweis
of the State, and above all laws of the legislature,
which cannot change their privileges or give
them new. The supreme court of the United

University of Oxford, by Mr. Viner. To this appointment
we owe his excellent commentaries; but since his time, the
chair of common law has become wholly a sinecure. A
young man who is intended for the bar cannot learn enough
at the university; and for other people, Blackstone is more
than sufficient.

States is of this sort. Its composition and its jurisdiction being fixed by the constitution, cannot be altered; and, on more than one occasion, in which the Congress had thought proper, by a law, to confide to it additional functions, the court declared itself incompetent, and considered the law as nul and void. In almost all the States there exist courts of this kind, but you will not expect me to give you a detailed account of the legislation of the twenty-four States; they are, moreover, so much alike, that in describing to you those of the United States, and pointing out the more striking differences, you will be able to form a general idea of the whole.

In general, the constitution, after having established the supreme court, leaves it to the legislature to establish, distribute, and modify the inferior courts according to the interest of the moment. This is necessary in a country in which the progress of civilization is so rapid ; for otherwise it would happen that vast and populous countries would be without tribunals, while there would be too many of them in the place by which colonization had commenced. The law which creates these courts, called statutory courts, is the condition of their existence, and regulates everything concerning them: it belongs to themselves, however, to explain this law and apply it, always well understood under the superior sanction of the supreme court. All the courts of the United States, except the supreme court, and nearly all the state-courts, are of this kind; and, for the most part, also, courts-martial, both military and naval, courts of chancery or equity, and corporation courts. Courts-martial originate in the regulations for the government of the army and navy, and correspond exactly with councils of war. Courts of equity do not exist in all the States: in some they are established by the constitution; in others, their powers are confided to the ordinary judges. As to the corporation courts, they are granted by the legislature to the large towns, and are intrusted with the summary jurisdiction within the city, and to settle trifling civil actions which do not exceed a certain sum, which varies in each particular case. All these courts may be abolished, modified, and reconstructed, by the *fiat* of the legislature.

The courts existing from time immemorial, distinguished by the name of common-law courts, are like those which administer justice in England; the origin of the King's Bench is lost in the darkness of time. I think, but am not however sure, that the court of Common

Pleas, which sets at Philadelphia, has existed likewise since the colonization of the country, without having been created by any law: it is, perhaps, the only court of record so situated in the United States; but all justices of peace are so. These latter constitute the first step in the juridical hierarchy; their existence is anterior to any constitution or law: their functions, both civil and criminal, as well as their jurisdiction, are determined by the common law: they are the same in England as in the United States. It is true, that their political or administrative functions vary, as well as the mode of their nomination, and the sum to which their civil jurisdiction extends. These different objects are defined by the constitution or the laws of each State. All justices of peace in the States belong in common to the United States, and exercise their functions in the federal courts; they are the only magistrates who possess this double capacity.

Another aspect under which to consider the different courts is, with reference to their dignity: they are divided into courts of record and not of record; the former are furnished with a register or record, which is supposed to report faithfully and uninterruptedly all that is said and done by or before the court from its commencement. The truth of the record cannot be questioned or contradicted in any case; and I have seen a party put out of court because, by a mistake of the name, he had been described as dead upon the record. This is the absolute truth; any body may inspect the record by paying the registrar, and may take extracts under the seal of the court, which are valid, unless an error of the copyist be proved, or a diminution of record. All the civil and criminal courts are courts of record, and as such, possess, in virtue of the common law, the power of imprisonment and fine for any contempt which may be offered to them, whether directly or by disobeying their orders and decrees. Thus, as soon as a constitution or a law establishes a court, and says that it shall have a record, it gives to it, at the same time, a power clearly defined by the common law. Courts-martial, justices of peace, and some corporation courts, are not courts of record; every thing in them is supposed to be done orally, and they do not keep any register of their transactions. It is true, that justices of peace, in some States, are authorised to keep certain registers, but they do not possess the sacredness of the record, and are only considered as memorandums.

We come at last to the most important distinction between the different courts, namely, their jurisdiction. I will endeavour to explain clearly the difference between the federal courts and the state courts, observing, that an exposition of the jurisdiction of the former may be received as applicable to the latter; for the state courts have full and entire jurisdiction in every thing which, by the constitution of the United States, has not been restricted to the federal courts. I shall consider, then, first of all, the civil, criminal, equity, and admiralty jurisdictions of the federal tribunals, according as it is given to them, in place, person, and matter, (*jurisdiction in loco, in persona, in subjecta materia.*) I shall analyze, afterwards, the federal system of the United States, and show of how many courts it is composed, and their original and appellate jurisdiction: I shall then do the like with the courts of some States.

To begin, then: the civil jurisdiction *in loco* of the federal courts extends over the district of Columbia, in which Washington is situated, over the lands in which this jurisdiction has been ceded to the United States by a special Act of a State, and over all the immense territory belonging to the Union, and comprised out of the limits of the States. In all these cases, the courts follow the *lex loci* or local jurisprudence.   There is a little uncertainty as to whether the jurisdiction of the federal courts extends also, and up to what point, over the lands of the Indians, who are inclosed within the limits of the States.

Their civil jurisdiction, *in persona*, extends to any cause in which either the United States, or one of their officers as such, or a foreigner, are parties; to those between two foreigners or citizens of different States, and lastly, between a State and the citizen of another State.   The courts are still, in these cases, obliged to conform to the local jurisprudence.

Their civil jurisdiction *in subjecta materia* embraces all cases to which the constitution of the United States, treaties with foreign powers, or the laws of the United States, give place: and in this case, it judges according to the constitution and laws of the United States; all suits on the part of the bank of the United States, for instance, is carried before these tribunals, because it is a federal institution, owing its existence to an Act of Congress.   All disputes with the government of the United States, and about its revenue, belong equally to them.

In the United States, as in England, the criminal jurisdiction is confided to the same tribunals.   There is no civil court and criminal court district. Louisiana is the only State in which there is this distinction, and where there exists a tribunal of which the jurisdiction is purely criminal: all the other courts, as well state as federal, try, during the assizes, criminal and civil causes indiscriminately.

To bring a matter *in loco* within the criminal jurisdiction of the United States courts, it is necessary that the crime have been committed in the district of Columbia, or in places to which this jurisdiction has been ceded by a State; as is the case in the forts, arsenals, and dockyards, of the United States, or without the limits of the States, or lastly, in open sea: in all these cases, except the last, the court applies the penalty fixed by the local laws, in the last by the laws of the United States.

It is only in the cases of an ambassador or foreign consul that the criminal jurisdiction *in persona* belongs to the federal courts, and then they always try according to the local law.

Every action rendered criminal, or punished as such by the constitution, treaties, or laws of the United States, gives to their courts the criminal jurisdiction *in subjecta materia*; thus, therefore, rebellion against the United States, coining of false money, attempt on the safety of the post, &c. are crimes of which the cognizance is reserved to the federal courts, in which they are treated according to the laws of the United States. Keep in mind, that the United States courts, being created by a law, have jurisdiction only in cases comprehended in that law; and that, as every penal statute must be construed in favor of the accused, unless a crime be very clearly foreseen by the laws,—any outrage whatever against "the peace and dignity of the United States," (such is the technical phrase,)—they cannot punish it. The case would be different if they derived their power from the common law, because that has foreseen every thing.

Before stating in what cases the federal courts exercise a jurisdiction in equity, or chancery, (which is synonymous,) it is first necessary that I define what it is. Previous to the revival of letters, the priests were almost the only lettered persons: the church had almost exclusively profited by the discovery of the Pandects, and had incorporated them with the canon law. This law became, more or less, that of Europe, at the end of some centuries, except in England, where the feudal power of the barons, and the turbulent spirit of the commons, perseveringly resisted its introduction. From thence grew a continual struggle between the civil and criminal

tribunals, in which the common law was followed; and the ecclesiastical courts, which
decided according to the common law. This
ecclesiastical jurisdiction exists still in England
in cases of divorce, testamentary proofs, &c.;
but in the United States it belongs to the ordinary tribunals, except in South Carolina, and,
perhaps, also in one or two States which have
private lay-courts invested with this jurisdiction.
The lay tribunals, however, resisted, with success, the encroachments of the ecclesiastical
judges in England, and continually restricted
their jurisdiction more and more; but, in the
meantime, the English chancellors, who, in those
remote times, were always bishops, performing
at the same time the functions of almoners and
keepers of the king's conscience, (titles which
they still preserve,) claimed a discretionary
power, which is descended to their lay successors in all cases in which the ordinary laws provide no remedy. They were considered to render
justice, not according to fixed laws, but according to their conscience and natural equity:
hence the distinction always made in England
between law and equity. It may often happen
that the law following previous decisions, and
slow and certain forms, could not render perfect
justice to parties, and might even decide unjustly;

in all such cases, recourse is had to the chancellor, and he provides a remedy : he has therefore the power, by particular writs, to suspend
all suits in the courts of law, and even to suspend the execution of their decisions. He can
never, however, take cognizance of a question
of fact, but when it presents itself, he must send
it before a jury in a court of law, which reports
to him the verdict, and he then decides on viewing
the whole.   The chancellor proceeds alone,
without a jury, upon written depositions, taken
before commissioners : his power is considered
wholly discretionary ; but as the decisions
of his predecessors are preserved in books of
reports, he is obliged to conform to them, as well
as to the received forms of his court.   He does
not give judgment, but grants orders or injunc-
tions; and all contraventions are considered as
contempts of court, and punished by fines and
successive imprisonments, until they constrain
the refractory parties to obedience.   It would
be difficult for me to make you comprehend
this jurisdiction without giving you some exam-
ples : you should first of all be told that the
court of Chancery is always open, day and night,
while the courts of law are only open at certain
periods of the year.   If, for example, while I
have an action pending before a court of law

against some one, he is disposed, before the
time of trial, to evade the jurisdiction of the
court, by quitting the country; upon my petition
to the chancellor, he will issue a writ *de ne
exeat,* prohibiting the person from going away,
without satisfying him (the chancellor), in
contradiction to me, that my interests shall
not suffer by his absence; either by giving bail
for his return in proper time, or for payment of the
debt, in case of a verdict against him. If a dispute exists respecting the property of an estate,
and the party in possession pulls down houses,
cuts trees, or in any way whatever damages the
property, the chancellor grants an injunction "to
stay waste." So also he may, by an injunction
"to stay proceedings," prohibit a party from
bringing an action before some other has been
tried; or even, in case of manifest fraud, prevent the bringing of an action without his permission; or cause the suspension of an arrest,
in order to protect the rights of a third party.
In all cases concerning trustees and minors the
chancellor interferes, to see that justice is done
according to the intention of the testator or
founder of the trust. He may order the specific
execution of a contract, explaining what the
parties have equitably a right to exact of each
other, &c. &c.

The United States have no chancellor. Some
States have one; others have courts of chancery, with several degrees of appeal; others
have none; but in this last case, the powers
of chancery are confided to the ordinary judges;
so that if, on one side, as judges of law, they
take cognizance of an action, on the other, as
judges of equity, they prevent parties and
themselves from going on. This is the case
with the federal courts; they can order the
State courts, and those of the United States,
in following the juridical hierarchy. From what
I have said, it is easy to see that the equitable
jurisdiction of the federal courts is coextensive
with their civil jurisdiction, since it is, in fact,
merely supplementary to it; and, like that,
when it applies itself, *in loco* and *in persona*, it
follows the local jurisprudence.

We now come to the admiralty jurisdiction,
which belongs entirely to the federal courts:
they decide according to the universal maritime
law, and the laws of the United States pertaining to the matter; their manner of proceeding
in all cases, *in personam*, is that of the common
law, that is to say, by a jury, and the oral examination of witnesses; and in all cases *in rem*
by the forms of civil law, that is, without jury
and by written depositions. They are always,

however, obliged to conform themselves to the previous decisions of the courts which are superior to them in degree; so that even maritime law and equity are regulated by, and make part of, the common law.

No court can take the initiative in any matter except that of a flagrant insult to its dignity, so that every thing is unknown in a legal sense, until they are made cognizant of it by the required forms. The federal courts, therefore, never know what passes in the State courts, unless one of the parties come and put them in possession of the facts. But there exist many cases in which the jurisdiction of the federal courts and of the State courts is concurrent, for example, the civil jurisdiction *in persona*; for it is a privilege which the constitution affords to a foreigner to allow him to plead before the federal courts; and he may forego that privilege, by bringing his action before a State court, or not excepting to it as incompetent. The State court is not obliged to know him as a foreigner, but when once a case is before it, it is too late to object to its competency. Many of these conflicting jurisdictions, however, are not yet settled, nor will they be until they are severally brought under the consideration of the superior court of the United States.

All the territory of the United States covered

by the States, is divided into judiciary districts, in each of which sits a district court. It holds several sittings in the year, in different towns of the district, according to particular laws, which alter with the wants of the population; and besides that, it is always open as a court of Chancery and Admiralty. It is before these courts that every matter must be first carried. There is but one judge to each district.

Several of these districts united form a circuit, which has a circuit court, composed of the judges of united districts, and presided over by a circuit judge. This court sits in the different towns within its province, and its jurisdiction is limited to hearing appeals from the district courts, upon which it decides definitively, if the sum in litigation do not exceed 5000 dollars. Like the other courts, it is considered always open to litigants in chancery and admiralty, before the circuit judge.

Lastly, the seven circuit judges unite at Washington, the first Monday in January of each year, and constitute the supreme court of the United States, the highest tribunal of the country. It is presided over by one of the circuit judges, who has the title of Chief-justice. This office is filled at present by the venerable John Marshall, one of the most profound jurists

and most upright and enlightened of men who
have ever lived. It is perhaps to him and to
his virtues that this court owes much of the
consideration which it at present enjoys. The
power of this court is immense; it decides in the
last resort all doubtful points of the constitution,
and refuses to execute the laws of Congress and
of the States, when they are contrary. Hitherto
it has fully justified the confidence reposed in
it, and I regard it as the first authority in the
United States, and as that which will preserve
all the others in harmony as long as the constitution shall be the same. Its jurisdiction is
purely appellant, except in criminal cases,
against foreign ministers or consuls, in which
it has an original jurisdiction.

The district of Columbia and the territory
without the limits of the States, have particular
and provisional courts until they become States
themselves. The definitive appeal is always to
the supreme court of the United States.

In all the States, except that of Georgia, a
nearly similar system is followed ; the number
of degrees of appeal varies from two to three, but
in all there is a supreme court, or even two
where there exist separate equity courts; in
all the inferior courts sit, in different places,
several times a year, so as to bring justice to

N

the door of the litigants. Each State then possesses a legal unity, a tribunal which puts forth
the decisions of the common law of that State,
and expounds the laws of its legislature. But
the State of Georgia has no less than eight,—
the number of districts into which the State is
divided. In each there is a judge, who is
elected every three years by the people, and who,
holds, at different periods, in different quarters
of his district, two sorts of courts, ' inferior,'
and ' superior :' the first is a court of original
jurisdiction, the second one of appeal, in which
he is assisted by a special jury, (chosen by the
parties in a particular manner,) so that the appeal of a cause is heard before the same judge,
who is thus invested with the powers of chancery, and whose decisions in his district are
definitive, for there exists no supreme court.
There are then eight common laws in Georgia,
and still they change every three years!! an
absurd system which has not been long introduced, and cannot long continue among a nation
so enlightened.

All these courts of record, as well as those of
the United States, are intrusted to maintain and
carry into execution the constitution and laws,
and to prevent any encroachment. As I have
already remarked, the court can never take the

initiative before the injured party has put it in
possession of his complaint; but then the constitution and laws invest it with very extensive
powers, according to the common law, for their
defence. These are by-writs of *habeas corpus*,
of mandamus, and of *quo warranto*.

By the first of these writs, the court directs
any one who may be in possession of the person
of another, to bring before the court, on such a
day and hour, the body of such an one, or to
state the reasons which prevent him from so
doing. This writ is issued by the clerk, by
order of a judge, not only at the instance of
parties, but of the first applicant; it is always
issued without any delay. The person to whom
it is directed must produce the subject of the
writ before the judge. No authority may resist
the execution of this writ. If, therefore, any
one is arbitrarily detained by any authority
whatever, for instance, a young person shut
up by her parents in order to force a marriage;
a soldier by his officer, to constrain him to re-
inlist; a sailor detained on board after his time
of service has expired; an accused or criminal
debtor in prison longer than the law authorizes;
a negro arrested under pretext that he is a slave;
a nun shut up in a convent, &c. &c. In all
these cases, the wronged party, by him or her-

self, or an official defender, may demand this
writ, and be brought before the judge who decides upon the cause of arrest or detention,
and sets him or her at liberty if there be
reason.

The court, however, upon a writ of *habeas
corpus*, does not decide upon the merits of the
cause of detention, but solely upon its legality.
If, for instance, a writ of *habeas corpus* be addressed to a jailor, in order that he may produce a prisoner who complains of being ille-
gally detained; and that he answer the writ by
a copy of the commitment, showing that the detention is by order of a court having competent
jurisdiction, that is sufficient; for the prisoner
has other means of trying the grounds of his
detention, namely, by writ of error or bill of
exception; but if he be detained by order of
the executive power, or of a military officer, or
in any other illegal manner, the court causes
him immediately to be set at liberty; and moreover, he may bring an action for damages and
costs against his detainer, on the ground of
false imprisonment.

The writ of *mandamus* is granted to any person aggrieved by the refusal of a public officer,
or of a political corporation, to perform a certain
duty. It is at first granted, under an alterna-

tive form, to do such a thing, or state the reason
of refusal. It is only after a hearing of the
parties, that the court renders the *mandamus*
peremptory if there be reason. If, for example,
a person has a right to a piece of land, in virtue
of a law, and the administration of the public
lands refuses to give it to him; if a man has
been appointed to an office, and the officer intrusted with it refuses to deliver to him his warrant, to administer the oath to him, or to acknowledge him in that capacity; if a justice of
peace, or any other inferior court, refuses to exercise some power belonging to it; in all these
cases, the writ obliges them to perform it, unless
they can assign some legal ground of refusal.
But this writ is only obtained when there is no
other remedy, and is not applicable to judiciary
acts; for a superior court may even, in certain
cases, by a *mandamus*, order an inferior court to
pronounce a judgment, but not dictate what judgment. It is only in appeals or annulments that it
can take cognizance of the decision pronounced.

The third 'writ,' that of *quo warranto*, is a
writ by which the court demands, of any constituted authority whatever, by what warrant
it claims such or such power. Upon this writ
the court decides generally, and even in case of
usurpation of power, and if the demand of the

writ has been made by a criminal information,
it will pass sentence against the guilty party.
These three writs are the safeguard of the citizen's liberty, inasmuch as the first secures his
person against all arbitrary detention, the second
is a check on the negligence of the magistrates,
and forces them to execute the laws, whilst the
third prevents any encroachments of power. I
cannot imagine civil liberty in any place in
which powers analogous to those of these three
writs do not exist. Delay or disobedience to
any of them is punished very severely, as an
insult to the court; not by a fixed penalty, but
by imprisonments and fines prolonged and re-
peated until obedience is obtained. These
powers, though extended, are not dangerous,
because the courts have no initiative, and though
the son or the wife of the judge were to be ille-
gally arrested, he could not take cognisance of
it but at the instance of a third party.

Nothing can be more simple than the construction of an American tribunal. Those of
the United States are in general composed of a
single judge; this is also the case with almost
all the inferior State tribunals. The superior
court of the United States is, I believe, the
most numerous tribunal in the union. The
judges of the United States are appointed by

the president, with the consent and by the advice of the senate, hold their offices during good behaviour, and are not removable but by judgment of the Senate, sitting as a court of impeachment; for at any time that a judge or any other functionary of the United States, even the President himself, may give rise to complaints, founded on the exercise of his functions, in the judgment of the house of representatives, the latter transfers the case to the senate, which decides definitively upon the complaint, in depriving the functionary. This is the only judiciary function of the Senate which is not like the English House of Lords, the supreme court of justice of the country.

In all the states, except Georgia, where they are eligible and change every three years, the judges are irremoveable, except by judgment of the senate, or of the two houses of the legislaturo united. In the State of New York alone, every judge resigns at the age of sixty years, an arrangement which deprives the people of its best magistrates. Almost everywhere they are appointed by the governor. In some States, however, they are elected by the legislature. They are every where very well paid (perhaps not enough, however), and enjoy great consideration and much influence.

The judge alone constitutes the court, but he cannot proceed without the officers of the court, which are, the clerk, the sheriff, and the counsel. The clerk, or registrar, is a very important personage. He it is who keeps the record and issues the writs and orders of the court. He is in general nominated by the judges or elected by the people, and is paid by the litigants for each official act. It is he who administers the oaths, of which there are a profusion in an American court.

But the sheriff (who in the courts of the United States is called marshal) is a very important officer also. He is the executive officer of the court, whether civil or criminal. There is one for each county, who is the officer for all the State courts within it. In like manner there is, in each district of the United States, a marshal, who executes the judgments of the court and serves its processes. My description of one of these functionaries will apply to the other. The marshals are appointed by the president; the sheriffs, in general, are elected by the people of the respective counties; however, in some States, I believe, they are appointed by the governors or the legislatures. These offices are very lucrative, but they involve a great responsibility, and the sheriffs are obliged to give

very heavy securities. Though the sheriff is a
person who goes but seldom from his office, and
acts almost always by deputies or substitutes,
of whom he has an unlimited number; it is he,
however, who is intrusted to make all sum-
monses and serve all writs, that is to say, to
communicate them to the parties, or to execute them when they are addressed to him. It
is he who sells the property of debtors, or arrests them, if they do not otherwise pay, and
gives possession of real property in dispute to
those in favour of whom the court decides. He
pursues and arrests prisoners, detains them, and
executes them if they are condemned. In short,
the court knows only him. He is responsible
to the court for the execution of these writs,
and must indorse upon each the " return;" in
other words, the result. For instance, upon the
back of a *capias ad respondendum* (a summons
to appear), he indorses either *"* executed such
a day, by giving a copy to the party, or to his
wife," &c.; or *" non est inventus,"* if he has not
been able to find him. So, upon a writ *de venditioni exponas,* he indorses, " I have sold such
property, on such a day, for so much, and have
disposed of the funds in such a manner;" and
so of the rest, whether civil or criminal. All
these writs, thus returned, remain on the roll.

He has the faculty, when the case is litigious, to make a " special return ;" in other words, to detail all the facts which have accompanied the execution or non-execution of the writ, in order that the court specify upon it. He is invested with a power which nobody can legally resist. He can arrest whom he will, seize and sell any property. He has under his orders, tipstaffs, constables, serjeants, records, jailors, and executioners, as many of them as he may require. He can not only demand the assistance of the army of the United States, or of the militia, but he may also call upon the *posse comitatus;* in other words, order all the inhabitants of the county to assist and support him. He has even been known to require the judge to descend from his seat to assist him in arresting some troublesome malefactor. In fine, he is the physical power of society; nobody resists him. But if he is invested with powers so considerable, he is strictly responsible for all that he does. If he is deceived, and arrests me for another, I sue him for damages and costs, and even criminally, if any rude treatment has been resorted to without provocation. I do not defend my property against him, but render him responsible for any damage which may result to me from his proceedings. The double responsibility of

the sheriff is so well balanced that neither property nor individual liberty is ever endangered
through it, and matters are much simplified by
being all united in one person. Besides these
functions, the sheriff also reports the result of
elections held in the county: in some States,
he is also receiver of the rates. These offices
are held in great consideration, are very much
sought after and are entirely paid by the
parties.

But however well constituted the court may
be, its walls would remain mute and deserted
without the lawyers. Tribunals and litigants
have certainly been invented for them, for they
are the parties who most profit by them. There
is in the United States but one class of lawyers,
who perform the functions of conveyancers, attornies, notaries, &c.; their legal title is counsellor at law. They are officers of the court,
and, as such, take the oath of good conduct,
and are subject to a disciplinary system. They
may be suspended, or even broken by the court.
They are admitted upon an examination, which
takes place in full court, without any previous
course of study being necessary.

The United States and the States employ a
counsellor in each of their courts, but that does
not constitute him a public officer: the United

States are his client, that is all. He appears in
all their civil and criminal causes, and as the
latter are always prosecuted in the name of the
United States, or of the people of the State, it
is he who pleads for them; but it is the people
itself, by its grand jury, who prosecutes. He
is paid like any other counsel, furnishing at
the end of each term his account for fees,
which the judge certifies. The office of attorney
to the United States is much sought after, because, besides being very lucrative, as the United
States are very good clients and payers, it
gives precedence at the bar; but that is all, for
the district attorney (as he is called) may be
suspended by the court, or even broken like any
other practitioner; neither is he prevented from
undertaking other causes, provided they are not
against the United States.

The attorney of the United States at the
supreme court has the title of attorney-general;
he is the head of the bar, the real minister of
justice. The courts being entirely independent,
equally of the executive and the legislative
powers, it is only as party that the former can
appear before them. All the district attornies
receive orders, instructions, consultations, from
the attorney-general. He is consulted by the
members of the government in all doubtful

cases. He orders or stops prosecutions in cases
in which the revenue or the United States are
concerned. But it is himself who pleads their
cause before the supreme court, and even before
the circuit courts when they are very important.
He is considered part of the president's cabinet
council.

But now that the court is constituted, I must
endeavour to shew it to you in action : but for
that purpose there must be a jury. Some time,
then, before each term, and after the formalities
required by law, which vary in each state, the
clerk delivers to the sheriff two writs of *venire
facias,* by one of which he commands him to
call a grand jury, and by the other one or two
lists of forty-eight petty jurymen each, taking
care to select *boni et legales homines.* The qualifications implied by this clause vary a little in
different States; however, they are in general
the same as those required for voting, that is,
being a freeman, of age, and paying any tax
whatever. To be of the grand jury it is necessary to be a housekeeper. The sheriff selects
the jury in rotation from a list which he keeps of
all those eligible within his jurisdiction, in such
a way, however, as that all parts of his county
or district may be as equally represented as possible. He consults also their convenience in

summoning those who have other business at
the place at which the court is held, and passing
over those that would be too much inconve-
nienced by attending. This, however, is op-
tional on his part, for those who are summoned
must attend.

On the day fixed by law, the judge and all
those who have business in court, or are attracted
by curiosity, repair to the court-house. No
particular dress distinguishes the judge nor any
body else. No soldiers of any kind are to be
seen there. A sort of rostrum constitutes the
bench of the judge; seats on each side are prepared for the jury. The clerk sits at a table immediately under the judge. The lawyers are
ranged round a table reserved for them in the
centre; the audience behind; the sheriff and
his people where they please. As soon as the
court is seated, the sheriff opens the court by
a proclamation uttered aloud. The noise ceases,
for what was before but an assembly of equal
citizens, becomes by the proclamation, a tribunal.

The sheriff having previously indorsed upon
the *venire*, the names of the persons he has
selected, the clerk calls them over. Those who
are not present are fined, or, if they have no
excuses, even imprisoned, for contempt of court.
He commences always by the grand jury. It

must be composed of more than twelve, and
less than twenty-four persons; in general from
sixteen to twenty-three.   When they have
answered to their names, entered within the en-
closure, and the judge has decided upon the
validity of the excuses which some of them may
have offered, and has appointed a foreman; the
clerk administers to them the oath, engaging
them to inquire into any breach of the laws
which may have taken place within the county;
and to represent it to the court, accusing nobody from malice, nor suffering fear to prevent
them from making accusations: and further to
keep strictly secret all that passes before them,
or that they may learn. This oath taken, the
judge delivers his charge, a sort of admonition,
in which he instructs them in their duties, communicates any changes that may have taken
place in the criminal law, and calls their attention more particularly to such or such a law,
according to circumstances.   That done, the
grand jury retire into the room prepared for
them.   They forthwith receive a report from
each magistrate of all persons accused, including those in custody, and those for whose appearance he has taken bail, the charges against
them, and a list of the witnesses in support of
them.   For although the   eriff, or even any

citizen may, upon legitimate presumptions, arrest
an individual, he is bound without any delay to
bring him before a magistrate, who alone can
commit or order him to find bail, and who is
responsible in damages and costs for an illegal detention. The magistrate examines the
accused, and the witnesses for and against. If
he believe there is ground sufficient for a trial,
he requires security for the appearance not only
of the accused, but of the witnesses; and produces them before the grand jury on the first
day of the next assizes. If there be no ground
for trial, he forthwith discharges the accused.

The grand jury is furnished by the district
attorney, with an indictment in the name of the
people of the United States, or of the jury
itself, according to the local forms; they examine
into its probability, hearing only the witnesses
in support of the charge, and without ever
questioning the prisoner, who may always re-
tract the confessions he may have made before
the magistrate. For it is one of the first maxims
of the common law that a prisoner may say
nothing against himself. If the grand jury
find that there is a probability of crime, the
foreman indorses upon the indictment, ' a true
bill,' but if they believe the accused innocent, he
writes, ' *ignoramus;*' and the prisoner is imme-

diately discharged. All these proceedings, as well as the examination of the witnesses, are, for obvious reasons, kept strictly secret.

But it is not only the magistrates who have the right of carrying complaints before the grand jury; this right belongs to every body, and is perhaps the most sacred of all civil rights. The charge remains secret until the grand jury have decided on the indictment, which the District Attorney draws up by their orders. In cases, also, of crimes against the United States, or the State, their attorney prefers a charge and an indictment in their name.

The grand jury have a right to call before them, under penalty of fine and imprisonment, all those whose evidence may be deemed by them elucidatory of the facts. When they have doubts upon a point of law, it is the judge's province to enlighten them. Their sittings continue from day to day, in a place appointed for them, until they have decided on all charges presented to them. Every day they lay before the court the indictments on which they have decided, and on the last day of the session make a general presentment. That is to say, they make a report on every thing which appears to them amiss in the present state of the county, not being however of a nature to furnish matter

o

for particular accusation. They say, for instance, that the roads are bad, that the police magistrates neglect their duty, that such a law, lately passed, does not fulfil its purpose, that such a measure ought to be adopted by the legislature. These presentments are considered as the expression of the wishes of the people, and the greatest attention is paid to them. They cannot pronounce an indictment, or make a presentment, without there being at least twelve of their number in its favour, whatever may be the number present. When they have made their presentment, they are dismissed.

While the grand jury is engaged in its inquiries, and sending prisoners before the court, the judge proceeds to the calling over of the names of the petty jury, to satisfy himself of their obedience to the summons; after which he calls on the causes. Here the practice varies a little as to forms, in different courts, but so little, essentially, that in speaking of the rules of the court in which I have practised, you may form a tolerable idea of the others.

In general the causes are called three times: the first to know in what stage they are, the second to fix the day of trial, and the third to dispose of them in one way or other. The criminal causes are mostly gone into first, in

order that no delay may take place in dis-
charging the acquitted prisoners; then the civil
causes, which must come before a jury; then,
lastly, the motions of form, questions of right,
and when the court has that jurisdiction, causes
in chancery.

Let us see the manner of proceeding in a
capital charge: the prisoner is brought before
the court under the guard and responsibility of
the sheriff; he stands before the judge, whilst
he is told that the country, represented by a
grand jury, charges him with murder.   The
indictment being read to him, he is asked to
plead; he answers that he is not guilty, and that
he will be tried by the country, that is, by a
jury; for if he does not answer, or if he confess
himself guilty, the court, after having warned
him repeatedly of the consequences, is obliged
to pass sentence upon him.   These are the only
questions which the court, or the jury, or any
body, have a right to put to the prisoner upon
the subject of the charge.

The next thing is to form a jury to proceed
to trial: the clerk calls the first on the list of
the jury, and placing him opposite to the prisoner, asks the latter if he will be tried by that
person; if he says yes, the juror is sworn to
decide between the people and the prisoner, and

he then takes his seat upon the bench, under the
protection of one of the sheriff's officers.   But
the prisoner may object to a certain number of
jurors (who vary from twenty to fifty,) without
assigning any reason, and as many as he pleases,
by giving a legal reason.   If, for instance, a
juror have been witness against him when examined before the magistrate; if he have been
sworn in the same cause in another term; if
he have formed and expressed an opinion of his
affair of a nature to prevent him from being un-
prejudiced; he may be objected to both by the
accused and the counsel for the prosecution;
but the latter rarely avails himself of this prerogative.   It often happens that the jury lists
are exhausted before the twelve persons required
have been found; in which case, the sheriff is
authorised to call "talesmen," that is, to take
the first persons to be had in the hall, the street,
the town, or lastly, in the county, until a jury
can be formed of twelve men, against whom
the prisoner can make no objection.   The
judge may be examined upon oath as to their
impartiality; and as soon as the twelve are
chosen, they are inclosed in their seats, under
the protection of the sheriff, so that nobody can
speak or communicate with them secretly:
that done, the counsel for the prosecution re-

peats the accusation to the jury, always in presence of the prisoner, details his evidence, and introduces his witnesses in proof. Every witness introduced is sworn to tell the truth, the whole truth, and nothing but the truth; he is afterwards examined by the party who calls him; when he has done, the other party cross-examines him; then the first re-examines him; and then the second does the same, and so on, until nothing more can be extracted: this order is always observed both in civil and criminal cases. The court and the jury may question the witness when they please, but in general they leave it to the counsel, who perform the task very well: it is here, indeed, that they display their talent and their professional tact, by which more causes have been gained than by eloquence and learning.

But before allowing the counsel for the prosecution to examine a witness, the prisoner's counsel takes care to make all possible objections; for the law of evidence, perhaps the most logical portion of the common law, is full of extremely nice distinctions on this subject. There are, according to this law, two things to consider in a witness: his competency and his credibility; his competency must be tried by the court previous to his examination before the jury, whose mind might be biassed by his depositions, though they might turn out not to be legal. If, then, he does not know the nature of an oath; if he is connected by ties of marriage with the prisoner; or if he have a pecuniary interest, however small, in the issue of the cause, he cannot be heard.

As to the credibility of the witness, that is entirely for the jury to decide, by giving to his evidence what weight they think proper; besides, some questions cannot be put, for a witness must only depose to what he has seen or heard in respect of the matter; he cannot express an opinion; he cannot report hearsays; he cannot be forced to say anything against his own honour or interest. Thus each new witness, and each question put to him, often gives rise to a discussion in which the court alone decides, without any interference of the jury.

If one of the parties thinks himself wronged by the decision of the court, he may protest in writing, and the judge is obliged to sign it: this is called filing a bill of exceptions for the decision of the judges, which does not prevent the cause from going on, but becomes a question of law, to be tried by a superior court, and a means of setting aside the decision.

After the counsel for the State has concluded

his exposition and the examination of his witnesses; the counsel for the prisoner produces
witnesses for the defence, and examines them, in
contradiction to the other side, in the manner I
have already described. Frequently the hearing of witnesses on each side lasts several days,
during which, the jury are bound not to separate, not to speak of the matter, or listen to any
thing on the subject. The accused, as well as
the State, can compel the attendance of the
witnesses necessary to his defence. This is done
by a writ of *subpœna,* which is an order of the
court to the witness to hold himself ready to
give testimony in such a matter, under penalties
of fine and imprisonment sufficient to bind him.

The hearing of witnesses concluded, the
counsel for the prisoner recapitulates the contradictory evidence, and puts forth all his means
of defence. In general a prisoner employs
several lawyers, who speak one after another,
the youngest commencing, and the eldest, or
principal, concluding. Afterwards, the counsel
for the prosecution replies; then he may be
again answered; but it is always the accuser, in
criminal matters, and the plaintiff, in civil, who
has the last word. The pleadings ended, the
judge sums up the whole matter to the jury,
explains to them the law which governs cases

of the kind, and, without prejudicing their opinion upon the facts, points out to them that which they ought to receive as the law. This summary is called the judge's charge. The parties may take a "bill of exception" to the legal opinion it manifests.

And now comes the decisive moment, that which makes the heart of every prisoner beat, for in capital cases he must be present. This is the moment in which the jury retire to deliberate: they are conducted out of court by one of the sheriff's people, in whose charge they remain. They are shut up in a room furnished with a table, pens, ink, and paper, and a jug of water. When once a jury is thus shut up, nobody is allowed access to them, nor none of them can go out until they have unanimously agreed on their verdict. According to the old common law, they remained shut up until they were agreed; but in case one of the jury was to die of hunger, thirst, fatigue, or otherwise, or if he escaped, the cause could not be decided by the eleven others, and it would be sent before another jury; hence arose the modern practice of permitting the withdrawal of a jury, in cases where their agreement is impossible. This, however, is not considered necessary before a jury has been shut up, at least, twenty-four

hours, and often more; for as long as the judge
has reason to hope that they will agree, it is
his duty to keep them locked up: but when he
is convinced that unanimity is impossible, then
the list of the jury is called over, and dismissed
in due form; the proceedings are void, and, at
the next sessions, or immediately, if the parties
consent, a new trial is recommenced before another jury. This, however, seldom happens: in
general, after a time, of various duration, the
jury declares its verdict; if not guilty, the
prisoner is immediately released; but even if he
is found guilty, he has still many chances of
escape.

The counsel for the prisoner may move for
another jury, and a new trial, in all cases in
which any defect, as to competency, may have
been discovered in any of the jury; or if any
of the witnesses against him have been found
to be perjured or suborned since their deposi-
tion; or if, by some accident or ignorance, the
prisoner has been prevented from making use
of some important evidence; the judge is then
invested with a discretionary power, which,
however, he is bound to exercise, according to
precedents, to grant or to refuse a new trial; if
he grants it, every thing that has been done is
annulled, and it is necessary to begin again.

The defendant may also "move in arrest of judgment." This motion is grounded upon irregularities of form, or on " bills of exception," which must be tried by a superior court. The courts of appeal, in these cases, decide only upon the law, never on the ground of action; and if they differ from the inferior court, the matter is re-heard by another jury, but before the same judge, who is bound to conform to the decision of the court of appeal on the contested point.

It is very important to observe, that all these advantages are restricted to the defence; for the people's attorney cannot take advantage of them. If a prisoner is acquitted, there is an end of the matter: he cannot be tried again for the same crime. The law even carries its clemency so far that, in any capital matter, an accused person cannot have his life put in jeopardy but once for the same thing: it is considered exposed, by every appearance, before a jury, under a capital charge. If then, in this case, a jury grant a new trial, or a superior court annul the decision of an inferior, the accused is immediately released, by pleading " *autrefois convict*," (tried before,) for his life cannot be put twice in jeopardy.

It is upon this humane provision of the law

that the motion for " quashing the indictment"
is grounded. The common law requires a minute exactness in an instrument on which the
life of a citizen depends ; the smallest error is
fatal to it. Not only the counsel for the prisoner, but any barrister acting as *amicus curiæ*,
may point out defects which vitiate an indictment ; but this is useless until a prisoner has
been before a jury, since, as his life has not
been in danger, another may be found, (as is
often done, even after a verdict, in cases which
are not capital ;) whereas, after every thing has
been exhausted for the defence, if an error of
form, however insignificant, is found in the indictment, the accused is discharged. And this
is the law which some people have been pleased
to represent as a law of blood ! It is impossible
to afford more protection to the life and honour
of the citizens against arbitrary power than is
done by the common law of America, and I may
say also of England. The maxim of this law is
that it is better to let a hundred guilty escape
than to punish one innocent person.

But if the jury find the prisoner guilty, and
there is no defect of form, neither in the pro-
cedure nor in the indictment, the judge pronounces sentence, and nothing can save the prisoner but the pardon of the president or the

governor, according to the court in which he has been condemned. You see, then, that criminal justice is very expeditious ; for if a man be arrested to-day, and the grand jury be sitting, he may be accused to-day, tried to-morrow, and nothing can prevent his being hanged the day following, unless he asks for time to sue for pardon. In general, however, prisoners are allowed to postpone their cause to the next term, but that can be done on their application only. If by the fault of the state-attorney, or by any fortuitous accident (such, for instance, as not being able to form a jury), the trial has been put off for three successive terms, the prisoner is entitled to his discharge. But he may be retaken on a new indictment, for there is no time limited within which the people must prosecute, and he cannot save himself by pleading " *autrefois convict,*" since he has not been before a jury. The people's, or district attorney, is invested with the power of declaring that he will not proceed *(nolo prosequi),* whenever he may see that the charge cannot be sustained ; and it is his duty to abandon it, in order to prevent useless expenses, as well to the prisoner as to the State.

In civil causes, justice is less expeditious : it requires at least two terms to try any action.

The common law, by a system of perfect analysis, has divided all civil inquiries into certain
categories, and for each injury it has provided
a particular remedy. It is necessary, therefore,
to follow very strictly the form of action established for each category, and not waste time
and labour by taking out a writ for one form
of action which belongs to another. The Sybil
must be consulted according to the rules of
her temple, and then she will always answer
justly, quickly, and with astonishing exactness;
but if you come to put foolish questions to her,
she will either remain silent or drive you from
the temple, put you out of court, or, to speak
to you in her language, declare your action a
non-suit; you will then have the costs to pay,
and may recommence fresh actions for the same
injury until you have knocked at the right door.

Actions are divided into personal, real, and
mixed, according to the nature of the thing
claimed. The first and last alone are in use; the
complicated forms of the second having caused
their abandonment in practice. The first are very
numerous, as the action of *assumpsit*, the most
common of all, by which you demand damages
for wrong done in not fulfilling an engagement;
the action of debt, by which you demand the
payment of a debt; of *detinue*, if you claim per-

sonal property which another has converted to
his use; of trover, if, instead of the thing itself, you demand only damages and interest in
its stead; of trespass, *quare clausum fregit*, to
be indemnified for any damages done to your
property by the defendant, his servant, or his
cattle; of trespass *vi et armis*, when the injury
for which you claim damages has been done on
your person, or proceeds *ex delictu;* of trespass on the case, for any special damage sustained, whether in consequence of slander, libel, seduction, &c., &c.   It would be too long
to enumerate them all.

The mixed actions are much less numerous:
they are resorted to only to decide questions of
real property.   The only actions of this sort in
the United States are that of ejectment, to decide the right to real property; and that of
trespass, *quare clausum fregit*, which decides on
the possession.

It is impossible to imagine a cause of complaint for which the common law has not provided a form of action, but it is necessary to be
well acquainted with them, and be well exercised in analysis, to apply them properly. When,
therefore, the attorney has heard the complaint
of his client, cleared away the mist of eloquence
of the interested party, stripped it of all super-

fluous matters tediously narrated, and has at
last found the gist of the action, he prepares
a memorandum containing the names of the
parties, the sum demanded, the nature of the
action, and the signature of the plaintiff's attorney; this memorandum is sent to the clerk
of the court in sufficient time before the opening
of term, so that all the formalities required by
law, and which vary in each State, may be observed.

Upon this memorandum, the clerk prepares
a writ " *de capias respondendum.*" This is an
order from the court, enjoining the sheriff
to summon the defendant to settle the demand
of the plaintiff, or to appear before the judge
on the first day of term, to answer the complaint. It is in general by this writ that all
personal actions commence; however, in many cases, where there is a fear that the defendant may withdraw his person and property from the jurisdiction of the court, the
suit commences by a " writ of attachment :"
this is an order given to the sheriff to seize the
property of the defendant, and hold it at the
disposal of the court. This writ, however, is
never granted but upon the oath of the plaintiff,
that his demand is just, accompanied by an
undertaking, with bail, by which he engages to

indemnify the defendant for all damages which
may ensue to him in consequence of the attachment, if his demand should be rejected by
the court. The defendant, on his side, may
always obtain replevy from the seizure of his
property by the sheriff, by engaging, with bail,
to reproduce it whenever required. The duty
of the sheriff, as soon as he has received these
writs, is to execute them immediately, and to
return them to the clerk on the first day of
term, after indorsing upon them the result of
his proceedings.

Besides the memorandum, the plaintiff's attorney must send to the clerk, before the first
day of term, his declaration, setting forth, according to prescribed forms, from which it is
dangerous to deviate, the injuries upon which
the plaintiff's demand rests. The form of these
declarations varies greatly, according to the
sort of action adopted and the facts of the case;
but there is never any necessity to state the real
details of the matter : it is sufficient to state, in
the received forms, the general facts which authorize the bringing of the action. It is only
when the case comes into court that the full
details of the affair are entered into. The rules,
however, which regulate these matters are so
delicate, that the greatest care is necessary to

avoid mistakes, of which the immediate consequence would be to put the plaintiff out of
court.

The defendant's attorney, after this declaration,
must answer it, either by pleading or demurring;
a demurrer is an answer by which the defendant
admits the facts of the case, but denies that
these facts give any legal right to the plaintiff to
sustain his action either at all or in the manner
in which he has brought it. A 'plea' is an answer
by which the defendant denies a part of, or all
the facts of the declaration. The plaintiff has a
right to reply to each of these two answers. The
defendant may reply to him again: all this in
writing, and according to received forms. They
arrive at last, after dissecting and dividing the
question, at a complete contradiction; this is
what is called 'issue.' These issues are of law
or of fact. If they are of law, they are tried by
the court alone; but if they contain facts, the
cause goes before a jury.

It is therefore only after the parties themselves
are agreed upon the point in dispute in their
affair, that the court takes cognizance of it. The
first term is what is called an ' appearance,' the
judge merely calls the cause to ascertain that
the parties are in court; if they are not, there is
default, and the court gives judgment imme-

P

diately. If the parties answer, they are allowed
until the first day of next term to demur, plead,
answer, reply, &c., but it is necessary on this
day that they be agreed upon the point in
dispute between them, and terminate all written
pleadings. If at this stage the cause depends
upon a contested fact, it is immediately carried
before a jury, just in the same manner as I have
described to you in the criminal causes. In
the same manner, the plaintiff's counsel commences by the exposition of his case, and the
examination of his witnesses. The defendant
produces his, and answers him; the former con-
cludes; then the jury retires, and is shut up
until they give an unanimous verdict. The
same forms after the verdict take place; the
same means of appealing from it are allowed,
except that this right belongs equally to both
parties. You will observe that, in all cases,
whether civil or criminal, the examination of
witnesses is always oral and before a jury. The
predilection of the common law for this species
of evidence is such that written proof is only
admitted when supported by oral. Before reading a letter or a note to the jury, it is necessary
that they be admitted by the adverse party, or
that the signature to them be proved by a
witness. It is only the seal of the United

States, and that of their courts, which do not
require to be proved. In like manner the laws
and customs of other countries are proved by
the testimony of witnesses who know them.
Immediately after the judgment, the clerk gives
to the sheriff the writ necessary to its execution,
whether a *fieri facias, venditioni exponas* or
capias ad satisfaciendum, according to the nature
of the case. It is for the sheriff then to execute
the judgment, but in that he must be guided,
always under his own responsibility, by the
plaintiff. These " writs" of execution may, however, be suspended or annulled by other writs,
either of the same court, a superior court, or a
court of equity; for example, by a writ of
supersedeas, or an injunction to stay proceedings.
The justice of these writs is discussed again,
either before the courts of appeal or those of
equity who have granted them, in such a way,
however, as that the superior courts are never
troubled, but with questions purely legal, entirely
relieved from the mere facts. These are the
decisions which are collected in books of reports,
and form the common law.

In courts of equity the practice is entirely
different, and resembles that of the cannon law,
to which the courts owe their origin. There
exists no form of action; every complaint, of

whatever nature it may be, is brought there by
a petition to the chancellor, stating all the facts
of the case in the fullest manner, without established forms, and under the oath of the petitioner
who prays that the defendant may be obliged to
answer upon oath. If the Chancellor thinks the
complaint reasonable, he orders the defendant
to answer, or he authorises the examination in
writing of witnesses, by commissioners, whom
he appoints *ad hoc*, and who must report to him.
The parties may answer and reply, propose or
demand new witnesses, until they be agreed on
the point in dispute between them; then the
chancellor, having read the documents, listens
to the pleadings in open court, and decrees
accordingly.   But it must be remarked that a
court of equity can never decide upon a question
purely of fact, unless upon the admission of the
parties themselves; in any other case, it must
send that question before a court of law, with an
order to try it by a jury, and report to it the
result.

I have tried as well as I could to explain to
you the judiciary system of the United States,
particularly in the details of practice, which is,
I think, the least known. I have been very
long, and I fear tedious, but you will allow that
the subject is not lively or very easy to strew

with flowers.   Courts composed of a single
judge, of which all the business is confided for
execution to a single man, are so different in
their construction from those of Europe, that it
has been necessary to make you acquainted
with them before speaking to you of the laws
themselves, and to examine them under a moral
and political view.   Before terminating this
letter, let me again remind you that I have no
book of authority before me, so that you are
reduced to take all I tell you on my word, for
it would be impossible for me to quote from
memory.   I believe, however, that I have not
committed any error of importance.

LETTER SEVENTH.

OF THE LAWS.—*The Common Law preferable to Codes, its greater susceptibility to improvement ; Oath-taking, present state of American Law on the subject ; alterations in the Common Law since the Norman Conquest, consequent on the changes in property ; uncertainty in the Law more apparent than real, and not an evil if real ; facilities in the United States of putting supposed improvements to the test ; state of the Criminal Law ; origin and explanation of the term " Benefit of Clergy ;" punishment of Death, the desirableness of its total abolition considered, Transportation the best substitute ; punishment of misdemeanors ; Libel Law ; Libels against the Government disregarded ; private defamation ; Laws relative to Real and Personal Property ; divorce ; recovery of debts ; state of crimes ; cheapness of justice ; fondness for litigation ; Arbitration ; respectability and talents of the American Bar.*

Brussels ; February, 1832.

PERFECTIBILITY, that quality which distinguishes the white man from every other species of men and of animals, ought to be found in all political institutions ; for without it, they cannot long

fulfil their objects.   In truth, institutions must
either keep pace with the human mind in its
progress, and become modelled upon the habits,
wants, and opinions of the time present; or else,
being in opposition to all these, must unavoid-
ably be broken up, and give place to an inter-
regnum of disorder and anarchy, until new institutions, in harmony with the time, be established.   It is this faculty of following and
adapting itself to the progress of society, which
eminently distinguishes the common law, and,
generally speaking, any law founded on custom,
as opposed to written codes of law; which, being
unsusceptible of enlargement, cannot but impede
the progress of society, until eventually it can no
longer support the yoke, and therefore is forced
to break it.   But there is a great distinction to
be made between a code standing as a limit to
legislation, and a code only intended to serve
as the starting point of a custom.   In my
opinion, a code of the first sort is always perni-
cious; and the other is at least useless and dangerous, in giving to the possible errors of those
who form it an authority not liable to be contested.   This opinion, I am aware, is not that of
Europe, it is far even from being general in the
United States: people often imagine that, if
they had a written code, they could dispense

with lawyers. I had, in my study, a copy of
five French codes in a little 12mo. volume, and
many times my clients have observed, as they
looked at it, "people must be very happy in that
country, since every body may know his rights
without consulting lawyers, merely by reading
this little book ;" and they would compare it
deridingly with some hundreds of volumes
which composed my yet very incomplete library.
In writing to you, I need not dilate on this gross
error. The French codes, although perhaps the
clearest existing, are mere Hebrew to those
who have not made them their study. All that
class of persons of whom I am about to speak to
you, desire what is called a codification, in other
words, they desire that, without changing the
provisions of the law, every thing useful should
be extracted from all these immense folios, be
digested in a single statute, under legislative
sanction, and the rest be thrown into the
fire. The lawyers themselves are divided in
opinion : lazy people, who dislike research or
mental labour, think that, by this means, they
should be put on a level with profound lawyers,
who have always a conclusive precedent to cite,
in answer to all they can advance. Other
lawyers, very learned, but imbued with the philosophical principles of the encyclopædists, wish

to simplify and give regularity to the law, by reducing it into a single formula. This party has triumphed in the State of Louisiana, where a code has been adopted, half Roman, half common law; but it is considered only as a starting point, and already a vast incrustation of common law has been formed upon it.

The most learned jurisconsults of the United States, however, prefer the common law simply as it exists. ' Have we not,' say they, ' digests and elementary treatises upon each part of the law, and upon the law of each State ? These books, it is true, are not invested with legislative sanction, and so much the better; for the names of Blackstone, Comyn, Deane, Ingersoll, &c. cannot consecrate an error, or arrest the progress of legal science, whilst a legislative Act would do so. Suppose it is now discovered that such an opinion of a great lawyer, or such a decision of a court, was erroneous, and productive, in practice, of great injustice, the superior courts would have no difficulty in correcting it, and substituting, in its place, a new decision, more suited to the present wants of society. In this manner, the improvements in legal science are made slowly and imperceptibly, but always at the precise point of time when their want is felt; whereas, if the law were written, and invested with legislative sanction, a new law would be necessary to alter it, and this would not be made until long after the abuse had become insupportable.'

I will mention some instances of this necessary improvement of the common law; as regards oaths, for instance. Formerly, those only who were of the communion of the holy Catholic church were allowed to make oath ; no heretics, Jews, or Pagans, and, with much stronger reason, no Infidels enjoyed this privilege. In course of time, however, and in proportion as England itself became protestant, all Christians were admitted to swear upon the Gospels. As commercial relations extended, the Jews were next admitted to swear in their way ; and afterwards the privilege was allowed to Turks and Pagans. The Quakers, not being willing to take an oath, their simple affirmation was accepted in law. The English law at present, I think, is that any man who believes in a future state of rewards and punishments, may make oath, if he pledge his future existence to the truth of what he advances. By this arrangement, unbelievers and pure Deists are prevented from giving legal testimony. In some States of the Union, where much bigotry still remains,

as in the New England States, the courts follow these decisions; so that when a witness is
introduced, the adverse party may ask him—
" Do you believe in the existence of God or
of the devil?" and if he answer in the negative, his testimony is rejected. In the South,
however, there has lately been a very important
decision, by the court of appeal of the State of
South Carolina, which, without deciding whether the oath of any one who does not believe
in a future state may be received, says that
these questions upon belief cannot be put to a
witness; because that would be obliging him,
perhaps, to accuse himself of something to his
shame, namely, forcing him to avow his unbelief. This, then, is the law, at the present moment, in the southern States. But I will tell
you what it will be ere long throughout the
Union, as soon as the question shall be brought
before the federal courts. By the constitution
of the United States no belief is necessary, in
order to be admitted or elected to any office
whatever; but by law any magistrate or officer,
before entering upon his functions, must swear
to support and defend the constitution and laws
of the United States. But now, if the oath were to
be rejected under pretext of unbelief, that would
be rendering a religious belief necessary, in or-

der to be appointed to an office, which is evidently contrary to the constitution.   The question has not yet been brought under consideration, and the courts are not going to contrive
difficulties beforehand; but as soon as that takes
place, the courts will decide in this manner. Mr.
Jefferson, for instance, was wholly an unbeliever;
he said, wrote, and printed so, a thousand times,
as you may see in his works, long before he was
elected president of the United States.   If, at
his installation, the chief justice of the United
States had refused to administer the oath to him,
the courts would have been applied to for a writ
of *mandamus* against the chief justice, ordering
him to proceed to the administration of the oath:
the question would then have been debated in full
court, and the law would have been fixed.

There can be no doubt that, in a generation
or two, the oath will have lost all religious
character before the United States courts; and
be considered only as a solemn assurance, made
according to ancient forms, and consecrated by
prejudices and forgotten opinions; but if application was now to be made to the legislators to allow
oaths to be taken by unbelievers, (which, as you
have seen, is in fact the law,) what religious
disputes would be raised in the bosom of the
assembly!   A law of this nature would not

pass until after many very stormy debates, and happening suddenly, would make a sort of revolution in jurisprudence, while the slow and progressive changes of the common law obtain the same result, without agitation, and without offending any body.

At the time of the Norman conquest the common law entirely adopted the feudal system; it is, perhaps, even to this race very remarkable in judiciary annals for their litigating spirit, which they implanted wherever they obtained a footing, that the common law has, perhaps, owed its greatest development. At that time the only riches were lands and castles, or personalities annexed to them, such as flocks, &c.; commerce did not exist, or was confined to some Jews and Lombards. The common law of that period concerned, therefore, only real property, regulating all cases of acquisition, succession, and confiscation of feofs, with the greatest and most minute exactness; then, real actions only were known to it: and if you consulted it upon personal interests, the judges of the King's Bench sent you away with the maxim, *de minimis non curat lex,* for your consolation.

It was the interest of the feudal aristocracy to preserve property in their families; thus all the law was directed to secure entails. Compare this state of things, not with that of America, but solely with the actual state of England, where the lands and crops, in a word, the real property, forms but a very inferior part of the wealth of the country; its manufactures, its forges, its mines, its ships, the immense amount of its capital, are the true sources of its prosperity. It is not therefore now, when commercial transactions are in question, involving more considerable interests than any Norman baron ever possessed, that the present judges may answer, *de minimis non curat lex.* Thus as I have said, real actions have been entirely abandoned, and personal actions are the only ones in modern practice. But this immense change has been made without agitation or revolution, by the slow and constant progress of the common law, following, as close as possible, the steps of national industry. In England an old aristocracy still exists, a party clinging to the past, and struggling vigorously against every improvement, so that the common law crawling along only follows at a distance the social progress. The difference which still exists, for instance, between real and personal property, the difficulties with which the transmission of the former is still surrounded, the difference made between an instrument signed only and one signed and sealed, are so

many remnants of feudal barbarism; but in
America it is not so: the common law is almost
on a level with our wants. In that country, in
which activity in all branches of employment is
the order of the day, the lawyers must exert
themselves like the rest; and if, on one hand,
the surface of the country is covered with cause-
ways, canals, and rail-roads, if the towns are
filled with libraries, colleges and universities, if
the Indians are repulsed, the deserts subdued,
new harvests created, and transported to mar-
kets unknown a few years back, if the empire
of superstition is dying out; on the other hand,
the courts of justice, the supreme power of the
State, is continually employed in improving the
common law, and rendering it worthy of a nation so rich, industrious, and enlightened. And,
indeed, why should more formalities be required
to sell an eighth of public land, which cost me
100 dollars, than a horse, which has cost me
500; than a bank share, which may be worth,
perhaps, 10,000; or than a fine ship, which
has furrowed every sea, and of which the price
may amount to 50,000? Why make a distinction between heirs and administrators or testamentary executors, since all entail upon real
property has ceased, since nothing hinders me
from leaving my property, of whatever nature it

may be, to whom I think proper; when, if I die *ab intestato,* my property will be partaken equally by all my children, and equally subject, whether real or personal, to the payment of my debts? Thus these distinctions begin to vanish rapidly, and the time may already be foreseen when it may be said of the American common law, compared to that of England, *pulcra mater, sed filia pulchrior.*

Let the legislatures employ themselves in passing laws financial, political, and of a local and temporary interest; but for God's sake let them leave to the wisdom of the courts the settlement of the details of the civil and criminal laws; let them not interfere but when the latter take the wrong road, and then only to rectify and put them into the right path.

It is the fashion in the United States, as in England, and I believe every where else, to complain of the uncertainty of the laws, but is this reproach well founded? I anticipate your answer, that it is not under the authority of a code, but that it is under that of a custom or common law. I will answer you, first, that frequently the uncertainty of the laws is only apparent, not only to the ignorant eye of the vulgar, but even to the more practised one of the lawyer. The client is naturally blinded by

his own interest, and the attorney, however well
informed, however learned, he may be, when he
has employed his meditations in finding good
reasons for his client, thinking but little of those
of his adversary, is apt to end by persuading himself more or less that he is right, and to blame
the uncertainty of the law when a decision of
the judge shows him his error.   And, in short,
the judge himself, between two counsel supporting
contrary opinions by the most ingenious arguments, must find himself extremely at a loss to
decide; and he too accuses the uncertainty of
the law, for what is only want of perspicacity in
himself, or inability to resist the eloquence of the
parties.   It is the human mind which is imperfect, and which always sins in the application of
the finest theories; we should lay the blame on
it, and not on the imperfection of the law.

But this uncertainty, supposing it to exist, is
it a misfortune? It is an old remark that 'the
letter killeth, the spirit giveth life.' Well, under
the administration of the common law, we have
the spirit of the law without the letter.   How
much crying injustice, indeed, would result from
the literal application of the articles of the best
code? Thus, in countries governed by that system,
do we not see the courts constantly employed
in explaining the letter of the law, so as entirely

Q

to change the sense? but under the authority of
the common law, this uncertainty is a great
good, for it invests the courts with discretionary
power to perfect the law; and then do not
forget that, according to my lord Coke, common
sense is a part of the common law. See how
these matters are managed in an English or
American court: the counsel on both sides exhaust themselves in learned subtleties and perfectly contradictory citations; the judge is in the
greatest perplexity, he does not know which to
think right; but the plain people of the jury
having listened attentively to the witnesses,
without understanding a single word of what
the counsel have been saying, withdraw, and in
a few minutes return quite astonished to find
themselves agreed upon a question which per-
plexes the court. Their verdict cuts the knot,
it carries always with it an inherent character
of justice which wins it acknowledgment and
convinces at once. The judge, all aghast, is
obliged to concur in it, and has now only to find
good legal reasons, authorities, and precedents, to
confirm the opinion of the jury, which from
thence becomes law itself, and settles subsequent
cases, until the social interest again requires an
aiteration in the law or the custom.

I do not recollect, in all my practice, having

seen more than one or two cases, in which, according to my cool and deliberate opinion, the American courts have not decided according to the real merit of the causes, and in an equitable and just manner between the parties. Between the learning of the judge and the plain good sense of the jury, perhaps the surest means is attained of arriving at the most equitable decision of a matter.

The varying nature of the common law makes it difficult to give you an exact picture of its present state in America; for if the judiciary organization vary in every State, the common law varies much more. I must begin by passing over the State of Louisiana, the system of which is wholly mixed, and is still on its trial. From what I have heard, however, it tends every day to an approximation with the law of the other States. This is, indeed, generally, the spirit of American jurisprudence. Twenty-four free governments existing together in the best intelligence, and united by ties of language and institutions nearly similar, are continually making experiments to ameliorate both their moral and physical condition. If the experiment succeed in one State, it is soon imitated by all the others; if it fail the new theory is as quickly abandoned. I have already stated, that the reports of the supreme courts both of England and of the United States, as also of each State, were received in all the courts as documentary information; it is therefore impossible that a new improvement can take place any where without its being known and imitated. Nor is it the courts only who contribute to this end; the legislatures themselves being composed in great part of lawyers, who often practise in different States together, feel the same tendency towards harmonization and general improvement. In giving you, therefore, the principal features of American law, it is possible that my picture may not exactly resemble the laws of any particular State, but it will have the general physiognomy of them all. Wherever I may be sensible of the existence of any striking differences, I will, however, point them out.

Laws may be divided into three great classes. They are either political, regulating the interests of the citizen towards society, and as such, establishing his part therein, and the obedience he owes to the government of his country; or criminal, defining the acts which society condemns and forbids, and the manner of punishing them; or, lastly, civil, regulating all the transactions of individuals with each other in their private capacities.

The political laws, presented under different points of view, have already formed the subject of the preceding letters, and will be further adverted to in those which follow. As I have before stated, the constitutions of the United States, are written and you can very easily procure them. The commentaries which I might add would only bear upon points of detail, which could in no way interest you.

The criminal law is derived from two sources, the common law and the written law. From time immemorial the common law has given technical definitions of different crimes, and has attached to each a particular penalty; but in its infancy these definitions savoured of ignorance, and the penalties it inflicted were stamped with the barbarism and cruelty of the time. The penalty of death was prodigally lavished, not only against high treason, wilful murder, manslaughter, maiming, arson, rape, burglary; but even for horse and sheep stealing, counterfeiting the seal of the State, of money, (which is considered treason,) bank notes, and many other signatures, public and private; in a word, for every thing bearing the definition of felony.

If I am not mistaken the number of crimes or offences punished with death amounted to more

than sixty; but the judges soon found a way of
bringing the law to a more humane practice. The
method adopted was certainly an odd one, but
it illustrates strikingly the spirit of the age. At
first the clergy were granted an exemption from
all punishment. This privilege was extended
afterwards to all those who, even without being
in orders, belonged, in however slight a manner,
to the church. Lastly, but for one offence only,
to all those who were clerks therein, or in other
words, who could read: but to secure their not
claiming the *privilegium clericale* or benefit of
clergy twice, they were burnt in the hand with
a hot iron. This privilege of the clergy however, never extended to high treason, murders
and some other offences; so that felonies, all of
which were formerly punished with death, became divided into two classes. Those which
were "clergiable," that is, for which the clerical
privilege could be claimed, and those to which
that privilege did not extend. In course of time
the proof of being clerks was dispensed with,
and every body, whether he could read or not,
was allowed to enjoy this privilege. At last, by
a law of George the First, the judges were at
liberty to transport to America those who were
found guilty of "clergiable" crimes, and the
mark was suppressed. By other laws made in

the time of George the Third this new system
became regular, and imprisonment, forced labour,
transportation, fines, and whipping, were substituted for the penalty of death in all cases in
which, according to the ancient common law,
the clerical privilege had been obtainable; so
that although, even now, the English common
law pronounces the penalty of death in a great
number of cases, in practice these enactments
are modified in almost all, by the "benefits of
clergy," and by the laws which regulate its
application.

In almost all the States of America, the definition of crimes given by the common law is
preserved. And every lawyer must comprehend
the wisdom of this measure, by reflecting on the
difficulty of elementary definitions, how important it is that they should be rigorously
exact; and further, that this exactness cannot
be obtained, however explicit the law may be,
but by a long course of expositions and judicial
decisions. A few States, however, have altered
these definitions, and have adopted an entirely
different nomenclature; all on the contrary have
passed laws fixing a penalty to each offence,
and it is only in cases in which a crime has been
forgotten in the statutes, that it can be punished
by the common law.

In almost all the States the penalty of death

has been suppressed, except for high treason, piracy, wilful murder, arson, and rape. But in some, Pennsylvania for instance, it has been entirely abolished, and solitary imprisonment for life substituted. The same system is upon the point of being established in Louisiana and in some other States, and all the lawyers in the Union are divided upon the great question, whether the penalty of death ought to be continued for atrocious crimes, or be entirely abolished. The new system has been some time on trial in the States which have adopted it, and the others will probably be guided by the results. For my part, I see many inconveniences and no advantage in suppressing the penalty of death entirely.

The partisans of this system forget that the object which society should propose in punishing, is not to strike the criminal or to avenge itself, but rather to prevent the renewal of crime, in others, by the example of the criminal's punishment, and in himself by putting him out of a state to repeat it. The effect which the punishment produces upon the condemned himself is a consideration altogether subordinate, and which cannot enter into the account, all things being otherwise equal. For crimes which leave room for hope that the guilty may yet be reformed, the American penitentiary

system, of more or less prolonged solitary con-
finement, moderate labour, moral and religious
instruction, continual looking after and discipline
at once active and severe, is certainly the best.
But there are other actions by which man
declares himself openly at war with society, and
which leave no hope of reformation; and when
even that might be possible, society would run
too great a risk by putting it to the trial.   He
is become dangerous, and ought to be put out of
the condition to do injury.

If an impending rock threaten to crush my
house, the sole problem for me to resolve
is how to get rid of it in the most sure, expeditious, and economical manner.   If the
rock were endowed with feelings, I should certainly try, if there were several ways of ac-
complishing those three objects equally well, to
choose that which was the least disagreeable;
but it would not be until after I had put my
house in safety, that I should think of its ease
and convenience.   And so of the man who
has put a life in danger, who has compro-
mised all the dearest interests that man can
have in society, by a conspiracy to overturn the
form of a popular government, he who has not
only had the will, but almost the power actually
to make war against civil society; such a man

is dangerous, and it is the interest and duty of society to rid itself of him. This reasoning applies also to those who are guilty of wilful murder, piracy, or arson, crimes which in themselves comprehend all others. I think that these four cases are all for which the penalty of death should be retained.

The friends of the penitentiary system answer to this, that by shutting up a man alone for life, in a dungeon, he equally ceases to be dangerous to society, and suffers much less. I deny both propositions. There is no dungeon so secure from which a man may not escape, or which may not be forced, either during popular commotion, war, or earthquake, or a fire. What a pretty effect would either of these events produce should it open the Philadelphia jail, and turn loose upon society some hundreds of the most infamous villains the world ever produced? For moral depravity is always in an inverse ratio to the causes which lead to crime; and they who become criminals in a country of liberty, abundance, and happiness, such as the United States, are without doubt more depraved than those who groan under oppression, abide in ignorance, and pine for want. What! shall we expel far from our houses, far from our cities, the filth therein produced, and yet, at a great

expense, build sumptuous edifices, to heap up
carefully and treat with tenderness all the corruption and pestilential excrements of civil society? and should we not fear contagion? and
should we go on expending our money, lavishing
our care and our time to so vile a purpose?
This very building might serve for an asylum,
or an hospital; this very bread, steeped in the
tears of the innocent, might support the widow
and the orphan; and it is from them it is with-
held, not, as the friends of the penitentiary
system tell you, to alleviate the misfortunes of
the condemned, but to prolong their torments
during long years of trouble and agony, at a
great expense, and without any benefit to society.
Let every one put his hand upon his heart, and
say honestly if he would not prefer being executed at once, to remaining alone in prison
without any hope of release.   And let him then
reflect whether it is not a sentiment of mistaken
humanity, which would prefer substituting perpetual imprisonment to the penalty of death.

The only means of suppressing the penalty
of death, in my opinion, is by substituting transportation.   This system has in later times been
greatly improved in the English establishment
at Botany Bay.   Why do not other nations
seek some distant and lonely shores, where

colonies might be established upon the like
principles ? Crime would thus be rendered
subservient to public good, by enlarging the
sphere of civilization, and opening a new source
of commerce to offended society. But then the
penalty of death must be retained in the peni-
tential colony, as the only means of managing
a society so depraved; and in the mother country
also, but solely for the punishment of those who
returned before the period of their transportation
expired. Thus the refuse which society casts
from it, instead of being destroyed or heaped
up in sheer loss, would serve to fertilize and en-
rich new and distant lands. It is to this system,
probably, that all nations will come at last;
but then it should be extended to all crimes,
whereas in England, the penalty of death is retained in far too many cases.

In all the States, offences not involving the
penalty of death are punished by close confine-
ment of various durations, in prisons well secured, and under an excellent system of discipline;
the prisoners are employed in labour of different
kinds, and a part of the profit resulting from it
goes to themselves. They are kept separate
from the prisoners for debt and those not yet
found guilty; for the legal maxim is, that a
man must be treated as innocent until a jury

has given a verdict against him. Committals to prison before trial are extremely rare, for it is only in capital cases that magistrates can refuse to release an accused person upon bail. His detention, therefore, does not depend upon the arbitrary will of any body; it is a grand jury who, at the next session of the court, puts him on trial or discharges him. The district-attorney cannot appeal, *a minima*, from its decision. The accused may insist upon being tried as soon as possible; and the only discretionary power to which he has to submit is that of the committing magistrate; but even in that case, if the magistrate either require excessive bail, or refuse to admit him to bail, he may always appeal to a superior judge, even during the vacations, either by a writ of error or an *habeas corpus*, and afterwards bring an action for false imprisonment. Society is empowered to prosecute by the means I have stated, not only crimes, but misdemeanors, *(delits correctionels,)* such as insults, assaults, nocturnal riots, offences against public decency, bad state of the highways: in short, any thing which disturbs the peace of the citizens is a proper subject for an indictment, according to the common law; to which the written laws have merely given additional efficacy, by particular enactments. But

this does not deprive the offended party of the
civil remedy; he has always in these cases his
action for damages for what he has suffered. The
criminal action belongs to society, and takes
place on the complaint of the grand jury,
although the offended party may not desire to
push matters so far; but the civil action is
entirely his own affair.

One of the most striking illustrations of this
double action is in the case of the law of
libel. Any publication against good morals, or
against the character of a citizen, of a malicious
nature, and calculated to disturb the peace,
whether true or false, is an offence of which a
grand jury can and ought to take cognizance.
This is the only crime, as regards the press,
known in America; for any body may say or
print what he pleases about the government.
The innumerable papers printed every where,
even in the smallest village, are perfectly free,
and may be published without any permission,
or entering into any security. In case of condemnation, the punishments are fine and imprisonment; but it is seldom that a grand jury
brings an accusation of this kind, unless the
publications are of a very scandalous nature,
and directed against the private character of
citizens, or of peaceable and respectable women.

As to political characters, people may always print what they like, because it is never supposed to be done from malice, but to enlighten public opinion in its choice.

But a person defamed by any publication whatever, may, besides the criminal accusation, bring an action for damages. The defendant, however, in this case is allowed to prove the truth of what he has published; which would be no defence in a criminal action. Damages are either general, as those obtained for general defamation, or special, if the plaintiff can prove that, in consequence of the libel, he has sustained any loss whatever.

Even slanderous words spoken furnish ground for a civil action, but it is necessary that the fact falsely imputed be of a nature, if true, to have constituted an offence punishable by law; or, that the slander has been the immediate cause of a specific injury. These sort of actions are also extremely rare in the United States, particularly in the West and South, where, in general, parties prefer fighting the matter out than troubling the law.

The liberty which pervades all the institutions of the country is found also in the laws which regulate real property, both as to its possession and transmission. Every one is master of his

own property. He does with it, in his life-
time, what he thinks proper; at his death he
leaves it to whom he will. The dotal system
does not exist. In general there is no marriage
settlement. All the personalties possessed by
the wife at the time of marriage, or acquired
by her afterwards, belong by law to the husband;
her real property remains her own, but the husband is the guardian of it, and she cannot dispose of it without his consent. Children succeed in equal proportions to the father or the
mother dying intestate. In default of descendants, property goes to collaterals, then
ascends. The husband, however, surviving the
wife retains a life interest in all her real property, whilst the wife, in the same case, is entitled only to a jointure of one third of this same
property. It happens, however, sometimes that,
by a marriage settlement, the husband acknowledges to the wife, a certain fortune as being
hers, to descend to the children, or, in their default, return to his family; but these cases seldom
occur, and only when the wife is much richer than
the husband. In general she takes her chance
with him, for better or worse, for by law the
wife and the husband are but one person. They
cannot give evidence in favour of each other.
In almost all actions brought by the wife the

husband must join. The American law, in accordance with good morals, does every thing to fortify and give sanctity to the marriage tie, that first element of all society. In many States divorce *a vinculis matrimonii* does not exist; in others it is pronounced, in some particular cases, by the courts of chancery, which decide upon applications for separations *a mensa et thoro*. But generally the manner of obtaining a divorce is by an extra-judicial measure, by a petition to the legislature, which passes a particular law for each case, after an examination by a commission, and hearing its report. Legislators are, however, much averse from these special laws, and require a very strong case to be made out.

In Louisiana, where the dotal system prevails, all landed property is shackled in a very complicated manner, and it is hazardous to buy it without knowing the genealogy and history of the families of the possessors; otherwise, when you least expect it, you will be beset by the descendants or creditors of a married woman claiming her dower, who may turn you out of your own house. This system does not prevail in the other States of the Union. You may buy in perfect security if you first ascertain, by an inspection of the registers, that there are no mortgages on the land, which you may do in half an hour. Besides, the seller always guarantees the property he sells, and it is against him, and before a court of equity, that the purchaser has his remedy.

As to personalties, the possession is always a proof *prima facie* of property, and as to the validity, unless it be stipulated, the maxim of *caveat emptor* is of full force.

The means of securing the payment of sums lent is first by mortgage, but it is necessary that it be clear and registered; without that it is of no force against future creditors. It can never vitiate the rights of previous creditors, as a *bonâ fide* sale would do. Only bricklayers and carpenters have a tacit mortgage upon the houses they build until they are paid for their work. The second means is by a deed of trust; that is, a sale or gift of the property to trustees for a specific purpose. For example, to secure the payment of a debt on a fixed day, I give or sell a house, or a piece of land, to a third party, on condition that the life interest shall remain mine, but that, if the day arrives, and I do not pay, he shall sell it for the benefit of the lender. It is in general by this form that the property of married women is secured in such manner as it may not be confounded with those

of the husband, and sold for his debts. It is
also in this way that the property of almost all
corporations, such as churches, colleges, masonic lodges, &c. are possessed. When the courts
of chancery try very complicated cases, in
which many parties are concerned, they often
order all the property under consideration to
be vested in this manner in trustees, to wait,
together with the produce, and be subject to
the ulterior decision of the court. A deed of
trust, as well as a sale, may be declared frau-
dulent, if it has been made with an intention
of deceiving creditors; but, to do this, the frau-
dulent intention must be clearly proved.

All goods, whether personal or real, go to
creditors. The United States are the only pri-
vileged creditor. After all these goods have
been sold, or if the debtor refuses to declare
them, he may be imprisoned for debts in almost
all the States of the Union. The constitution
of the United States has authorized Congress
to pass a general law upon bankruptcy, but
that has not yet been done. In the meantime,
however, most of the States have Insolvent Acts,
by which the honest debtor, who has delivered
up all his property to his creditors, must be set
at liberty on making oath that he has retained
nothing; and he is not liable to further arrest.

In some States, the property he may subsequently acquire is his own; in others, it belongs
to his former creditors, wholly or in part. Imprisonment for debt, then, is only employed as a
coercive means of forcing the dishonest debtor
to discover and deliver up his property; for he
who is innocent may always go out of prison,
by swearing that he has got nothing; unless his
creditors prove that he swears falsely, which
would be a very serious case of perjury, and involve penalties of a very strong and degrading
character.

Generally speaking crimes are rare in the United
States: this is greatly owing to the education
of the people, but above all to the abundance
which prevails, and the total absence of misery.
Crimes against the person are more frequent in
the new countries than in the old States. Attempts upon property, on the contrary, are almost unknown in the south, the west, and the
country places; whilst crimes against the person are more frequent there. Homicide is very
frequent, but deliberate murder is seldom heard
of. In a free country, still a little homely,
every one feels his individual consequence, and
takes upon himself the redress of an insult. In
the more civilized parts of the Union, particularly those in which religion prevails, the prac-

tice of duelling is nearly unknown; but in the south and the west, it is very frequent among the cultivated classes. Upon the shores of the Atlantic, duels take place with as much etiquette as in Europe; but in the western forests they are less ceremonious. At the very moment of dispute, parties draw their weapons and attack each other; the usage of the country is even to let them do so, for any one claiming assistance would be covered with infamy. Frequently, if the quarrel is of long standing and implacable the parties warn each other not to go out unarmed, for at the first meeting they are determined to do themselves justice. Juries in general are very indulgent to duels, and even to rencontres (as they are called), when every thing passes fairly; but they are very severe against anything like murder. Country people generally settle their differences with the fist; sometimes, also, they bite each other's noses and lips, particularly in the west, where the manly population, proud and independent, have a particular relish for fighting in any way they please. Very seldom indeed a great crowd assembles, on any occasion, without a battle taking place before its separation. But these conflicts are always at fistycuffs, and concealed weapons are never employed in them.

In the Atlantic States, morals· are different, and tend rather towards crimes against
property. Robberies by open force are rare,
but pilfering and cheating are very common.
The American sharper is a perfect adept in his
profession; for, as it cannot be want which im-
pels him to crime, in a country so happy as
America, it must be inclination, passion, the
genius of theft, which involve him in it, and
every day reveals new and altogether original
modes of cheating. The career of people who
resort to this profession is in general, however,
but of short duration, for the police of the
United States is so well managed, that nothing
criminal can escape that argus with thirteen
million eyes.

Indeed we are all police agents and spies. If
a conspiracy against the State comes to my
knowledge, I am eager to impart it to the sovereign; I do not leave him ignorant of what I
may have been able to learn of the opinions of
his servants; and the sovereign always rewards
me according to the importance of the intrigues
I have confounded. The people is the sovereign;
the newspapers the means which I adopt to
apprise him; and my reward awaits me at
the next election. There are no *gens-d'armes*
or town-serjeants with us; but if a robbery or
a murder is committed, any citizen may arrest

the party *in flagrante*, and take him before the nearest justice of peace or magistrate, who commits him in a regular manner or releases him on bail until the next assizes, after hearing the depositions pro and con. If the criminal, however, has succeeded in escaping, the report soon spreads through the country. In the taverns, at church, at market, in all public places, in short, the affair is talked of. All who have any information to give, take care to give it; but if he succeed in evading immediate pursuit, on the representation of the parties interested, the governor publishes a proclamation in the newspapers, promising a reward to whoever will deliver him up, and containing a description of his person, and any other clues that may have been procured. The proclamation becomes a subject of conversation in all the taverns, and every stranger, coming from the place where the crime has been committed, is sure to be questioned and scrutinized thoroughly. Recently, a man at New Orleans, who had killed his wife, was arrested upon the borders of Canada, where he tried to save himself, conducted back to New Orleans, and condemned. Nothing can escape the systematic publicity of this universal police, and the only way to escape being betrayed is to have no se-

crets. In the great southern towns, where there
are many blacks, there is in general organized a
municipal armed guard, to watch during the
night; but this guard, far from inconveniencing
the citizens, on the contrary, submits to the first
white who comes and saves him from the necessity of patrolling himself.

It is true that it sometimes happens, not often, however, that an innocent person is arrested for a guilty, (and does not that happen also
at Paris?) but, in such cases, he is amply indemnified: this gives occasion to a new lawsuit, of which the number is very considerable.
Law expenses are moderate; the temptations
to go to law continual, and the taste of the
people certainly tends to litigation. It is a singular thing that the descendants of the Normans
have everywhere retained their fondness for going
to law. This taste is observable in Italy in the
kingdom of Naples, which was conquered by
them; in the English nation, who submitted to
the same yoke; and in the French provinces,
where they were first settled. The rest of Italy,
Scotland, Ireland, and the rest of France, do
not partake of this litigating spirit. The descendants of the English have brought it into
America, where it is characteristic. You can
hardly find any one who has not had a lawsuit

in the course of his life. This may also be
partly attributable to every one being more or
less engaged in business, and to there being no
idlers or people exclusively devoted to pleasure.
For the rest, going to law does not hinder dining together and mutual visiting.

Another cause, also, which must increase the
frequency of lawsuits, is the immense number
of lawyers we have among us. Every body is
more or less versed in the laws; for every body
is sworn and goes to the assizes, as elsewhere
people go to the theatre. Those who know but
little of law, always think themselves sure of
their matter, and immediately consult an attorney, to whom they represent their cause so
well as to satisfy him of its justice. Besides, a lawyer, as you know, is very easily
persuaded by his client. Owing to the number
of lawyers, their fees are very trifling, excepting
those of the great luminaries of the bar, which
are very considerable. So that going to law is
a cheap amusement; and, indeed, what would
life be without a little contradiction? How
many a planter would be consumed with ennui, if
he passed his life raising cróps, all fine, and varying
only in degree! His days, so bright and golden,
would be all alike, and oppressively monotonous.
But, by good fortune, his neighbour's horse just

makes an excursion into his field. Quickly an
action is brought of *trespass, quare clausum fregit;*
or a passenger beats his negro, or seduces his
daughter or his servant,—immediately follows an
action of *trespass, vi et armis per quod servitium
amisit;* or, better still, while on a journey he
discovers a cart or saddle which he had lent to
a friend in the hands of a third party; forthwith,
an action of trover, or *detinue.* It often happens, also, that parties are uncertain about their
right, and then they arrange to carry it amicably before a court.

Arbitration is much resorted to in the United
States, but the litigants gain nothing by that;
for although, before carrying the cause before
arbitrators, they engage to abide by their decision, there are always so many ways of evading
the engagement, that it amounts to nothing;
and besides, the cause is pleaded before arbitrators, by lawyers, and in the same manner as
it would be in full court.

The bar of the United States is a very distinguished body. It is even the first body in
the State in the consideration of the people.
There are three professions which are called
learned, and which confer degrees: these are,
the faculties of law, medicine, and divinity; but
whilst the two latter lead to nothing, the bar

leads to every thing. It is the real nursery of statesmen, and it is in it that the people seek their legislators and governors. In a theocracy, the government is in the hands of the priests; in a military despotism, in that of the generals; in a country governed by laws, it is just that their interpreters and ministers govern. Thus are we well governed, and I regard this influence of the lawyers upon the government as the best guarantee of our liberties. It is to this point that Europe will come, in proportion as liberty shall be better understood there.

Oratory is much cultivated in the United State: every body speechifies. Written speeches are unknown, both at Congress and in the courts; and therefore we have orators. I have just heard those of Great Britain; but I must say conscientiously that there is nobody in parliament like Messrs. Clay, Webster, Wirt, Berrier, Hopkinson, Haine, &c. If the latter had subjects half as interesting as those discussed in parliament, with what lustre would they not shine. But that time will come, and ere long, Congress, like the British parliament, and the old Roman senate, will become *arbitrer gentium.*

LETTER EIGHTH.

OF THE ARMY, THE NAVY, AND THE INDIANS.—
Visit of Lafayette, and enthusiasm of all clas-
ses on that occasion; formidable appearance of
the militia; the regular army, its composition
and government, how augmented in case of war
and reduced in time of peace; military schools;
recruiting; repugnance of the people to the ser-
vice; tyranny of the officers; General Bernard's
system. THE MILITIA; *its composition; com-*
parison between the militia of the towns and
that of the west and south; description of a
mounted rifleman; the author's campaign with
a small army of them against the Indians; vo-
lunteer companies; several descriptions of them,
and of their modes of proceeding. THE NAVY;
ship-building; facility of producing a great num-
ber of ships; probable difficulty of finding sail-
ors; no impressment; officers; privateers; mer-
chant service; allusion to the wars in which
America has been engaged; wars with the In-
dians; probability of the eventual extinction
of the Indian race; observations on the distinc-
tions of race among mankind; inferiority of all
to the European whites; speculations on the ef-

fects on colour and faculties produced by crossing the races ; in what way the Indian race will at length disappear; lands allotted to the Indians called " reserves;" complicated question between the Creeks and the Cherokee Indians and the State of Georgia ; the United States a party to it ; interference of the missionaries ; Mr. Munroe's plan to obviate the difficulty—colonization of the Rocky Mountains ; serious objections to the plan ; speculations on the future proceedings of the Indians, and of the government of Mexico ; the Bushmen and the Emperor Francis of Austria.

Brussels; February 1832.

IN 1825, when Lafayette made us his triumphal visit, he was everywhere received as the guest of the nation.   What miracles did he not witness !   He had an opportunity of comparing the state of the country, as he had left it fifty years ago, with what it then was, and might attribute the difference entirely to the republican institutions by which we are governed.   He saw the country as nobody had ever before seen it, and as it has not been seen since.   Everything assumed a holiday appearance; the towns were repainted at his approach; the roads repaired ; everything put on an air of youth and peculiar freshness ; the magistrates went before him, the people welcomed him with enthusiasm,

he was held up as a model to the schools collected in the streets he passed through. From
many towns, deputations of the handsomest
ladies of the place were sent to the frontiers to
embrace him, and give him welcome in the
name of the sex. He was obliged to stand god-
father to all the children born upon his road; to
hear as many sermons on Sunday as there were
churches of the different denominations; to eat
as many breakfasts and dinners daily as it
might please the various corporations and societies to invite him to; to drink as many glasses
of wine as he met thirsty persons; and to make
as many speeches as he met fine talkers, which
is not saying a little.

But, of all he saw, nothing astonished him
so much as to behold, in the most peaceable
country upon the earth, more than 1,100,000
men, completely armed and equipped. Indeed
everywhere upon his road, and even some hundred miles right and left, the militia was assembled, and came to present themselves to
him under very formidable appearances. He did
not know the state-governors except in military
accoutrements; and many were the merchants,
lawyers, and planters, whom he saw only as generals or colonels! Here he might see and admire the institution of a national guard in its

highest point of perfection, for all this immense armed force was nothing but the militia.

The army itself, in time of peace, is inconsiderable. Under the ancient federation, it was composed of contingents, furnished and fully equipped by the States, but, under the present constitution, the States may not keep up bodies of troops under arms in time of peace. The army is essentially federal, and its concerns entirely within the prerogative of the president and Congress.   Its organization has varied many times during the last ten years; under the presidency of Mr. J. Adams, it was reduced to less than 3,000 men, and during the last war it was carried beyond 100,000. At present it is composed of about 6,000 men, divided into four regiments of artillery and seven of infantry, and commanded by two brigadier-generals and a general-in-chief with the rank of major-general. The organization of the regiments, the manœuvres, and exercises, are entirely in the French manner, although the word of command is given in English. The soldiers are very well dressed, fed, and lodged. The army is distributed upon a line of some thousands of leagues all round the Union; the artillery occupies the coasts of the Atlantic; the infantry those of the Gulf of Mexico, and the frontiers of the

Missouri and Arkansaw. Upon this frontier a small post of fifty men has been planted, at some hundred miles from civilization; and it is necessary that it should be settled, fortified, and maintained there among the Indians, who are frequently hostile.

The war department is under the direction of the secretary at war, who does not belong to the army, for with us the accumulation of employments is not allowed, and there are only officers in actual service. The United States do not grant pensions but to those who are obliged to quit the service on account of serious wounds, or to the widows and orphans of the deceased. The army is organized agreeably to a law which directs that it shall be composed of a major-general, two brigadier-generals, a colonel, chief of the staff, &c. &c. It cannot, therefore, contain more officers than the law ordains. Those who are in the service are disqualified from being elected or appointed to any office whatever, while they remain in the army. All the officers are appointed by the president, *with the consent and advice of the senate;* and he possesses the constitutional power of dismissing them all, although I am not aware that this power has ever been exercised. Generally, however, in time of peace, promotion

strictly follows length of service. If war broke
out, Congress would pass a law to augment the
army and determine its extent and form. The
president would then fill up the appointments
according to his discretion, whether by select-
ing from the old officers who served in the last
war, advancing officers in the existing army, or,
finally, calling into the army officers of the militia, or people distinguished by their patriotism
and possessing the confidence of the new levies.
After the war, the Congress, in like manner,
would pass a law to reduce the army and determine its model; then the reductions in each
rank would be effected without giving any pension or privilege whatever to those who should
resign or be disbanded. After former wars Congress made a division of public lands among
the officers and soldiers thus disbanded, and
the same measure would probably be adopted
again.

When an officer gives in his resignation, he
immediately ceases to form part of the army
and becomes nothing at all. The only thing
he retains, and that only by courtesy, is his title.
Thus, for example, the actual president, Andrew
Jackson, who is usually called General Jackson
has long ceased to be a general. He receives
no salary as such, and has no control over the

army. However, in his capacity of president,
he is commander-in-chief of the sea and land
forces.

The army is recruited by voluntary enrolment,
so that in time of peace it is very indifferently
composed; for what citizen is there who cannot,
by very moderate labour, earn more than the
pay of a soldier. Besides, the love of liberty,
and the repugnance to all constraint, indispose
the people to enlist. It must be admitted also
that the tyrannical conduct of the officers to the
soldiers contributes not a little to disgust the
people with the military service. This conduct
is a consequence of the sort of men who enlist,
but it also reacts upon those who would enlist,
and repels all decent people. In war time it is
otherwise; the ranks are filled immediately with
volunteers who enlist that they may serve their
country, make a campaign, and partake of its
glory and dangers. The officers soon see that
they have different materials to deal with, and
alter their system of discipline accordingly.

The present army must be considered only as
the model, or the nursery of one more considerable; it is, as it were, intended to preserve
the tradition of military usages and regulations.
The officers who compose it are in general very
good, and, in the event of a war, would be imme-

diately promoted to superior ranks, and distributed among the new regiments that would then be raised; these would be most in want of good subalterns, a class who constitute the support and sinew of every good army.

The maxim of the United States is to be prepared for war during peace; and therefore nothing to that end is neglected. A school upon the system of the polytechnic school of Paris, is established at West Point, near New York, where some hundreds of young people receive quite a military education. On quitting, they have the choice of entering into the army as officers or of adopting a profession; most of them do the latter; but at the first signal they would be ready to rejoin the flag, and would make excellent officers. Many private colleges have adopted the system of education at West Point, and at present a great many young people are educated in an entirely military manner. By these means the manœuvres and management of arms will be as generally known to the future generation as the catechism is to the present.

But besides this attention to matters regarding the personal qualities of the army, the United States have established numerous military arsenals in which the arms and artillery are finished and preserved. The manufactory, how-

ever, of arms and powder, as well as every other
species of industry, is wholly free in the United
States. I believe even that the government has
no iron-foundry, but supplies itself, ready made,
from private factories.

The last war having shewn that the existing
fortifications did not fulfil the purpose expected,
Congress adopted a system of fortifications of
great extent and fulness of design; and during
fifteen years its execution has been pursued
with activity. This project is mainly attributable
to General Bernard, and never, perhaps, did an
officer of genius design a scheme at once so vast,
comprehensive, and original. It will immortalize
the general.

The real military force of the United States,
however, does not consist in its army, but in its
militia. Until a certain age, which varies in
different States, every citizen forms part of it;
for as the army belongs to the federal government,
so the militia depends wholly on the States.
Preachers, schoolmasters, doctors and some
other persons are exempt from it. The Quakers
and other religious sects who refuse to fight
must pay the disciplinary fines or march. Persons holding offices in the United States are also
exempt, as well as magistrates, in time of peace.

In each State the governor is commander-in-

chief of the militia. It is his province to put
them in motion, whether on the demand of the
president in case of a general war, or of his own
accord if the urgencies of the State require it.
The officers are elected by the privates, except
the generals, who are usually appointed by the
legislature or the governor. The organization
and uniform of the militia are the same as those
of the army ; and from the moment of its being
called into active service it is paid like the other
troops of the United States. The law fixes a
certain day in which it is assembled to manœuvre,
and the colonel or captain may call them out
oftener to exercise or elect officers. These assemblages are always more or less military
holidays.

It is necessary to make a great distinction
between the militia of the new countries and
of those parts of the Union which have been
long inhabited, particularly the large towns
in the north-east. There they are composed of
mechanics and labourers, tradesmen's clerks,
and apothecaries' shopmen, all people totally
unfamiliar with the use of arms or military
habits. In general they exercise pretty well,
especially in making a variety of theatrical evo-
lutions, of no utility whatever, and for which
they have a great taste; but if, in the midst of a

parade, the rain comes on, you will see them scamper away with singular agility. However well diposed these might be, they would not be able to sustain the privations and marches of a campaign. You will tell me that the battle of Baltimore was gained by this sort of militia. Very true, but it was at the gate of the city. The American is brave; he is above all distinguished by a rational and reflecting courage; it is never in this respect that the militia may be impugned. But at the battle of Baltimore, the citizen-soldiers went out from their houses, having breakfasted and shaved as usual; if they had been obliged instead of that, to bivouac in the mire for a single week they would have been knocked up before meeting the enemy. Herein is the great advantage which the militia of the country have over those of the town. The men who compose the former are accustomed to the inclemencies of the seasons. They all go hunting, and are familiar with the use of a gun. It is true they are not so smartly dressed; that they do not exercise so well; are a little more turbulent; but all this does not hinder them from rendering better service before the enemy.

But to judge of the militia you should see those of the west and south. A regiment of mounted riflemen, men inured to all the fatigues

and privations of the almost savage life of a first
settlement; mounted each upon his favourite
horse; armed with his trusty carbine, to which,
not seldom, he and his family have been indebted for a dinner in time of need; these are
people who make a sport of all fatigue. To them
a campaign is really a party of pleasure. They
know the woods, can find their way by the sun
and the bark of the trees, whether to track an
enemy or a stag; their dogs assist them here,
for each has his dog with him. They have no
uniform, every one comes as he is, for his daily
labour, with some new extra covering spun and
wove by his wife from cotton planted by himself. A hat of twisted palm-leaves protects his
person, blackened by the smoke of the bivouac;
an otter skin artfully folded and sewed contains
his ammunition, the means of kindling a fire,
and his little stock of tobacco; a wallet behind
his saddle carries provisions for himself and
his horse. The animal himself is as little fasti-
dious as the master. A few handfuls of maize
per day suffices him, but in the evening, on
arriving at the camp, he is unsaddled, unbridled,
and two of his legs fastened together, then he is
left in the woods where grass in abundance very
soon invites him to a frugal supper. No great
discipline among a troop like this; no regular

exercises: every one makes war for his own account, and as if by instinct. It is a hunting party on a large scale; these, however, were the most distinguished troops in the last war, and who repulsed the English at the battle of New Orleans.

I have myself made a campaign with such men, an army in miniature, three hundred men strong. It was commanded by a brigadier-general. I went out as his aid-de-camp, forming myself the whole staff of the army; I returned colonel of a regiment: few periods of my life have left me more agreeable recollections. I shall never forget, one moonlight night, fording the Whitthlicootchie at midnight, lighted by our fires, and the still stronger but much more distant light of the woods, which the Indians had kindled in order to cover their retreat. This great river, in all the majesty of virgin nature, flowed between two perpendicular banks of rocks near sixty feet high. A narrow path led from each side to the ford. The moon reflected in the silver waves, and their almost phosphoric clearness was only interrupted by the long black line formed by the army marching in a single file. We remained nearly six weeks in this way, on horse-back all day, encamped at night in the woods. We met the Indians only three or four times, but their footsteps swarmed around us, and it was manifest that we were continually encompassed by them. One night they attacked us in our camp and lost two men. One day they disputed a ford with us, and three among them remained on the field of battle. At last seven were taken upon a little island at the mouth of a river, were tried, and acquitted by the jury. The cause of the war was the massacre of a white family, under circumstances of unheard-of cruelty. Six white children from two to twelve years old, were burnt alive, and the father massacred. It was to arrest these murderers, to force the other Indians to retire within their limits, to secure, in short, the tranquillity and peace of our families, and save them, perhaps, from a general massacre, that we took up arms. We completely succeeded.

The half-savage sort of militia of which I am now speaking are only found, as I have already mentioned, upon the borders of civilization. They would form, perhaps, the best troops in the world, if they were well disciplined and exercised; but that cannot be attained without keeping them some months under the flag. It is, therefore, always a probability that on a level country and during the first year of a war, these militia would be beaten by regular troops; but the case would

be very different after the second campaign,
and even after the first in trackless woods, without magazines and resources of any kind.

Besides those I have mentioned, there is another sort of militia in the United States always
ready to take the field, whose equipment, arms,
and exercises, are quite unexceptionable; and
which is commanded by experienced officers
withdrawn from the army since the last war.
These are the volunteer companies.   All those
who are found united by professional ties or
family connexions associate together to form
corps of this sort.   The act of association,
duly drawn up and approved by the colonel
of the regiment to which they are attached,
settles their formation, their uniform, the modes
of electing their officers, the admission of
members, their retirement, &c.   These companies frequently possess very great property,
and the conditions of admission are sometimes
very difficult.   The honorable Artillery Company
of Boston, for instance, possesses a small arsenal
and a very fair *material* of its own, and I believe
that it costs nearly a hundred pounds to be
admitted into it.   In every thing pertaining to
their discipline and internal affairs, these companies are entirely independent of the officers
of the regular militia, but they are under their

orders when they are called into active service;
in general, however, they are employed in de-
tached expeditions. Their uniform is entirely
of their own choosing, so that there is no great
town without several companies of sharp-
shooters in the costume of Scottish highlanders,
who have been made very popular by the novels
of Sir Walter Scott. The merchants, on their
part, form companies whose uniform consists of
white pantaloons, blue frock, round hat, and red
morocco belts. The French, or their descendants,
unite also on their part, give the word in their
language, and adopt the bearing of some of the
old guard, or that of the French national guard;
every where there are Irish and German companies. A very singular effect is produced by this
medley, but it excites emulation in a high degree,
and these volunteers would be choice troops any
where. Besides, the exercises common to all the
militia, in which they are obliged to take part,
they meet to manœuvre or shoot at a mark as
often as the captain pleases to call them out.
Once or twice a year some volunteer companies
of a town go with all the apparatus of war to
visit the neighbouring towns. The necessary
funds for the expedition are subscribed by the
members of the corps, and remitted to the
quarter-master, who precedes them and orders

268

the lodgings in a perfectly regular manner. All the volunteer companies of the town to which they repair go out to meet them, and give them a dinner. They perform manœuvres in common, make acquaintance, dance, give invitations, and exchange promises of reciprocal visits; and thus these occasions become also one of the means which contribute to attach and connect the people of the different States among themselves.

All these military movements are made without any communication of them to government. One of the large caps of a company, is seen from a window some morning, the wearer is struck with the fineness of the weather, and recollects that he has nothing to do that day. Without more ado, he runs to the captain and proposes a military promenade; the idea pleases the latter, the drums are sent for, they are beat through the town, and the corps assemble. Although this command emanates officially from the captain, he could not take upon himself so important a measure without the consent of all the company; as soon, therefore, as it is assembled, the matter is discussed: the majority of votes decides what shall be done: the minority submits, or pays the fine; and when once the resolution is adopted, the captain sees it carried into execution with an

air of authority not unlike a little despot. In
the midst of the most profound peace, in a state
of political tranquillity which admits not the
suspicion of a commotion, a stranger is perfectly astonished to hear the drum beating on all
sides; he goes out; he meets nothing but armed
men, running to join their flags; companies
already formed moved about on all sides; he
thinks he is dreaming; he saw no soldiers the
day before, and can only account for their
presence by supposing the town has been taken
by assault during the night. He is soon, however,
reassured, by the air of indifference and security
with which the quiet townsman regards, inno-
cently passing, all this military pomp. Nobody
even can answer his inquiries, as to the cause or
object of this general movement; and, indeed,
in the northern towns, there is scarcely anybody
but the little negroes or mulattoes who attend
the parades or care about them. Nobody else
is idle; for the white little rogues are at school,
and envy in this, as in many other things, the
independence of their brethren of the sooty
complexion.

The great towns, such as Philadelphia and
New York, each reckon perhaps ten or twelve
thousand of these volunteers. They are constantly ready to march, are perfectly well equipped
and exercised, and render great service in time of

war. The principal objection to them is that they
are with difficulty brought to give up the immediate defence of their homes; for being almost
all young men of family and property, they have
too close an interest in their native town to be
fond of removing from it. Taking into consideration the peculiar position of the United States,
this is not, however, of any very great importance.
There is, indeed, but a single frontier to defend,
that of the Atlantic.   All the points of debark-
ation are covered by forts defended by the regular army: immediately in the second line, are
the great towns defended by volunteer companies
and their regular militia; then the heart of the
country has its militia, or levy *en masse.*

There would be no occasion, therefore, to put
the militia of the great towns in motion until
after all these should have fallen into the power
of the enemy, and then there would be no
difficulty.

There is, besides, another defence, to which I
have not yet adverted, it is, however, that on
which we most rely—I mean the navy. To our
navy were owing the greatest triumphs of the last
war; for, although young, it has beaten the English in every sea, and its successes have astonished Europe. It is not, however, very numerous; we have at present, I believe, scarcely
a dozen ships of the line, but they are very fine

ones. Naval architecture, whether for merchant-men or men-of-war, has made immense progress in America. By a very simple invention, frigates have been rendered almost as strong as ships of the line, and ships of two decks equal to those of three. It consists simply in suppressing the gangway and continuing the quarterdeck and forecastle from end to end. The deck is constructed strong enough to support pieces of a caliber equal to those for battery.

This construction has been just adopted for an immense ship building at Philadelphia, and ready to be launched: it has a hundred and eight covered ports and thirty-six upon deck. It is the largest ship ever built. Moreover, government spares no expense in naval structures; accordingly, they are very splendidly built, and the almost indestructible quality of the wood now employed exclusively in the navy, affords a presumption that it will ere long raise itself to a high state of splendor, and to a numerically imposing force.

Although the ships of the United States are but few at present, their number may be increased with the greatest rapidity. There are eight or ten naval arsenals ready, whenever required, to build a great number of ships. In each of these is a great many creeks, many of them covered, and immense warehouses of timber and rigging. Further, in the city of New York, Philadelphia, and Baltimore, there are building-yards for ships of war, belonging to private individuals. They have already, since the last war, built several ships for account of the government, in addition to which there are those which formed the fleets to Columbia, Peru, Spain and Mexico, Brazil, and Buenos Ayres. They lately built two ships for the Greeks; one was sent to its destination, and the other, bought by the American government, now forms part of its navy. Some time ago the Russian government bought a superb cutter at Philadelphia, and I have no doubt that the private dock-yards of the towns of the Union could furnish annually twenty frigates of the first class, completely equipped, without reckoning what the government yards could do. The government is so sure of its resources in this respect, that it does not desire to increase the number of its ships during the season of peace we are now enjoying.

The maintenance of ships in ordinary is very great; whatever care may be bestowed, an old ship is never worth a new. Among the ships of the American navy there are none of no value. England is far from being able to say

as much. It is the sole power with whom we
may have a maritime war. In a month's time
all our navy would be armed and ready to
dispute the approach to our coasts; and before,
as it were, a fleet of a dozen ships of the line
could come and attack us, our arsenals would
have poured forth a dozen ships quite new,
and prepared to meet them. Besides, great
improvements are every day making in naval
architecture, and the last ship built is almost
always the best; there is therefore a great
advantage in having all the materials ready,
instead of putting them in hand at the moment
when they are wanted.

The only difficulty the United States would
experience in the equipment of a fleet, would
be in finding sailors; for the English system of
impressment does not prevail. The crews are
enrolled voluntarily, and at a rate of pay always
above that of merchant-men, and hitherto there
has been no difficulty. It is, however, to be
feared that at the moment of a war, when a
great demand would take place, as well for the
navy as for innumerable privateers, which would
offer, besides the lure of high pay, the hope of
rich captures; it is to be feared, I say, that
some difficulty would be found in completing
the crews. In spite of that, there is one consi-

deration, which restores my confidence; it is, that no war can be undertaken that is not sanctioned by the will of the majority; an unpopular war cannot take place with the United States, and if the people wish a war they will find the means to carry it on.

It must be acknowledged that the war service does not offer great attractions to people of so turbulent a character as American sailors. In truth, the discipline on board ships of war is very severe; more so, perhaps, than in any other service, and I believe that is necessary to make them forget republican equality, which could not be allowed at sea without the greatest danger.

The officers of the navy are very numerous, particularly in the inferior grades; these grades are the same as in England. The officers are not all actually employed, either on board the ships, or in the arsenals, dock-yards, &c. There are some of them waiting orders, who have been directed by the ministers to repair to such a station, and to hold themselves at the disposal of government; they receive their full pay, but no provisions. Others are absent on leave for a limited period. Lastly, others are quite out of the service, receive no pay, and remain in that state until they apply to government to

put them again into active employment. When
they are thus retired, they may dispose of themselves and of their time as they please. Many
of them, for instance, command merchantmen
in the China trade; or devote themselves to
any other species of industry. As soon, however, as an officer becomes part of the navy
in any way whatever, he cannot be elected or
appointed to any office.

In time of war, American commerce, whioh
is in a great measure paralysed, furnishes an
immense number of privateers. The schooners
of Baltimore, during the last war, were dread-
fully injurious to English commerce, and even
spread themselves between England and Ireland.
This system would operate much more destruc-
tively now, if hostilities were to recommence;
for the merchant service is at least doubled in
extent since ten years ago, and the recollection
of the immense fortunes made in this manner
last time, would be an encouragement to embrace this system of war, immediately after its
declaration.

The merchant service of the United States is
immense; it extends over every sea. To those
who have seen the packets which go from New
York to Havre, London and Liverpool, it would
be needless to say that they are the finest vessels

afloat, whether as it respects internal construction, or sailing and accommodations.   These
packets, in short, are excellent travelling inns
between Europe and America; one may live in
them as well as on shore, for the same price, and ⟨
have the passage for nothing. The safety of this
mode of conveyance leaves nothing to be desired, for upon 2,160 voyages that these packets
have made during ten years, only three have
been lost. Their rapidity is inconceivable; I
recollect having seen some years ago, at New
York, on the 4th of January, the president's
message delivered at Washington, on the 1st of
December, printed in the Liverpool newspaper
of the 16th of the same month. This, however, is out of the common course; the average
time is twenty days from America, and twenty-
five to go there.

The United States have hitherto had but two
wars with European powers, for I do not reckon
the declaration of war in 1798, which was
not followed up. These two wars were with
England, and in both the advantage remained
wholly with the Americans. I am aware that
the English boast of having taken Washington,
in the last war, and burnt the capitol; but this
fine exploit, which at the time made so much
noise in Europe, has only to be known in its

details to be appreciated at its proper value.
The city of Washington, although the official
capital of the United States, was at that time
only a small town of seven or eight thousand
inhabitants.   The English troops who were
afloat in the Chesapeake, favored by the tide,
ascended in the night one of the rivers which
bear their tribute to this immense bay, and
landed, in the morning, some miles from
Washington.

They marched immediately upon the town,
where they found no resistance, for the two or
three hundred marines who were there had
evacuated it at their approach, and were gone
to Bladensburg, six miles on the Baltimore
road.   After having burnt the capitol, or rather
the few moveables found there, for the freestone
walls are not so easily demolished, the English
army marched to Bladensburg, where it defeated the marines and some militia who were
with them.   Strengthened by this advantage,
it continued its route upon Baltimore, where it
was completely beaten by the militia of the
town, and had its general killed. This expedition, which cost large sums to England, and
was intended to make a powerful diversion in
the central States, entirely failed of its object,
and was completely destroyed in less than a

week after its landing. The burning of Washington was even of service to the American
cause; for this act of vandalism, joined to the
horrors and cruelties committed by the English
army on its march, effectually silenced the
party opposed to the war, and by uniting all
the nation in a sentiment of vengeance, increased a hundredfold the strength of government. The expedition of the English against
New Orleans was still more unfortunate; but it
must be admitted that they had some success
in Canada, success, however, which could
lead to nothing, and which was entirely owing
to the opposition of the federalists to all the
measures of government, and to the refusal of
some of the New England States to put their
militia in motion upon the demand of the president. But to what purpose is it to examine
into these two campaigns in this manner?
Does the conquered ever allow himself to be
so?   And in the midst of contradictory reports,
the best means of judging of the success of a
war, is the result. In her weak state, when
reckoning not more than five millions of population, without government, finances, army or
navy, America obliged England to acknowledge
her independence; and George the Third was
obliged to receive at his court, as the first am-

bassador of a future rival power, that same Mr.
Adams, who had been denounced as a traitor
and a rebel. It is but fair to admit, however,
that the assistance of France contributed greatly
to the success of this first struggle. America
would have succeeded alone, but it would have
been at the expense of much greater sacrifices,
and much more time. In the second war who
had the advantage? Was it not again the
United States? Which of the two parties
made concessions at the time of the treaty of
Ghent? certainly not America; England acknowledged her limits, and expressly renounced
the rights of searching her vessels and impres-
sing her seamen. Now, this was the ground of
the war.

I do not think the United States will be for
a long time engaged in an European war: they
are now too strong to fear any power, and any
nation having a maritime trade would see it
infallibly destroyed by seeking to enter into
strife. I think then that on this side, long
years of peace are before us. But the republic
is constantly engaged in petty wars with the
Indians, whom it is continually pushing further
from its frontiers. An attack on their part
brings on a war, a treaty, a cession of territory;
the conquered territory is speedily sold and

populated; the white man and the red man
again come in contact; disputes, a new war, and
a new cession of territory follow; and so it will
go on, until the tide of civilization reaches the
shores of the Pacific ocean, and the Indian
race is extinguished.   Nothing can save it.

For myself, who am not a philanthropist, I
frankly avow that I think this result is very
desirable.   It is a question, like many others,
which is not the least understood in Europe,
and upon which people deliberately talk non-
sense, treating it with that morbid sentimen-
tality which was so much the fashion among
the philosophers of the end of the last century.
When two races of entirely different men are
found together upon the same soil, they must
necessarily either become amalgamated, or one
of them become subject to the other, or be destroyed.   Let us begin by examining the first
of these alternatives: that which has taken
place in all conquests.   The Jews are the only
people who have continued to live in an insulated
state.   The barbarians who invaded Europe
soon mixed with the conquered; the Tartars
did so with the Chinese, and that was at all
times the system of Roman policy; but then,
lastly, there was in all these cases a parity
of race; they were white or yellow men, gifted

with an equal degree of intelligence; and if
some little difference existed among them, it
was solely the fruit of accidental causes, and
produced by climate and manner of living;
there existed no radical difference in the race,
in the species.

Different parts of the world were originally
inhabited by distinct races of men; each of
these races possessed a lower or higher degree
of perfectibility, and civilization with them pro-
ceeded until the intelligence of a race reached
its utmost development: thus, we see the
negro race (to judge of it by the geological
state of the continent it inhabits, probably the
oldest upon the globe,) has never been able to
pass the savage state; they live upon the coasts
of Guinea, in Nubia, and in Abyssinia, in the
same manner as they did in the most distant
times of which history has preserved the remembrance; and then, as now, they sold one
another as slaves. The actual state of civilization among the Hindoos is exactly the same
as in the time of Alexander; and it appears that
long before that time they had arrived at that
state of equilibrium between their wants and their
faculties. It is the same with China; and the
Arab race, which, although white, is very different from ours, presents the same spectacle : at

the time of Abraham and Ahasuerus, it had
arrived at the same level. The European race
alone have not yet reached the limit of its perfectibility; nor can we foresee how far that
extends. To it only the treasure of civilization
has been confided; and to it must its extension
be owing, until it covers all the surface of the
habitable globe. Our race, however, is not
pure; it is the happy result of many cross
breeds, but having little variety among them.
Now, it becomes a question, whether in crossing
our race with another less perfectible, the cause
of civilization would thereby gain or lose. It
is useless reasoning to establish opinions in
support of which we cannot bring proofs from
past experience. My opinion, however, founded
upon the knowledge I have of many mixed
races of men in America, is that we have nothing
to gain by this mixture; moreover, the experiment is making, and making on a larger scale
than any experiment hitherto tried since the
existence of the world.

At St. Domingo whites and blacks will have
completely disappeared in two or three generations, and at the end of some others the population will be entirely composed of mulattos of
a uniform complexion. The same fate attends
all the Antilles, with this difference, however,

that each of them will have a different colour,
according to the proportion which existed in the
elementary colours.   In Mexico the red race
predominates, there are many whites and few
negroes. The Mexican colour will be therefore,
after some generations, a proportional medium
between these colours. All South America is in
the same condition, each State, however, having
these elements in very different proportions.
There will be, for instance, a much greater difference between a Mexican and an inhabitant
of Guatimala, (where the negroes and the red
people are in equal number and infinitely superior to that of the whites,) than between an
Englishman and a Spaniard of the present day.
That will always tend to separate more the
different States of South America, although all
sprung from a common source, and united by
ties of language and religion.

But whilst the experiment of crossing the
races is making upon so immense a scale, I
wish that the contrary experiment, that of preserving our white race in all its purity, and
placing it in the most favourable circumstances
for developing all its intellectual and physical
faculties may not be abandoned.

Whilst the inhabitants of the Antilles shall
gradually become savage, and abandon the use

of stays and small clothes; whilst South America shall fall back in its civilization, as it has already done since it has shaken off the yoke of Spain; whilst ancient Europe, a prey to its internal disputes against its kings, nobles, and clergy, consumes itself in vain efforts to get clear of the obstacles which those superannuated institutions impose on its civilization; whilst it is itself menaced every day with an invasion of Basquirs and Calmucks, I love to anticipate, in the future, the white man as free, perfectly unshackled in his industry, his thoughts and his genius springing forward upon a virgin land, fashioning it to the requirements of his new civilization, continually thriving and causing to flourish there peace, abundance, luxury, and the arts. But to obtain this great result, it is necessary that the race remain pure; the forest must disappear to make room for the regular streets of great cities, and the red man who can only live in the woods must disappear with them.

The second alternative is not possible, or at least cannot be accomplished for some years. It is what the Spaniards did in all their colonies: they had subdued the red race and reduced it to complete slavery, but that slavery was not of long duration; the amalgamation soon took place, as it always will when the commerce

between the sexes of two different races is productive. Besides, it would be altogether useless
for the United States to entertain, for an instant,
the notion of subduing the Indians. Those of
the Islands, of Mexico and Peru, were cowardly
and soft, and could be moulded to slavery, but
the North American Indian is a warrior and
wild to the last degree. You may kill him or
put him to the torture, but make him work or
draw a cry from him, never. Those even among
them who are half-civilized and cultivate the
ground, do not do it by their own hands, but
by those of their negroes. This hatred of labour
is observable even in the mongrel issue of the
Indian and the white; I do not know one who
exercises a manual profession, and those among
them who have received a good education select
the road to idleness and become preachers
rather than work in a counting-house or at the
bar.

There remains, therefore, but the third alternative, that of exterminating the race. But let
us begin by understanding each other: do not
suppose that I wish to justify the massacres
committed by the Spaniards at St. Domingo
and Cuba; do not think that I would preach a
crusade against the red man, and make the
forest resound with the cries of my victims: no,

no, I speak of terminating the race not the individuals, and the experience of the United States has proved, that the best means of attaining that object is to treat the Indians well, and to give them a taste of civilization. Individuals thus live in peace and prosperity, and the race goes out. The plan which the United States have followed hitherto, when they have conquered a savage people, has been to enclose it within an extent of fertile land ten times more than sufficient for the wants of an agricultural population. In this park, called a reserve, and into which the entrance of any white man is interdicted, they are furnished with cattle, implements of husbandry, and a forge; and missionaries have permission to establish stations there, consisting of fine and very productive farms. Nothing hinders these Indians from being happy and enriching themselves, and indeed they do in general live very happily; they let their cattle wander in the woods, and derive food from their flesh. Sometimes the women cultivate little corners of land, make deer-skin shoes ornamented with glass beads, and little baskets which they sell to their white neighbours; the men hunt, and sell their fur-skins: but in spite of all this, at the end of two or three generations, these tribes entirely dis-

appear. Thus far I have spoken of the northern
tribes, in the south the case has been different.
The Indians thus enclosed, consisted of considerable tribes, and already sufficiently moulded to
the usages of the whites to have frequently made
the Spanish governors of Pensacola, St. Augus-
tine, and Mobile tremble. They carried on with
some English merchants, established in those
towns, a considerable traffic in fur-skins, and possessed a great many cattle, and, above all, fugitive negroes from the United States, whom they
had appropriated. Many whites, escaped culprits,
or fugitives from justice, went and settled among
them, allured by the safety which Indian hospitality offered them; by the privilege of marrying
as many wives as they pleased; and more than
all, by the ambition of playing a principal part
in the politics of these tribes: their marriages
produced a great number of mongrels, some of
whom were very well educated. These people
and the chiefs who possessed many slaves, as
well as the missionaries who instructed them,
made fortunes; whilst the mass of the tribe
diminished in number, like the Indians of the
north, placed in the same circumstances. Every
thing would have continued to go on quietly in
this manner: the Indian race would have been
extinguished in these reserves; the chiefs and

the mongrels become rich proprietors of the
soil and citizens, blended with the whites, would
be as mere drops in the ocean, altogether unin-
fluential upon the race.

Besides, in proportion as the intercourse
takes place between the white men and the
women of colour, and the white women retain
all their purity, the white race does not suffer;
while, on the contrary, any mongrel or mulatto
born is so much gained upon the enemy.

Unfortunately the great southern tribes, such
as the Creeks and the Cherokees, are found
chiefly on the territory of the State of Georgia.
This State formerly extended from the ocean to
the Mississippi; but it has ceded to the United
States all the country to the west of a certain
line, from which have since been formed the States
of Tennessee, Alabama, and Mississippi.   This
cession was made to the United States against
their guarantee of the right of property which
the State of Georgia possessed and reserved to
itself over all the vacant lands within its limits.
On the other hand, however, when the Indians
were enclosed in their reserves, the United States
engaged towards them, by a solemn treaty, to
defend them against any aggression, and to
ensure them the enjoyment of these reserves
unless they voluntarily renounced them.   The

State of Georgia, which is certainly the most
ill governed of the Union, has adopted a very
singular mode of disposing of the public lands:
instead of selling them and making them an
item of its revenue, it every year puts them up
in a lottery for all citizens who have attained
their majority; so that there is among the
people of this State, who are naturally very turbulent, a devouring hunger after the public
lands. All the other lands which belonged originally to the State having been disposed of in
this manner, there now only remains the reserves of the Indians, which contain some
millions of acres. The State of Georgia, relying
upon its contract of cession with the United
States, claims the property of these reserves, and
the right of disposing of them. The Indians, on
their side, relying upon their treaty with the
United States, do not consent to be dispossessed.
Up to this point the matter would not have been
difficult to arrange; for though these Indian
tribes, settled in Georgia, form a population
of fifteen thousand souls, there is not, perhaps,
more than a hundred families among them,
(almost all of mixed blood,) who are settled upon
the soil, and cultivate it with their Negroes. They
might have been easily indemnified by granting

U

to each family in possession as much land as it might desire. The rest of the nation cares very little whether it be in Georgia or on the other side of the Missouri; it has no interest in the soil. But what comes to complicate the question, and render it a very serious one, is that these mongrels, having at their head a certain John Ross, a man of much merit, very well educated, and ambitious, conceived the idea of erecting themselves into an independent nation, giving themselves the phantom of a representative government, and establishing laws and tribunals: I say a phantom of a representative government, because this government exists only in name, and is only the means by which Ross and his associates avail themselves to throw dust in the eyes of the philanthropists and simpletons of the north. The fact is, that under the shadow of this phantom, he and his colleagues govern the Indians in a perfectly despotic manner.

Now, it is impossible for the United States or the State of Georgia to suffer an independent government to be established in the very midst of the Union. The Indian colonies are not considered as foreign powers; their right over any land of which they make no use is not acknowledged; they are considered as

only occupying, temporarily, the districts they
inhabit, under the protection and guardianship
of the United States. This question is rendered
still more serious by the part which the Missionaries play there. These are the people
who, in order to preserve the fine farms they
have raised, blow discord among the whites,
and stir up the religious societies, of which I
have spoken to you, to take the part of the
Indians.

To solve this difficulty, and prevent the like
in future, Mr. Munroe, during his presidency,
proposed a vast system which, although it has
not yet been wholly adopted, has, however,
served as the general basis of the proceedings
of the United States towards the Indians since
that time. It is as follows:

Between the Missouri and the Rocky Mountains, which separate the great valley of the
Mississippi from the Pacific Ocean, there is an
immense country in which the whites have
scarcely began to show themselves. The eastern side of the Rocky Mountains is very well
wooded, and equals in fertility the western side
of the Alleghanies; but from the foot of the
Rocky Mountains to the Missouri the country
presents nothing but an immense plain, slightly
undulated, like the sea after a tempest, and wholly

destitute of wood. The ground is, however, very
fertile ; a grass of perfect beauty grows everywhere about in abundance ; the banks of the
rivers, great and small, which water the plain in
every direction, are the only points which present a narrow border of wood ; but for a fuller description I must send you to Cooper, who has
given one in his novel of the Prairie. This country is occupied by innumerable horses and wild
buffalos, which serve both for riding and food to
very numerous tribes of Indians who have not
yet been subdued. Mr. Munroe proposed to invite
all the Indians inhabiting the east of the Missouri to pass over to the other side of that great
river, where the United States would ensure to
each a " reserve" in perpetuity; and would establish among them one or more governments
similar to those of the territories ; until such
time as these nations became sufficiently advanced in civilization to form States, and take
their place in the confederation.   By this
plan, the immense prairie would be interdicted
ground to the whites, and the new States,
which must soon be formed on the two sides
of the Rocky Mountains, would find themselves
separated from their brethren of the east by a
red population. This result must, however, take
place in part; for as the countries destitute of

trees offer much fewer facilities to new setlements than the forests, it is probable that the woods on the⁶ eastern side of the Rocky Mountains will be peopled before the prairie which separates it from the Missouri.

The United States have already succeeded in transporting many Indians to this prairie; and now, in all the treaties they make with them, it is always there that they direct the steps of the emigrants. The mongrels of Georgia having refused to treat in any way with the government of the United States for a cession of their lands, the government has commenced individual negotiations with the Indians; and, in spite of the penalty of death pronounced by the laws of Ross against those who consent to emigrate, some thousands have availed themselves of this resource, and the rest will probably follow their example: when, therefore, there shall remain nobody in the "reserves" but a few of the headstrong chiefs, and the nation in mass shall have emigrated, the State of Georgia will quietly take possession of the contested territory.

But this plan of Mr. Munroe, however specious it may appear upon paper, is surrounded with the greatest dangers. The tribes who inhabit the prairie are very different from those

of the sea-coasts. They are much more numerous, much more inured to war, and do not yet
know the power of the white man. The single
nation of the Siouts reckons ten or twelve
thousand warriors on horseback, armed with
lances and arrows, true Tartars of the western
plains. Now I take it for granted, that if a
force like this, led by an enterprising man,
such as Ross, were to rush in upon civilization, it would do incalculable mischief to the
United States before there would be time to
collect forces together to exterminate them. I
think that, well conducted, they might arrive
even at Washington, as the Gauls arrived at
Rome. At present, these nations do not know
their own power, are disunited, and cut one
another's throats in continual wars. They only
attack the extreme frontiers of the United
States separately, and with no other object
than the pillage of some new settlement. They
will be easily conquered in detail; and if the
plan followed hitherto was continued, each inclosed in his "reserve," and surrounded with
white men, in the course of a few generations
they would be extinct or absorbed. But if civilization continues to drive them before it, the
population will soon get condensed; instead
of remaining ignorant of their strength, they

will be informed of it by the already half-civi
lized Indians that have been transported among
them. Let them but organize a government; get
among them people of ability, and gifted with as
much enterprise as Ross; and you will soon see
new swarms of Huns, guided by another Attila,
come thundering over western civilization. In
the last war, did not the famous chief, Tecumtze,
assisted by his brother Francis the prophet,
succeed, under English protection, in preaching
a crusade, and forming an alliance against the
whites, among all the tribes, who, from the
lakes of Canada, where it rested upon the Bri
tish possessions, went even to Florida, and
there received assistance from the Spaniards?
It was this league which obliged General
Jackson to seize upon the Floridas, and it is in
consequence of his victory in 1818 that the different tribes are found each penned up in an
insulated state, and carefully separated from the
prairies of the west. But if thirst for their
lands, and the little annoyance which these in-
convenient tenants occasion to their neighbours,
should now decide the government on making
them emigrate in mass, the red league, but a
hundred times stronger and more powerful,
would be soon re-established; and government
would see itself engaged in a secular war which

would oblige it to keep on foot a very considerable regular army, to sustain immense expenses
for its maintenance in a desert country, which
would retard the progress of civilization towards
the west, cover its frontiers with pillage, con-
flagration, and massacre; and only terminate
in the extermination, by fire and sword, of one
of the two races.

And who can tell to what extent this Indian
league would find support from the Mexican
government?   Already the two civilizations,
Mexican and American, begin to meet.   A ca-
ravan trade is established between St. Louis
and Santa Fé, in New Mexico.   On the sea-
coast, Mr. Austin, a conqueror of a new sort,
is busy drawing the Texas from the Mexican
Union to throw it into the American federation.
His mode of conquest is quite original: it consists, under the authority of the Mexican government, of importing into a territory dependent thereon, a population entirely American.
As soon as it becomes sufficiently numerous to
form a State, it may, if it please, declare
itself independent of one federation and reattach
itself to the other.

But you will ask me, perhaps, what can
Mexico do in its present state of complete dis-
organization, and torn by internal discords,

against a nation so well organized and compact
as the United States? Agreed, not just now;
but the state of anarchy which now afflicts
Mexico may not last always. Among the number of generals who now contend for power, and
make and unmake elections at the point of the
bayonet, some man of genius will arise, who
will pull down all his rivals, put an end to discord, destroy the republic, and establish a military government; it is towards this point that
all Spanish America gravitates. As soon as he
shall have established internal peace, it will be
necessary, in order that he may not be overturned himself, to employ the army in distant expeditions. It is not the Indians that he will
attack: there is nothing to be gained by making war upon them, and besides they are his
natural allies; more than three fourths of the
Mexican army is red, and who knows if he will
not be so himself? It will be the Texas that he
will wish to reconquer, but by force; and if he
were seconded by the Indian league, he might
put the United States into a very dangerous
position, or at least draw them into a very long
and disastrous war.

But let us hope that the happy genius which
has hitherto watched over the cradle of our
republic will continue to protect it; that it

will succeed by wise measures in preventing the league of the savages against civilization; in escaping the massacres which would be the consequence of it; in extending the peaceable conquests of civilization, even to the Pacific ocean; and in maintaining peace with its Mexican neighbours, whose gilded misery is far from being matter of envy. But to attain these results it is absolutely necessary, by little and little, to exterminate the red race, at the same time preventing the sacrifice of individuals; on the contrary, preparing as much happiness for them as the state of civilization of which they are susceptible will permit them to taste.

How now! I hear the simpletons and anti-quaries exclaiming; will you destroy a race; not leave a sample of them, except those which shall remain in the museums of the naturalists? I hear them crying out against the cruelty of my views, and requesting as a favour, that at least a poor little red colony may be preserved, that · it may be seen, some thousand years hence, how the ancient savages were made. First of all, I think, with Buffon, that nature does not know species, but rather individuals; it is with the happiness of the latter that we should concern ourselves: in doing so, we are sure of securing the happiness of their race, which is only a metaphysical being.

What then? supposing we could by a legislative measure prevent the birth of hunchbacks and cripples, would you not wish to do it? As to curiosities, I have little taste for such as have no other merit, and I confess I do not partake in the taste of the Emperor Francis for the Bushmen. You must recollect that about 1820, when the frigate which had conveyed the Emperor of Austria's daughter to Brazil returned, it brought over a family of Brazilian savages, as a present from the Emperor Don Pedro to the Emperor Francis. The latter received these foreigners with much kindness, and conceived for them the tenderest friendship. He had a pretty little hut built for them, in the midst of a small wood in the palace garden, where they were perfectly free, (Austrian fashion!) enclosed within iron rails. The good Emperor passed whole hours in their company, and marvelled greatly at their smallest actions. It was said publicly in Vienna, that the Holy Alliance had had them brought over to serve as a model of the degree of civilization to which Prince Metternich wished to carry the civilization of Europe: I cannot vouch for the truth of this, not being in his confidence, but it is certain that a family

of Hungarian adventurers took a fancy to play
the Bushmen. They reddened their bodies,
pierced their lips and ears, and run sticks
through them, like their prototypes. The father,
who retained his colour and usual dress, made
an exhibition of his sons and daughters in a
state of nudity, but painted red, for so much
money. Spoken to in German, they answered
in the Bushman tongue. A live cat was given to
them, which the lady strangled with admirable
dexterity, and the family devoured it perfectly
raw. To see them make this repast, the charge
was double. I do not know how many meals
they had in a day; but, after having collected
a hundred thousand florins *Wiener Warung*,
they decamped, informing the good people of
Vienna of the trick they had played them. A
play was made of it at the *K. K. P. Leopold
Stadt Theater*. Now I ask you whether there
was not as much pleasure in seeing these Hun-
garians eat a cat as if they had been genuine
Bushmen? And what is there so curious and so
attractive in the Northern Indian, that he should
be made so great an object of interest? Do not
judge of them by the descriptions of Cooper,
who has always tried to make gentlemen of his
Indians; who has even given them very delicate
sentiments towards the fair sex, quite out of

nature. The wife of an Indian is his beast of
burden; in travelling or in the field she it is who
carries on her back all the baggage; and sho
is beaten by every body, even by her children.
As to the Indian, he is physically brave, morally a coward; he is patient from necessity;
moreover, some of them have a good deal of
natural sagacity.

It is said that the presence of the whites is
injurious to the Indians: I deny it; they are
more happy now than they were before the
colonization of America. Instead of hunting
with bows and arrows, they have now guns;
instead of going stark naked in the snow, or
ill-covered with skins of beasts, they are now
dressed in good stuffs, and provided with good
blankets, which serve them for cloaks; instead
of fasting when their shots fail, they have now
cattle, which saves them from famine. Each has
now his steel, his knife, and his hatchet; I
will even say they have all combs; but I shall
not dilate upon that subject, because, in their
case, they are but a useless ornament.

LETTER NINTH.

Of the Finances.—*Comparative " cheapness" of the American and European governments: economy defined; sources of revenue in the United States,— the Post-office, sale of public lands, fines and confiscations, dividends on shares in Banks and .public companies; United States Bank; principles which ought to regulate different nations in their commercial policy, foreign and domestic; impolicy of the American system with regard to the tariff; revenue and expenses of the different States; Philadelphia, extraordinary legacy left to it by Mr. Girard, probable consequences on the prosperity of the city; expenditure of the United States, payment of the national debt and interest thereon; different projects for the disposal of the surplus revenue consequent on the speedy extinction of the debt, difficulties attending all of them; want of capital in America, universal adoption of the credit system, every body speculates; supposed case of a New England carpenter; fluctuations of fortune common in America; extension of the banking system, paper currency in circulation generally; protecting influence of the United States Bank over the*

other Banks; Insurance companies; companies
for other purposes; complaint of the unfair dealing
of the Americans not warranted.

Brussels; March 1832.

I HAVE observed, for some time, a discussion
going on in the French journals, as to whether
the government of the United States is really
as cheap as it has been represented. General
Lafayette, assisted by Mr. Cooper and General
Bernard, have contended, and supported their
arguments by figures, that taxation is incomparably less in America than in France. I am
also entirely of their opinion. But to support
it, I must adopt another method. Not having the
necessary documents to establish a rigid comparison between the state of the American
finances and those of the governments of Europe,
I cannot recur to figures to support my opinion;
and if General Bernard, like a strict mathe-
matician, has faithfully raised the projection of
the American financial system, I am going to
give you the picture of it. I am perfectly sensible
that there is a great disadvantage in treating a
question of finance without figures; notwithstanding, I am going to attempt it, for I am
reduced to do so by the total privation of docu-

ments; and although my memory might furnish
many figures, it could not be with the exactness
which a subject of this kind requires.

Mr. Hume, a member of the English Parliament, was the first who brought into fashion
the term "cheap government." At first, minis-
terialists and oppositionists found the expression
excellent, and piqued themselves on admiring
it; but it was soon discovered that "cheap government" was nothing but a pass-word for
republican government, and from that time,
those who desired neither a republic nor republican institutions, became outrageous, not only
against cheap government, but against economy
itself. At last, one writer carried his prejudices
against this mode of government so far, that in
order to deprive the partisans of liberty of what
they considered their best argument, and force
them, as it were, into their last retrenchment,
he undertook, *mirabile dictu,* to demonstrate
that monarchical government was cheaper than
the government of the United States. I shall
not follow him in his reasonings, because that
has been already done by the persons referred
to, better than I could do it, and besides it
would lead me too far. But I may observe,
that any comparison between the expenses of
the two countries is materially affected by the

value of money in the respective countries;
thus, for example, when I give, in Florida, 1
dollar and 25 cents a day to a carpenter, besides his board and lodging, it is very clear that
1 dollar and 25 cents is only worth in that
country what a carpenter's day's work is worth
in France. It is then clear, that if I pay nearly
6 francs per day to a labouring man who
would cost 2 francs in France, I must pay
in the same proportion the salaries of all employed in civil and military offices; and that,
although they may receive a more considerable
quantity of metal, their expenses being greater
in the same proportion, they are not better paid
than the same persons in Europe, who receive
nominally less. The difference in the relative
value of money in the two countries is a common factor, which augments the figure of
equation without changing its value. This applies to all those employed in inferior capacities in the republic, to those who are paid for
their subsistence, and whose salary is considered
only as a compensation for what they forego
by not employing their time elsewhere. But in
Europe, besides this class of persons employed,
there is another, who are paid, not according to
what they do, but according to what is required
to keep up the dignity of their rank. This

class has no existence in the United States; the 25,000 dollars per year allowed to the president is the only instance that can possibly be considered as of the same sort of expense.

But let us first inquire what is understood by economy? Is it the having ten bad servants, ill paid and serving ill, or rather the having but one good one, doing more work than the ten together, although costing as much as them all. Economy in government consists in paying liberally as many good hands as is absolutely necessary for the service, and not one more; it consists in not stinting the necessary expenses, but in not permitting any useless ones, under any pretext. Suppress luxury in the government, replace it by the solidity and good qualities of the materials, and you will have economy, and the tax-payers will have the consolation of knowing that nobody fattens upon their spoils.

Another error into which the author who has attacked the financial system of the United States has fallen, is in believing that all the revenues of the United States, or even of the States, come from taxes; whilst, in fact, much of them is derived from property belonging to the nation, and which, consequently, does not weigh at all upon the tax-payers. In order to understand this, it will be necessary to analyse the different sources from whence the governments draw their revenues.

The post-office is the first branch we shall examine. This immense department, which extends like a net from one end of the United States to the other, and propagates the latest news with inconceivable regularity and safety, even in parts of the country which are hardly inhabited, is under the direction of the postmaster-general, a sort of minister, not forming part of the cabinet. There are more than eight thousand post-masters, each of whom have an account current opened with the department, and which is made up every three months. The mail is forwarded by contract, in stages, which also convey passengers; their construction and convenience vary greatly according to the state of civilization in the different parts of the country. The contractors are paid by drafts on the different post-masters, and the surplus of the receipts is paid into the banks of the United States to the credit of the post-master-general. The postmasters are compensated for their trouble, first, by the right of franking their own letters, both those they write and those they receive, as well as a daily newspaper; and further, by a commission which varies from 30 to 10 or 12 per cent.

upon the gross receipts, and which, however, in
no case may exceed a certain sum. They can in
no circumstances contract for, or be interested
in, the conveyance of the mail. The postage of
a letter for 400 miles and upwards is 25 cents.
A newspaper for the same distance costs only
1 cent and a $\frac{1}{2}$, and a pamphlet $2\frac{1}{2}$ cents per
printed sheet. These rates are reduced as the
distances diminish. The post-master-general
after paying all the contracts for the conveyance
of the mails, and providing for all the expenses
of the central departments, pays further into
the hands of the treasurer of the United States,
a very considerable sum every year. Of this
source of revenue, however, I only speak from
memory; for the object proposed by government in this department, is not to create a
receipt, but rather to ensure prompt communication between all parts of the republic. Indeed,
besides the post-masters, the privilege of franking is common to the president, the vice-presi-
dent, the heads of the different departments and
all the members of Congress. The journalists,
far from being shackled by government, enjoy
also the right of receiving all their newspapers
free; and the senators and representatives make
so good a use of their privilege that, during the

session of Congress, there goes out from Washington from thirty to forty thousand franked letters every day.

I have spoken in another letter of the sale of the public lands. They form a source of considerable revenue, and the administration is confided to the commissary of the land office, who resides at Washington. But the receipts from them are effected by particular receivers placed in each district, and who, after paying the various drafts of the government, and deducting a commission of 5 per cent. on the sales, which commission may in no case exceed 2000 dollars, pay in the rest to the banks of the United States, to the credit of the treasurer.

Fines and confiscations are also a branch of the receipts, in general an inconsiderable one, but sometimes, through fortuitous circumstances, increased by very large sums. Many crimes, are, as I have mentioned, punished by a fine which goes to the benefit of the United States. Confiscation, properly speaking, does not exist, that is to say, the property of any individual can in no case devolve to the State in consequence of a criminal condemnation. But by an ancient odd custom, derived from the common law, any inanimate object which has caused, accidentally or otherwise, the death of an individual, becomes, under the name of *deodand,* the property of the State. Thus, in any indictment for homicide, (*meurtre,*) care is taken to specify the value of the weapon used by the criminal. This value, however, is always nominal in important cases, for the absurdity of the law is too palpable, and it is probably to this very absurdity and to the manner in which the courts evade it, that its non-repeal must be attributed: for instance, a steam-boat, which had caused the death of an individual who was caught under its wheel, was valued at 10 dollars. I only speak, therefore, of *deodands* from memory; but in all cases of contraband, not only the articles introduced fraudulently, but even the vessel which brought them, becomes the property of the United States. A number of cruisers is organised for this purpose; these are schooners of the finest construction and of a very superior sailing. They belong to the United States but do not make part of the navy, they are under the financial department. The captains and crews are deeply interested in the seizures they make, which, however, must be declared valid by the courts of admiralty.

The dividend received by the United States for shares in the United States, belonging to them,—and for those which are subscribed from time to time, in the different road and canal companies, presents another item of receipts, which, though not very considerable just now, may easily, as I am going to explain, be very considerably augmented.

Many States have already adopted this system. The State of New York, for instance, draws an immense revenue from its canal, and the State of New Jersey from some oyster establishments which its government has formed on the sea coast. They are farmed out every year and produce such large sums as to have allowed of the reduction of many taxes in that State, and will eventually, perhaps, render it possible to repeal them entirely.

The United States joint stock company is established under the sanction of the United States, to receive deposits, discount bills of exchange, lend upon mortgage, or upon deposits of commercial value or precious metals, and lastly, to give circulation to a paper currency, which being at any time convertible into specie, can never fall below par, and which, on the contrary, by the facility it offers for transmission, is often above. The United States hold a very large proportion of shares, and as such, have a voice in the nomination of the directors and presidents who govern this institution. It transacts all the bank business of government; but, as a compensation for this privilege, it is obliged to have funds ready for it in its different branches without making any charge. It is intrusted also with the payment of the interests of the public debt, as well as of the portions of its capital which become redeemable. This institution has rendered the greatest service to the commerce and industry of the country, as I shall explain to you hereafter.

The United States often subscribe for a certain number of shares in the companies which are formed in the different States, to make roads and canals. It is not that they could not make them at their own expense, but, generally speaking, there are many reasons opposed to their doing so. In the first place, this power could only belong to them in virtue of an article in the constitution which authorizes them to do every thing which may conduce to the general good ; a sort of vague provision, similar to the fourteenth article of the charter, which might serve to cover many usurpations, if the federal government should wish to usurp, and if the State governments had not always their eyes open. It is necessary, therefore, before the United States can undertake a public work within the limits of the States, or authorize a

joint stock company to do it, that the work be
acknowledged to be one of general utility, and
that a majority of the States, at least, draw a
direct advantage from it. Anything, therefore,
which tends to improve the harbours, and render
them capable of receiving numerous ships of war,
or to facilitate the navigation of the great waters,
suffers no impediment; for it is the province of
the United States to regulate external commerce.
Anything which tends to facilitate the military
defence of the country is in the like case; but it
is very doubtful whether the United States have a
right to establish a toll, or authorize a joint stock
company to do it. Anything they might erect
would, therefore, be so much sunk money, returning no interest. The States, on the contrary, as
masters of the soil, may do within themselves
whatever they choose, and are exceedingly jealous on this point. Indeed a new road may often
ruin the capital of a neighbouring State, and it is
quite clear, that the citizens of any State may be
desirous to direct public works towards an object
of local utility, and in competition with works
which their neighbours may be executing. A
last consideration is that works of public utility,
which would only be profitable to a single town
or a single State, would be made at the expense
of all the others, which would certainly be

unjust. But if so many reasons are opposed to the United States claiming the power to undertake works of public utility, whether directly or by the medium of joint stock companies under their authorization, nothing hinders them, when once the government of a State has authorized the formation of one of these companies, from subscribing themselves for any number of shares whatever. They have already often done so, and with advantage, and I hope they will continue.

The great source, however, of the revenue of the United States are the customs: they form nearly nineteen twentieths of the whole receipt. The constitution of the United States has reserved to the federal government the power of regulating external trade, and establishing duties upon importation ; but it has forbidden the imposition of any shackle on internal trade, and the establishing of any duty upon exportation. The tariff of duties also must be the same for all the ports and frontiers of the Union. In each port, and upon the frontiers of Canada, collectors are intrusted with this administration. They are paid by a commission upon the sums they collect, which, however, may in no case exceed a specified sum. Besides collecting the duties, it is their office to

register newly built vessels; to give certificates
of birth, called protections, to sailors; and to
take care that the lighthouse and floating lights
are kept in proper order. It is from them, also,
the captains of the preventive service, the lawyers of the United States, and the district mar-
tials, receive instructions for everything concerning the suppression of contraband trade. The
funds they collect must be paid into the banks
of the United States, to the credit of the treasurer. These are posts of great consideration, are
much sought after, and, in commercial towns,
give great influence to those who fill them.

The duties collected upon many articles are
very considerable, but they never fall heavy upon
the merchant ; the government always allowing
a credit of three, six, nine, and twelve months,
according to the amounts ; so that, in general,
the merchandize is already sold before the duties
are paid. Productions imported to be re-exported
pay nothing, and those manufactured in the
country to be exported under a new form, receive
on their export a premium proportioned to the
duties which the raw material paid on its introduction. I have mentioned that exportation is
entirely free, as well as the transit from one port
to another, whether by sea or by the interior.
No town duty or excise, (*octroi ou droits reunis*,)

can be exacted, but all imposts are accumulated upon importation. They were already very heavy, when, in 1825, the manufacturing interest succeeded in getting them much augmented, so that in many cases they are ncw equal to a prohibition. The manufacturers profited greatly by this state of things, which permitted them to sustain the competition of English manufactures, without diminishing their price and in inferior quality ; but, unfortunately, all the manufacturers are on one side of the Potomac, whilst the consumers are on the other: this, at least, is the case for the greater number of articles. The southern States, which produce only tobacco, cotton, sugar, and maize; and who buy every thing with the proceeds of these productions, found, therefore, much to complain of, when they saw the price of stuffs rise, and their quality fall off, just at the moment when the immense increase in the production of cotton operated in reducing the value of their principal dependence. It was, in fact, their interest to furnish themselves where they could do it cheapest; whether the manufacture was English or American was perfectly indifferent to them. In vain was it attempted to persuade them that the protection granted to the manufactures of the north would soon put them in a situation to create a market much more advantageous for them than those of Europe : experience has since confirmed the perfectly accurate calculations of those who were opposed to the tariff; and the southern States now find themselves reduced to the necessity of consuming productions of an inferior quality and at a very high price, in order to put the northern manufacturers in a situation to make very great profits at their expense. This state of things is unjust, and cannot last long without wholly destroying the prosperity of the southern States. Accordingly, they opposed it with all their might; but, carried away by their passions, their opposition was conducted in such a manner as to do them more injury than the tariff itself. They began by denying the constitutionality of the law which fixed the new tariff, and pretended that Congress had no right to lay on imposts to protect a particular industry, although it might do so to create a revenue and supply its wants. The State of South Carolina carried irritation to the highest point, and, forgetting its usual sagacity, talked even of separating itself from the Union: vain words, which were eagerly seized on in England as an evident proof that the Union of the States cannot last; but which in itself threatens no danger, for the remedy

would be a hundred times worse than the evil
which they wish to obviate. These southern
States, since the passing of the new tariff, have
adopted a line of conduct decidedly hostile to
the northern States, and above all, to their
manufacturing interests.   They tried, for instance, to reduce their consumption as much
as possible, using only coarse stuffs manufactured in their families, and strenuously
set them against any sort of amelioration in
their habits, or imitation of the industry of their
northern brethren.   It is very clear, however,
that conduct directly opposite would have been
proper for them; and since the tariff established
an unfair advantage in respect to the American
manufactures, they should have been the first
to turn it to account by establishing manufactories in the south; which, if not able to
sustain the competition of the English manufactures without the tariff, might always, at
any rate, have been able to compete easily
with those of the north.   Indeed, in the south,
there is nothing to prevent the employment of
negroes in this labour, which seems even much
more suitable for the women than that of the
field; and the price of manual labour would
have been much less than that obliged to be
paid in the north.   It is true, that formerly a

negro could be employed in agriculture more
profitably than in any other way; but those
times are passed, and the value of the productions of the soil is reduced to such a degree that
I think there would now be much advantage in
withdrawing a part of the labour employed in
agriculture, and devoting it to manufactures.
In this way, production, which is too great at
present, would be diminished, and the profits
secured which have been made upon our raw
materials, by the English or by the inhabitants of the north.   But the southern States
have followed quite a contrary course: they
have declared war against every thing bearing
the name of manufacture, industry, or tariff; and
if they continue, in ever so small a degree, the
same line of policy, they will infallibly see themselves overcome by the people of the north, in
whose hands all the capital will soon be con-
centrated.

The inhabitants of the north, moreover, or
at least the party among them in favour of
what they call the American system, also push
their admiration of a protective system much
too far; they have been desirous of forcing industry, by high premiums, to produce objects
which nature itself has appeared to reserve for
other climates and other times.

If all the nations of the earth were equal in industry; if all possessed an amount of capital proportioned to their population, the wealth of the different nations would be found to be in a direct ratio to the fertility of the soil and the beauty of the climate. But the different degrees of civilization to which the various nations have attained; the schools of policy, above all, of the respective governments; and the disparity existing between the amounts of capital amassed, have entirely destroyed this natural proportion. It is to the renewal of this proportion, it is to the destruction of all commercial and manufacturing monopoly, that the progress of enlightenment tends. But this result will not be equally favorable to all nations; for those who, by their geographical position, are naturally poor, will be obliged to disgorge wealth and renounce power, which the ignorance of other nations has permitted them to acquire. As a general position, the freedom of commerce will be then all in favour of nations naturally rich. But, however, in the present moment, and as long as an inequality of industry and capital exists, a protective system is necessary to the more favored nations, in order to force them to take the rank which nature has assigned them. Italy, for instance, the richest of all the countries

of Europe, now finds herself almost wholly
without industry, and tributary to all others.
Her oils and her barillas are sent to Marseilles
and return in soaps. Her silks and her cottons
seek manufacturers in Switzerland, Lyons, and
England, and return to Italy, in a manufactured
state, to find consumers. The commerce of Italy
is carried on entirely by foreign vessels. If
she were free, the first care of a good government would be to replace her in the first rank
of European industry and commerce; and to
that end the only means would be to establish
a tariff duty of such strict severity that the
nation should be obliged to go bare or establish
manufactures; that once done, industry once
established, there would no longer be any
danger in repealing the tariff, and establishing
an unlimited freedom of commerce. Capital
would by that time have learned to flow in the
new channels opened for it, and nothing afterwards would be able to turn it back. Freedom
of commerce would by then have become an
advantage to Italian industry; at the commencement, the same freedom would have killed
it, or rather have prevented it from being born.
England, on the contrary, is naturally one of
the poorest countries of Europe; but a multitude of causes which it would be too long to

enter into, but which may be reduced to two principal ones,—the natural industry of the inhabitants, and the excellence of her social institutions,—have enabled her to heap up a mass of capital unexampled hitherto in the history of man.

But whenever other nations enjoy the same advantages, her prosperity must fall away; for is is not founded upon nature, but upon factitious bases. In the present state of things, England preaches unlimited freedom of trade: in truth, she has nothing to lose. Let her diminish her duties as much as she pleases, for a long time the manufactures of no country will be able to compete with her; and the more other nations imitate her example, and believe in the doctrine she now preaches, the more they will see their progress in industry retarded, and the more her monopoly will be strengthened, and her fall delayed. In preaching freedom of commerce, England seeks to make dupes.

But it is not every branch of industry which should be equally protected in each country. Every land, every climate has its natural productions; and the natural industry of a country should be limited to their exportation in their highest state of manufacture. This is the sole end which a good government should aim at by a prohibitive system, and to protect the

young plant, until it acquires sufficient strength
and has struck its roots in deeply. If, for example, the English government imposed duties
only in order to protect industry and not to
create a revenue, which is, in my opinion, the
best of all systems, all duties upon the importation of wines, oils, colonial produce, in a word,
on every thing which she cannot now, nor will
ever be able to produce, ought to be wholly
abolished. This would greatly diminish the
cost of living, and render manual labour cheaper.
On the other hand, heavy duties should be
imposed upon the importation of any manufactured, or even raw articles which the country
could produce as well as the foreigner. At first
the protecting duty will create profits sufficiently
considerable to invite capital into a new chan-
nel; the success of one manufacture will lead to
the establishment of many others; the competition
thus produced will soon reduce the price below
those at which foreigners could deliver, and the
importation duty will become perfectly nominal·

From what I have said above, the United
States being, taken altogether, one of the
richest countries on the earth, I may seem
to approve the establishment of a strongly protective system, like that of the existing tariff.
That, however, is very far from being my opi-

nion. The people of the United States can be much better employed than in shutting themselves up between four walls, to breathe the corrupted air of manufactories. The forests invite them, the western roads are still open, and the tide of civilization has not yet been driven back by that of the Pacific ocean. As long as any of the country remains uncultivated, as long as nobody wants either bread or work, why, out of two occupations, the one ennobling man and increasing his strength, the other the condescending to play the part of a piece of mechanism; why, I ask, choose the latter? Why force capital to take this direction, except for particular kinds of industry, the productions of which are extremely heavy or brittle, such as iron and glass, for instance, and for which the expense of conveyance is almost always a sufficient protection? Why seek to establish manufactures? can we not always command those of the foreigner with our raw materials? Would it be a disadvantage to us if we wore only stuffs of English manufacture, and if the English people had eaten no bread that was not made from American wheat? We should thus have partaken, between us and foreigners, the different labours of civilization, in such a way as to retain to ourselves those which are agreeable and suitable to the dignity of freemen, leaving to others our refuse, and the employments which enervate and degrade man. The American system (as that of Mr. Clay and his friends is called,) is good in itself, but premature by some centuries. It has been the means of bringing into the market some fine manufactures, of which we are very proud. In some articles, the American manufactures may, even abroad, sustain competition with those of the English. But have we not bought these advantages by the sacrifice of a mass of comforts which the difference of the prices cannot pay? and by a commencement of moral and political degradation, as it regards those who have been forced to become in-door labourers, who, but for that, would be free and independent husbandmen of a soil cultivated by themselves and belonging to them? These truths begin to be felt, and it is probable that the American system will be but of short duration. We shall, perhaps, be obliged to return to it after all the public lands are sold, but, fortunately, that will not be for some time.

The different States have also their revenue derived in each of them from a different system of taxation. As I have already mentioned, they cannot lay on any duty upon exportation, importation, or transit of merchandise; but they

may impose direct taxes, capitations, excise on
the manufacture of liqueurs, patent-rights, &c.
They may also borrow money, employ their
capitals in public works, which become productive for them; and almost all of them avail
themselves of many of these means at once, and
sometimes of all.

In every county there are expenses to provide
for, for which the county court imposes taxes
upon the inhabitants; and in the towns the
corporation expenses are defrayed in the same
manner. The expenditure in some of the great
towns is even considerable. The revenue and
budget of the city of New York, for instance, are
much more considerable than those of the State,
and the taxes upon landed property there are
very heavy. Philadelphia is similarly situated;
but, owing to a fortuitous event, its financial
condition has been rendered very extraordinary;
and it cannot fail, in a very short time, to become one of the finest cities in the world: this
is worth explaining. A Frenchman of the name
of Girard, who left France in a state of extreme
poverty, (I believe as a ship-boy, or sailor at
most,) died there lately, at the age of ninety and
upwards, leaving a fortune of nearly a hundred
millions of francs, (nearly four millions sterling,)
which he had amassed during a long life of

industry, probity, and privations. He was a
very strong-headed man, much esteemed, and
lived in a very singular manner. He was regular
in his habits, without denying himself the gratification of any of his tastes, and expended his
immense income in public works and useful enterprises. At his death, he left, among other lega-
cies, ten millions of francs, (about £400,000,)
for the establishment of a college, on condition
that no priest of any religion should, under any
pretext, interfere in its management. But the
greater part of his fortune, more than sixty
millions of francs, (about £2,400,000,) he left to
the city of Philadelphia. It is impossible to foresee the start which a legacy like this, if well
administered, may give to this city. The interest
of this sum being much more than sufficient to
cover all municipal expenses, it is probable that
all the taxes will be abolished; this will tend to
augment the population of the city, and give an
immense advantage to its manufactures. Who
can calculate what roads, canals, and other
public works the corporation may be induced
to undertake? It will be in twenty years' time
that we shall see the fruits of this immense
legacy.

The chief item in the expenses of the United
States has been the payment of the capital and

interest of the debt contracted during the last war. At the time of the Revolution war, the United States, to supply its charges, and not being in a condition to make loans, was obliged to issue a paper-money similar to the French assignats. This paper, which was greatly depreciated during the war, was bought up at a late period at the market price, which was thought, but erroneously, to indicate a state of bankruptcy; for as this paper had been issued at par, had continued circulating, losing its value gradually though insensibly, the last holders did not lose more than the first, and their losses were exactly equal to the proportion they would have had to pay of any tax which might have been levied to buy up this paper at par; this, besides, would have given a very unfair advantage to the actual possessors of paper over those by whose hands it had before circulated. At the commencement of the last war, the credit of the United States was very low; they succeeded, however, in making loans, and since then have repaid the whole, within thirty or thirty-five millions of dollars, which will be paid in two or three years: the United States will then have an excess of revenue of twelve or fifteen millions of dollars yearly; and disputes have already com-

menced as to the way in which it should be
employed. The question is, in fact, much more
perplexing than it may seem at first sight; for
if the imposts were to be reduced so as to bring
the receipts on a level with the expenditure, it
would be the ruin of all the manufacturers who
have employed their capitals in this direction,
solely on the faith of the nation. I certainly
wish that the tariff may be greatly modified,
but gradually, and not in such a way as to produce any disastrous shock to manufacturing
industry, of which all classes, in one way or
another, would feel the effects for a long time
to come. One party proposes to divide the
surplus revenue among the States in a given
proportion; but there would be serious inconveniences attending this mode. The equilibrium
between the power of the state governments
and that of the federal government, would be
destroyed in favour of the former; besides, it
would be impossible to establish a mode of distribution which would appear equitable to every
body. Another party wishes that the federal
government should employ this money in undertaking great works of public utility. This
mode has also very many inconveniences, and
the independence of the States would greatly
suffer by it. A medium course will probably

be adopted. During the first years, this money
will be employed in completing at once the immense fortification-works on the coasts; which,
as I have told you in a former letter, have been
undertaken by the United States upon a gigantic sale. That once done, the government
will subscribe for a certain proportion in all the
companies incorporated for public works by the
States. In this way the government will see
every year accumulating a capital of twelve to
fifteen millions of dollars, in road and canal
shares, which will bring it in a heavy interest;
and that, in like manner, may be invested in
shares in new enterprises; so that, in case of
war, or any fortuitous event taking place,
which might require unforeseen expenses; instead of borrowing, the government will only
have to throw upon the market, and sell at the
price of the day, a quantity of shares sufficient
to supply its wants.

If the state of peace and prosperity in which
the Union is at present, should continue only
ten years longer, it will by that means, be found
raised far above all its eventual wants, and
may, in the course of time, undertake public
works, in comparison of which the Pyramids of
Egypt are but child's play.

To the eyes of the European, projects of this

sort seem gigantic, but in America they are
nothing astonishing. The government would
only do what many individuals and many corporations have done before it; in fact, the rapidity with which capitals augment in the
United States, surpasses all belief. The demand for capital is such, and the enterprises,
commercial, manufacturing, and agricultural,
are so numerous, that whatever may be their
amount, they are instantly absorbed. They
may always command from seven to ten per
cent. interest, and produce much more to those
who retain their property in them. What
cramps industry in Europe, is the super-
abundance of capital, whilst in America the
progress of industry has no other limit than its
scarcity. To obviate this inconvenience, it
therefore becomes necessary to adopt a system
of universal credit, and to allow, as it were, the
creation of factitious capitals. This means has
therefore been resorted to. All business is
done on long credit. For example, a merchant
will often buy, at three months, a cargo which
he knows must be necessarily sold at a loss,
at Cuba; but he will immediately find the
means of borrowing again the value of this
shipment, by giving it as guarantee. With
these two sums united, he will bring back a

shipment of sugar and coffee, and realize immense profits before the period arrives at which he must pay these two first debts, and his engagements at the Custom House for importation duties. All the dealers of the great towns sell to the country dealers at credits of six months or a year. These do the same with the planter. How many planters even have paid for their lands or their negroes with their crops or private undertakings! Every thing, in short, goes on by speculation; nobody lives upon the interest of his money, or on his yearly income; all is activity, enterprise, speculation, hazard. Very often immense profits are realized; at other times, a false calculation involves complete ruin; but, in the meantime, as the general capital of the nation augments immensely every year, which supposes that every one is thriving in business, it is very clear that the gainers in this general lottery must be more numerous than the losers.

A New England carpenter, for instance, who, like all the Yankees, has been well educated, leaves his little town, where he can have had no other prospect before him than that of being a carpenter all his life, and goes and settles himself in one of the new countries in the west, on the banks of some great river. Behold him

at first become a master builder; he undertakes
to build either private houses or public edifices
on credit; he himself gets credit from his workmen, and lives on credit in his lodging, at his
tailor's, &c.   He will be sure to thrive in his
business ; he will then buy a piece of land,
build mills or factories, and so become a miller
or a manufacturer.   He will accompany his first
shipment to New Orleans; will begin making
other commercial speculations, buy a steam
boat, settle in the great city, and, in consequence of a miscalculation, lose every thing;
but nothing will hinder him from beginning
again.   On the contrary, being known as an
enterprising man, who has already made a fortune and been unfortunate, he will forthwith
find some person or company, who will confide
to him either the erection of a house or the direction of a timber-yard, the management of
a plantation, or the command of a steam-boat;
so that he will recommence his financial career
from a more elevated point than he did before.

But let us suppose that he has undertaken the
management of a plantation,—there he is overseer; nothing can prevent him at this time from
economizing his salary, and making private
speculations, often at the expense of his master.
At the end of one or two years he will quit, well

or ill. He will then go into some new country,
settle on a small piece of land (at the passage
of a river, where he will construct a ferry) as a
victualler,—mechanist,—builder in its various
branches; he will render himself very popular;
become the influential man of his district, be
elected, first, an officer in the militia, then a
justice of peace, then a member of the legislature, and perhaps even a member of Congress.
There his mind, in collision with those of the
first men in the nation, will be sure to gain
something; continual discussions will enlighten
it; he will get fashioned to the manners of
the world; become a fine speaker if he was
not so before; and, in short, after returning
home, in two sessions he will get himself
received as a lawyer. Frequently ambition
and public business will make him neglect his
own; politics change, his party becomes the
weakest, he is not re-elected, and finds himself
reduced to his mere practice. It is now the
time to begin once more. But much more probably he now becomes governor of the State, or
director of the banks, and finishes his honourable and laborious career as judge of one of the
supreme courts. There are few, indeed, among
the most distinguished of the Americans, who
have not passed through many of these fluc-

tuations of fortune; who have not had three or four trades, frequently of those which in Europe appear most discordant. You may have known a man as a lawyer; you see him again at the end of a few years, at the other end of the Union, captain of a ship, or a planter, an officer, a merchant, and even sometimes a preacher ; in some instances he will have run the circle of all these; and although perhaps he has not made his fortune, whether owing to the fault of his stars or his own, the community, meanwhile, is always the better for his labour; for the tree which he planted in the desert will continue to bear its fruit, whether destined to assuage his own thirst or that of another.

To facilitate as much as possible this progressive movement, so rapid, and often so turbulent and irregular, the system of banks has been invented, and it is developed to the fullest extent of which it is susceptible. Money does not circulate in the United States, none is to be seen; it is close shut up in barrels and boxes, duly labelled and sealed; and only leaves the cellar of one bank to go in carts to repose in those of another. The banks issue notes for three or four times the value of the specie in their cellars; these notes, in the south, are sometimes for very small sums, even for 6¼ cents. In

some States they are never under a dollar, and
the United States Bank issues only those of
five dollars and upwards. These banks, the
number of which is infinite, are joint stock
companies, in shares; the shareholders elect
directors annually, who appoint a president,
a treasurer, and other officers of the bank, each
according to its constitution : these officers
direct all the business of the company, and receive deposits, discount bills, lend money upon
interest, in short, do every sort of business requiring the advance of capital. These banks are
bound to take up their notes in ready money, on
presentation.   They all have accounts open
with the rest.   Very often, the States are themselves shareholders in one of their banks.
Amidst the competition of all these institutions,
sometimes helping, sometimes thwarting one
another, the great Leviathan, the bank of the
United States, extends its branches and its
offices for discounts and deposits, from one end of
the United States to the other. This is the great
regulator of the entire machine which prevents
too violent shocks from taking place.   Before
its institution, many banks might suspend their
payments in specie, the value of their paper
became variable; the discount of one town upon
the other was unceasingly changing, and always

so managed as to produce immense loss to the government of the United States. Now all the banks are indebted to that of the United States. It takes upon itself the transmission of funds from one end of the Union to the other, for a discount which in no case exceeds 2 per cent., and which, in general, is at par for private persons. As I have already mentioned, it transacts the government business at par; the other banks are therefore obliged to reduce their discount, at least, to the rate of that of the United States bank, for otherwise they would get no business. All these banks cause an immense amount of capital to circulate with incredible rapidity. They give life, animation, encouragement to every thing, and form the distinctive feature in the American system of industry.

On the other hand, the enormous risks to which so many concurrent undertakings must necessarily give rise, are covered by innumerable insurance companies. They are also joint-stock, and constituted the same as the banks; there are some of them to meet every sort of risk.

Many manufactures, mines, and improvements of every sort, are also carried on by similar societies; who often combine the privilege of issuing notes with the other powers granted them by the legislature. Roads, canals, bridges,

z

rail roads,—in short, all public works are constructed and carried into effect in the same
manner. All these societies are corporations,
having a civil and political existence, and may
sue and be sued at law like any individual. All
of them employ lawyers, engravers, engineers, &c.
&c., and become an immense source of prosperity
to the small town in which they establish their
offices. Sometimes, indeed, they do unprofitable
business and fail, but that is very seldom.

It is common for foreigners, who have visited the
United States on business, to complain of the dishonesty they found in trade, and of the instability
of the fortunes acquired there. I think that this
is owing first of all to the bad choice they make
of their correspondents, and secondly, to their
going to sleep over their business. In fact, in
the midst of a crowd like this, where all are running towards the same object, it is necessary to
run also, and keep firm on your legs, if you will
not be passed in the race or upset. It frequently
happens that very fertile lands have been discovered in a locality; government sells them
at very high prices; speculators get hold of
them; a sort of infatuation takes place; the
population flock there in crowds; works of public
utility are commenced; shops start up on all
sides, the prices of land continue to rise: at

last a bank is established there, and every thing breathes prosperity. Suddenly one or more successive bad crops or yellow fevers, or the establishment of other settlements of the same sort, in a still more favorable situation, the spirit of change, in short, and the appetite for novelty, substitute discouragement for the original infatuation. The lands which had risen far above their real value fall below it; the population finding that they do not make their fortune fast enough, get disgusted, and emigrate as fast as they before run thither; all falls, in short, into a state of decay as singular and as fictitious as the state of prosperity which preceded it. These two states of things continue alternating until, after many oscillations, the new district is better appreciated, and its real value fixed in as permanent a manner as any thing can be in a country so progressive as the United States. Happy then is he, who, knowing the genius of the people and their institutions, as well as the geography of the country and its climate and productions, knows when to buy and sell at the right time; but woe to the European, without local knowledge, who shall act according to the advice of friends either interested, or really deceiving themselves. He is sure, in following the principle of Panurge, to buy dear and sell cheap, to arrive at the same result and be very soon undone, unless he have the courage, spirit, and flexibility which an American opposes to the blows of fate, and knows how, like him, cats, and parsons, always to fall upon his feet.

LETTER TENTH.

Of Manners, Fine Arts, and Literature.— *Competition the main principle of American society; glance at the St. Simonian system, that of the Americans a contrast to it; periodical press, its general diffusion and inferiority; independent character of all classes in the United States; different circles of society; society at New York, at Philadelphia, at Charleston, at Richmond, at New Orleans, at Washington; equality of condition in America, marriages, non-interference of the parents; matchmaking at Washington; changes in the habits of life after marriage; Saratoga; courtesies to strangers; freedom of American society from the affectation of high acquaintance so general in England; general rate of expenses of those who live in the best society; Fine Arts and Literature, deficiency of encouragement, particularly of the former; elementary systems of education; Architecture flourishes and is encouraged; music retarded by the straitness of manners; the Corps de Ballet at New York; consternation produced in the audience; prudery with regard to painting the human figure; unavoidable backwardness of the Fine Arts in the present state of manners; description of a public holiday; the Americans secure happiness in preference to pleasure; the right medium not yet attained.*

IF in the United States the government is
established upon a principle altogether new
and unknown, at least in its application—that
of the sovereignty of the people, in the strictest
sense of the word,—so also society and the relations of individuals towards each other are
based on a footing not less new; namely, competition. There is no sort of aristocracy of
birth: fortune gives no rights but to the physical
advantages it may purchase; but talent and
merit see no bounds to their reasonable ambition. Every body in our republican system is
rigorously *classed* according to his capacity.
You are about to conclude we are St. Simo-
nians;—no, my friend, do not mistake me. Can
you suppose that I, a white man and free, am
going to submit my reason to that of any of my
equals? Do you think that I will go and ask
some buffoon to class me, when I am sure of
conquering by myself that station, whatever it
may be, to which I am entitled in the scale of
beings? Do you think that I will go and acknowledge the Père Enfantin; or any other quack
to whom he may delegate his functions? I, who
am dependent on nobody, and free as the air
I breathe? Quite the reverse: the St. Simonian

system and the American system are the two
extremes of the diameter of human thought.
The one is based upon an absolute subjection,
a slavery much stronger than has ever existed,
since it extends even to the mind, and if we are
to believe certain reports, perhaps slanderous,
even over the most sacred affections; the other,
on the contrary, is founded on the principle of
the most absolute liberty: independence is its
result. The one will protect me against all
dangers, real or imaginary, and force me to
be happy, in its own way, even against my will:
the other launches me, young and hardy, upon
the waves of life, to sport as I please, extricate
myself from difficulties as I can, and be happy
or perish in my own way; for it is very certain
that without losing my identity I cannot be so in
that of another. Competition,—that is the secret
of the American system; every thing is to be won
by competition: fortune, power, love, riches, all
these objects of desire are attainable; it is for
the most skilful to go in pursuit of them. Just
as in the old fairy tales, those enchanted princesses are defended by dragons, vultures, roaring
lions, but still more, by rivals who crowd the
same path, and who will not be sparing of
a kick to assist you in tumbling down. Fortunately, however, in our land of plenty,

the princesses to conquer and deliver are sufficiently numerous to content all valiant knights, and even many of their squires; so that the combat is not so desperate as it might be supposed. There is room for every one at the banquet of life; and what is more, the table has no upper end, no seat distinguished by a canopy.

All men are born equal in rights and in chances of success; for if, on the one hand, fortune gives advantages to some; on the other, she withholds the spur of necessity, and thus greatly slackens their energy. All have equal chances of attaining every thing. The rich fool will not be less a fool, and cannot, but with difficulty, maintain his fortune against the attempts of the man of parts impelled by necessity. The man once engaged in any career cannot stop an instant, nor relax in his exertions, without being immediately passed by young rivals whose very names were unknown the day before. This continual competition, this perpetual struggle of all against all, maintains society in a state of activity which has the happiest results. Whatever may be the pursuit followed, every one is wholly dependent upon public opinion. This it is which reigns despotically, and 'classes' each according to his works, with strict disinterestedness and unerring judgment. But, in order that

public opinion may be duly enlightened, the
utmost publicity is necessary; therefore nothing
is neglected in the United States to effect that
object in every possible manner. The press is
entirely free. The publication of newspapers
and their circulation, so far from being shackled
by duties, securities, and stamps, or being restricted by the post, is encouraged as much as
possible. Consequently newspapers multiply.
Every town or village has, at least, one; and
every shade of opinion, however slight, is sure
of having its interpreter. Every thing is known,
every thing is discussed, every thing is explained, and the sole means in the United States
of not being discovered is to have no mystery.
Guided by a light so sure, the people form their
judgments, and are never deceived in their
verdict.

I am not inclined here to defend the American
periodical press. There are hardly four or five
good papers in the crowd; the rest copy these,
and shew very little delicacy in the means of
which they avail themselves to support their
opinions. But their virulence acts as an
antidote to itself; and besides, a personality
never remains without an answer, so that the
deplorable spirit which animates them, produces
no effect upon ears accustomed to hear the

reproaches put forth by opposite parties. At the time of the contested election between Adams and Jackson, the newspapers of the two parties assumed so virulent a tone, and published so many calumnies, that it was truly disgusting to look into them. Whoever believed them, might have sincerely commiserated the fate of the nation, obliged to choose between two such scoundrels as the candidates were respectively represented to be by journals of the opposite parties. It is proper to be just, however; the great difficulty met with in the United States, in the elections, is how to select among many persons of equal merit. The nation advances calmly in prosperity, without any of those concussions which give occasion to the display of talents of a superior order. It certainly possesses people of the first merit, and abundance of them, but it is almost impossible for them, in the present state of peace and tranquillity, to attain their proper elevation, above the rank of merit immediately inferior to them. The less, therefore, the difference is between two candidates, the more must it be exaggerated by the papers of their respective parties, who in that perform the office of repeating circles. The difference is so small that it would pass unperceived if it was not multiplied some thousands of times.

One of the most remarkable effects of this
publicity is the interest which every one takes
in the politics of the day; an interest which
produces a sameness in conversation, in whatever society you may happen to fall. The
hackney-coachmen talking at the corner of the
streets with a porter; the lawyer, the planter,
the preacher, dining together with a rich trades-
man, all speak of the same thing. The next
election, the measure now being proposed, whether in Congress or in the state legislature, or the
last lawsuit which attracted the crowd, form the
subject of conversation; it is treated differently
in the different circles, but still it is always the
same subject; and it is equally well understood
by all classes, for the newspapers are read by
every body.

It is easy to see that when there reigns in a
country such an unanimity of opinions, such a
similarity of intellectual tastes and occupations,
the differences among the classes which compose society are entirely chimerical. I do not
mean to say that there are not in the United
States several circles of society; that cannot be
otherwise in any polished society; but I do
mean to say, that the limits which divide them
are so delicate, that they melt into each other;

and that, if there are many circles, there are neither castes nor ranks.

The American is mild, polite, but proud, as it
befits a freeman to be; he does not pretend to
any superiority, but he will in no respect submit
to be treated as an inferior. Every one considers that he carries on a trade, that he may
live; and far from coveting idleness, he despises
it; he thinks all honest trades equal in dignity, although requiring, as they do, different
degrees of talent, he sees no injustice in their
being unequally recompensed. The servant of
a lawyer or a physician, for instance, perceives
no material difference between himself and his
employer, (for the word master is only used by
people of colour.) One brushes clothes, the
other pleads causes, or feels pulses, or preaches,
or judges, or makes laws, or governs—and all for
money. There is not so much difference: each
tries to do his duty in the best way he can.
Thus the domestic will be very attentive and
submissive. Whenever his situation no longer
suits him, he will leave his master; and in no
case will he suffer on his part either insult or
violence. Let him fall ill, or have a lawsuit,
and he will give his custom to his master,
pay him like any body else, and consider him-

self *quoad,* as having changed characters with
h, m.

This spirit of independence forms the grand
distinctive character between the English and
American manners; for outwardly and physically they are much alike. If, for example,
you go into what those who compose it call the
first society of New York, this circle is composed of tradesmen newly arrived at the summit
of Fortune's wheel, where it is very doubtful if
they long remain. They take advantage of
their fleeting days of prosperity to show off as
much luxury and folly as their situation will
permit them. All who have made a voyage to
Europe, try to ape the exclusive manners of
which they have been the victims on the other
side of the Atlantic; affect to value everything
foreign, and consider America as a barbarous
country, where nothing elegant has ever been
invented,—not even the galopade and *gigot*
sleeves. The first European swindler who takes
the trouble to pass himself off for a duke or a
marquis is sure to carry away all their suffrages,
until it pleases him to join thereto their purses.
Men of this stamp will pretend not to trouble
themselves about politics, or at least not to talk
about them; for it is a subject so vulgar and so
unfashionable .... in London! They try to imi-

tate the perfect nullity of conversation in that
city, and in general, assisted by their natural
resources, they succeed pretty well.

But apart from this society is that formed by
the merchants, shipowners, lawyers, physicians,
and magistrates of the city. This is truly American: they do not amuse themselves by apeing
European manners; among them, conversation is solid and instructive, and turns upon business and the politics of the day. Society in
New York is perhaps more tinged with European manners than in other of the great towns
in the United States; and that is very natural,
if we consider the immense number of foreigners
who reside there. It is the city which has most
theatres, (for it has no less than five,) and it has
had even an opera and a *corps de ballet*. There
is more dissipation and more foolish expenses in
it than in any other place. The principal street,
the Broadway, gives a striking impression of
America to the European on his landing. After
Regent Street, in London, it is the finest street
I know. The wide pavements, with their elegant shops, are, at certain hours of the day,
crowded with all the fashion of the place. All
the pretty women go there to take a turn, and
there the fine gentlemen are eager to meet them.
The foreigner reading his newspaper, in the

large parlour of the city hotel, sees all the *beau monde* defile before him.

Society in Philadelphia is much more quiet: the Quakers are a happy people, who give a look of repose to all the city.   Here there is no noise as in New York; the carriages are much fewer, the streets being so clean there is no occasion for them.   All the streets are alike, none, therefore, serves as a general promenade like the Broadway of New York.   Chesnut Street, however, is the best built, and there the fashionable people come to take their lounge. The library of Messrs. Carey and Lea is the place where you must take your station towards noon, to see this street in all its lustre.   The society of Philadelphia is much more enlightened than that of New York; the professors of the university give the tone, which communicates to it, perhaps, a slight degree, almost imperceptible however, of pedantry.   The winter parties are meetings of learned and literary people, including also citizens in any way distinguished: they are always open to foreigners, properly introduced.   Ladies are never present. The meetings are held on appointed days at the houses of different persons in rotation: science, literature, the fine arts, and politics, form the subjects of conversation, and in general much intelligence and urbanity are displayed. They are always terminated by a supper, and are calculated to give foreigners a high idea of the intellectual resources of that city.

But it is to Charleston that he should go to enjoy American society in all its luxury. There the various circles, composed of planters, lawyers, and physicians, form the most agreeable society I have ever known. The manners of the south have a perfect elegance; the mind is highly cultivated; and conversation turns upon an infinite variety of subjects with spirit, grace, and facility. The affectation of frivolity or of foreign manners is as completely banished as pedantry and religious hypocrisy; everything is intellectual, moral, and rational. Charleston is the ordinary residence of many of the most distinguished statesmen of the Union, who are always willing to explain their views to their fellow-citizens. Alas! why can I not recall the delightful hours I have passed in that society, without being reminded of the loss of that friend in whose hospitable residence I first knew it. He is no more, and Charleston has lost, for me, one of its greatest attractions.

The society of Richmond greatly resembles that of Charleston, and is as agreeable. In

Virginia, good society is spread more generally over the whole surface of the State than it is anywhere else, owing to the want of a large capital, which always serves to attract it, and gives the tone exclusively. Virginian hospitality is proverbial, and with great justice.

New Orleans forms a perfect contrast to all the other cities: here there is no intellectual conversation, no instruction; there are but three booksellers in a city of sixty thousand souls, and yet even their warehouses are composed of the refuse of the filthiest productions of French literature. But if there is no conversation, there are eating, playing, dancing, and making love in abundance. An institution peculiar to this city are the quadroon balls, where the free women of colour are alone admitted to the honour of dancing with their lords the whites; for the men of colour are most strictly excluded from them. It is truly a magical spectacle to see some hundreds of women, all very pretty and well dressed, and of every shade, from that of cream coffee to the most delicate white, assembled in superb saloons, to display their mercenary charms. The most respectable people frequent these balls, which are quite public, and where every thing invariably

passes with the greatest decorum. The gaming-
houses are also very numerous in New Orleans,
and have ruined many of the young people of
Kentucky, come to pass their carnival in this
Babylon of the west.

But the place in which American society appears to the greatest advantage is Washington,
during the winter. In summer the city is
almost deserted; it is then inhabited principally by the members of government and those
connected with the government establishments.
But the first Monday in December of every
year, is the day fixed for the assembling
of Congress. As the time approaches, the
senators and representatives arrive in crowds,
accompanied by their families, and followed by
shoals of solicitors and people having business
with Congress. The city seems full instan-
taneously. The ministers and diplomatic body
give entertainments; the members of Congress
give dinners in return; if the day passes in the
whirl of business, the night is borne away by
that of pleasure. The president holds a levee
once a week; this is to say, one evening in the
week he opens his house to all those who desire
to pay him a visit. Nothing can be more simple
than the etiquette of the head of the govern-

ment. The concourse of visiters is the only
thing which distinguishes these assemblages
from those of any other individual.

The conditions of life being perfectly equal
in America, parents have nothing to oppose
to the choice their daughters may make of a
husband. Thus it is a received maxim throughout the Union, that this choice only concerns
the young ladies, and it is therefore for them
to be prudent enough not to enter into engagements unworthy of their hands. But it
would be considered almost as an act of indis-
cretion on the part of the parents to wish to
influence their choice. Nothing in the world
can be so happy as the situation of an American
young lady from fifteen to twenty-five, particularly if she is pretty, as almost all are, and
has some fortune. She finds herself the centre
of general admiration and homage; her life
passes in holidays and pleasures; she is a
stranger to contradiction, still more to refusals.
She has only to choose, among a hundred
adorers, the one she thinks most likely to ensure
her future happiness; for here every body marries, and every body is happy in marriage. This
state of 'belle,' as it is called, is too attractive
to make young ladies consent to quit it too
soon; accordingly, it is not, in general, until

after rejecting many offers, and when they perceive
that their charms are beginning to lose something
of their empire, that they conclude by choosing
a liege lord. It is to Washington, in particular,
that the fine women of all the States come to
shine; a sort of female congress, in which the
charms of every part of the Union are represented. An ardent deputy from the south is
captivated by the modest charms of a beauty
from the east; while a damsel from Carolina
rejects the overtures of a senator from the north.
All, however, are not rejected, for at the end of
every session a certain number of marriages is
declared; they serve to strengthen further the
Union of the States, and multiply the ties which
unite all parts of this great whole in an indis-
soluble manner.

Once married, the young lady entirely changes
her habits. Farewell gaiety and frivolity. She
is not less happy, but her happiness is of a
serious character; she becomes a mother, is
employed in her household, becomes quite the
centre of domestic affections, and enjoys the
esteem of all who know and surround her. Society everywhere in the United States may be
considered, therefore, as divided into two very
distinct classes: that of unmarried persons of
both sexes, whose principal occupation is court-

ship, and the f....ling a suitable companion with
whom to make the voyage of life; the other of
people who have already made that choice.
You see in the corner of a drawing-room, people
of the latter class forming groups among themselves, and talking politics or business: they
will hardly address a word to the young girls
who flutter around them, unless it be to joke
them upon the success of some coquetish
frolic; the mothers are in another corner, chatting
together about their domestic matters, and receiving interested attentions from the admirers
of their daughters. But for these, and the
young men, a ball-room is a real field of battle.
They boast among themselves of the number of
declarations made, and refusals given, in the
course of the evening: a thousand little co-
quetries are played off to draw a young man
to declare himself, only to have the pleasure of
refusing him afterwards. All these little tricks
and skirmishes are perfectly innocent, for such
is the general purity of morals that no inconvenience is ever the result of them.

If Washington is the theatre of the winter
campaign, that of the summer opens at Saratoga: this is a mineral spring in the State of
New York, to which all the fashion in the
Union resorts, during the months of June, July,

and August.   The heat of the southern climate,
and the intermitting fevers which desolate the
plantations at this season, drive all the planters
towards the north; they go with their families
to New York, from whence they proceed up
the northern river, as far as Albany, go and
pass a few days at Saratoga, afterwards see the
great lakes; from thence, the fall of Niagara,
the great canal, the Catskill mountains, and
perhaps even push their excursion. as far as
Canada.   The State of New York is filled,
during the summer, with an immense number of
virtuosi, travelling for their health or pleasure.
At Saratoga, people live at large inns, horribly
ill accommodated, in small rooms six feet square:
but the principal parlours are very beautiful,
and the exterior of their hotels has truly a
monumental air.   People rise early, go and
drink, or make believe to drink, of the water of
the fountain; return to breakfast in common;
the papas and mammas are ready to die with
ennui all the day; the young ladies play music,
the young gentlemen make love to them: from
time to time some excursion is made in the
neighbourhood: in the evening comes dancing.
People are very soon tired of this sort of
life, which nevertheless has its charms for four
or five days.   It is at Saratoga that the lovers

meet, who parted, in the winter, at Washington, and it is at Washington they promise to be found again on quitting Saratoga: these places of mutual resort, and, more than all, the public and sociable manner in which people live at the waters, present every facility of augmenting the circle of acquaintance. In short, an American has friends in every town in the Union, who, wherever he may be going, ensures him, as well as those whom he may recommend, a hospitable reception.

In every town the principal citizens, those who are at the head of the place by their influence, fortune, or talents, consider it a duty to do the honours of their town to any stranger a little distinguished. As soon as they are informed, either by the journals or by public report, of the arrival of such a person in their town, they go to his hotel, pay him the first visit, and invite him to dinner. The visiter never leaves the table without receiving an invitation in the same manner from some of the guests, so that in a very short time he is enabled to make the acquaintance of all the society of the town. If there are balls or public dinners, he is sure of an invitation; and if he is a man politically influential or popular in any way, public dinners are given to him by subscription.

These civilities are returned by the traveller, as soon as he gets home, to any citizen of the town in which he has been so well received, who may come to visit the place of his residence; so that a round of mutual good offices is kept up, which connects still more strongly the different towns of the Union among themselves.

Moreover, the different professions, particularly the lawyers, are actuated by an *esprit de corps* which they turn to their mutual advantage. They associate together in the most friendly manner, and thus render their practice very agreeable; for however they may wrangle in court, nothing more is thought of the matter when they get out, and, in general, all the members of the same bar live in the greatest intimacy. The assizes are always a festival time, for not only the members of the bar residing in the town where they are held, but even the principal citizens of the place, make a point of inviting in turn the court, its officers, and all the bar.

What I have said of good society must be understood of all classes, observing, however, that in proportion as you descend, the people are less informed, the manners less elegant and refined, and the morals less pure. But the sort

of manners is always the same, and even down
to our slaves, every body gives tea-parties and
balls. The great difference between the American
and English manners, and which completely
characterizes the two societies, is the total absence in America of that spirit of social servility which, in England, forms so striking
a contrast with the free institutions that the
people so justly make their boast. There is
not a respectable man or woman in England
who is not constantly gnawed with desire to appear something more than they are. There is
no meanness that they will not commit to be
invited into a society a notch higher than their
own. The merchants and tradesmen do not
converse about the business, dinner, or ball
of their neighbour; but they have never done
talking of the dinner of such a duke, or the
rout of such or such a marquis, people whom
they are never likely to come near, and whom
they know only by name : everybody has the genealogy of the peers by heart, and they trouble
themselves much more about their alliances than
those of their own friends and acquaintances.
As soon as a stranger is presented, even to the
family of an eminent merchant, the mistress of
the house takes care to tell him over and over
the names of all the nobility who have done her

the honour of speaking to her; and fancies by
that means to give the stranger a very high
notion of her social respectability. This paltry
servility, which to me is in the last degree disgusting, has no existence in the United States.
There is not an American who would not blush
to seek an invitation, and he has too much pride
to acknowledge that any society is superior to
his own in dignity. The common workman, if
he is inclined, is found seated beside the rich
man at political dinners; and any decent female
may attend the subscription balls, whatever
may be her condition in life. On the contrary,
even, distinctions among the different circles are
maintained by the pride which every one feels
in not receiving obligations which he cannot
return: it is upon this ground partly that the
social equality discernible is founded.

    To enjoy life in an independent manner in
America, you must spend four or five thousand
dollars a year. Those who spend less do not
desire to live in a society in which they would
find themselves humiliated by their want of
fortune; and those who could spend much more
cannot do so without separating themselves from
general society altogether. Nobody spends
more than ten thousand dollars, whatever may
be his fortune. It is owing to this cause, that

the salaries of the inferior clerks, and others in the government, are much higher than those of corresponding rank in France, whilst the salary of a minister is much less.

In a country in which everybody is more or less occupied with business; where few persons are in a condition to live upon their incomes, or the interest of their capitals; it cannot be expected that the fine arts and literature should have received their full development. It certainly is not owing to the want of genius or taste in America, but of pecuniary encouragement; and as long as the work of the poet or the painter is less remunerated than that of the lawyer or the preacher, people will speak, and not write. Literature, at the present moment, is almost entirely oral, oratory being that branch of it which is the most advanced. The American Reviews, however, sufficiently shew, in the talent with which they are written, that it is not ability but time, which writers require. A man engaged in business may manage to snatch a few hours to write a scientific or literary article; but he cannot without injury to his proper occupations, undertake works upon a large scale. I am aware that we number among us authors distinguished in those kinds of literature which require lightness of style, and grace and fresh-

ness in the colouring; but these are exceptions
to the general rule; these are the insulated fore-
runners of a generation of literary men yet to
come.

Everybody is literary in the United States,
for everybody has received a good education.
Instruction is quite free. Westpoint is the only
college in which education is given at the expense of the government of the United States.
In some States, there are elementary systems of
education of great extent. The State of New
York, in particular, possesses those establishments upon a scale which has no parallel
in the world. The Universities, which alone
have the power to confer degrees, are incorporated by the State-governments, but they
are quite independent of them, appoint their
own professors, and follow the doctrine which
they prefer. Whoever can find pupils is at
liberty to establish a college, or a boarding
school, or any school whatever. The Jesuits
have two colleges, which are among the best
in the Union. There are two or three convents
of nuns, for the education of young ladies.
Every religious sect establishes seminaries for
the education of the ministers of their religion.

Some time ago two rival sects started up,
who are disputing on the subject of education:

the one wishes to continue the old system, and
make the dead languages and their literature
the basis of all education; the other, on the
contrary, desires to exclude the study of them
entirely, and confine education to the exact
sciences and positively useful knowledge. Each
of these two sects has its journals, its professors,
and its disciples, and we shall soon be able to
judge of the results they will produce. It seems
to me, however, that in a country in which every
thing tends so strongly to give a positive, and perhaps, too serious a direction to the mind, there
should be sometimes a sacrifice to the graces,
and that the blending of ancient literature could
not but add to urbanity of manners, and elevate
them greatly above their primitive austerity.

This observation applies still more strongly
to the Fine Arts.   That which deals with inanimate matter, Architecture, is arrived at a high
degree of perfection. The banks, the churches,
the capitals, the town mansions, the exchanges,
the courts of justice, &c., are all built with
much elegance and solidity, and, what is
more, they are perfectly appropriate to the
objects for which they are intended.   The
private houses are in general small, and much
more slightly built; this is owing to there never
being more than one family in the same house;

but they are all very convenient, and, in the
south particularly, there are many remarkable
for their elegance. Richmond and Savannah
may be mentioned as possessing many private
dwellings which are truly little palaces. Architecture has flourished because it has been encouraged; the other arts would do the same
with the same encouragement. But how make
presbyterian austerity, which still constitutes
the foundation of manners, particularly in the
north, renounce its nasal twang for the warm
and passionate music of our modern theatres?
All the young ladies it is true, more or less,
strum the piano, and sigh over romances. A
music-master, therefore, gains a livelihood, if
he aspire to nothing more; but when enough
is known for dancing, and burlesquing in
church singing some choice airs from Tancredi,
the highest perfection aimed at is attained;
namely, singing correctly, and playing in time.
As to expression, our ladies are too chaste to
think of including that in their singing, so that
the finest pieces assume in their mouths a tone of
icy virginity. Some years ago the waltz was
entirely proscribed from society; people only
danced quadrilles and Scotch reels. The waltz
was considered, at the time of its introduction,
as a dance of unheard-of indecency. The pulpit

held forth against the abomination of permitting
a man who was neither your lover nor your husband, to encircle you with his arms, and slightly
press the contour of your waist. What then
was the effect when *a corps de ballet* from Paris
arrived at New York! I was at the first representation: the appearance of the dancers, in
short dresses, created an astonishment I know
not how to describe; but at the first pirouette,
when the short petticoats, with lead at the
extremities, began to mount and assume an
horizontal position, it was quite another matter:
the women screamed aloud, and the greater
part left the theatre; the men remained, for
the most part, roaring and sobbing with ecstacy,
the sole idea which struck them being that of
the ridiculous. They had yet to learn the grace
of those voluptuous steps. And it is in a
country in which respect for morals and decency
is carried to such a point as this, that complaint
is made at their being no distinguished artists!
for God's sake, how can it be otherwise?

A painter or a statuary can never arrive at
the perfection of their respective art, but after
long study of the naked figure. It is indis-
pensable that they possess profound feeling of
the beautiful, that their mind suffer itself to
be carried away by all the illusions of love

before they can warm, with their glowing hands,
either the marble or the canvass. And how is
this to be done in the United States? Any artist
would lose his reputation if he disclosed, in a
picture, higher than the ankle or the elbow.
Even the ancient statues, deposited in the museums, are carefully veiled; and as to having a
living model, that would excite such an indig-
nation that the painter would be obliged to quit
the country. The artists and actors are married
people, perfectly respectable, living in the best
society and receiving company at home. The
least irregularity in their moral conduct would
cut them off completely. I knew an actress
even, who, having committed some slight im-
prudences, was excluded from society, and
obliged to quit the theatre, for neither actors
nor actresses would perform with her. The
very dancers must be moral: and yet it is
objected that we have no artists! But all this
is very clear; it is decency, chastity carried to
excess, which clips the wings of genius, cools the
passions, and breaks the pencil and the palette.
The proof that this is the sole obstacle which
prevents the Americans from rising in the arts
is that we have excellent portrait painters;
our engravers are as good as in Europe; but
for historical painting, the genius is wanting, it
has been frozen in the bud.

Great efforts are now making all over the
United States to foster the arts.   Every town,
great or small, has a museum of plaster casts
and daubs, dignified with the names of the first
painters.   But all this will not do.   The sentiment of the arts, that deep sentiment without
which genius can do nothing, does not and
cannot exist in the United States as long as
manners remain the same.   Take Phideas or
Apelles, drop them into one of our towns,
in the midst of a public ceremony, the 4th
of July, for instance, the anniversary of the
declaration of independence, one of the most
courageous and most rational acts that a nation
has ever performed.   First of all they will hear
the cannon roaring on all sides, the ships will
have all their flags hoisted, all the militia will
be under arms, the different societies, the different professions and trades, will form themselves
into a body to join the procession formed by the
magistrates and the militia.   It will repair to
some church, where a very grave man, dressed
in a black gown, with melancholy air, bilious
complexion, and lengthened figure, will announce
to them, in a doleful tone, that although their
ancestors may have signed that immortal declaration, they are not the less damned if they have
continued to swear or to dance on Sundays; and

B b

that it is not merely being free, but that it is necessary also to be Christians and elected in order to be saved. After that, another person, in some other place, will deliver an oration which, being the hundred thousandth and some odd, upon the same subject, will probably make the auditory yawn, although certainly a finer theme for eloquence never existed. After the oration comes the dinner, then the toasts, then the speech upon the events of the day, good at first, but falling off in quality in proportion as the consumption of the wine increases. Finally, everybody departs home, more or less tipsy, but fully satisfied with having done due honour to the anniversary of the independence.

Is there in all this solemnity nothing poetical, nothing which speaks to the eye or to the senses? Everybody (except the preacher, who wears a black gown) is in plain clothes or in militia uniform, unless the lodge of freemasons of the royal ark join the procession. Then there will be, it is true, King Solomon, in a scarlet robe and gilt paper crown; King Hiram, in a robe of blue, with crown of silver paper; and the High Priest of the Jews in his robes, decked with a dozen false stones upon the breast. There is nothing but this to break his uniformity; and the procession has rather the air of following a funeral than of celebrating an anniversary so important in the history of civilization. Do you sincerely think that, if our Greek artists had never seen popular rejoicings in any other way, they could ever have produced their great works ? It was with the soul still full of the games of the Palestra, where they had seen the Lacedemonian virgins struggle without superfluous vestments; it was, still covered with Olympic dust, got where every thing had spoken to their senses and to their imaginations; it was after taking part in the worship of Ceres or of Bacchus; it was, in short, on quitting the arms of Lais, of Phryne, and Aspasia; and it was by following their advice, and even that of Alcibiades, that the marble became animated, that the canvass spoke. As long as we have different manners, it is impossible to rival the productions of the Greeks.

But I am far from saying that the arts, and all the enthusiasm belonging to them, are worth the sacrifice of the modest virtue, which ensures peace to our firesides. I am far from advocating corruption of manners, and being willing to buy by their sacrifice a few pictures and statues which, after all, whatever enthusiasm they may excite in me, will never procure me a stock of happiness equal to that which every one in the United States draws from the social intercourse of his chaste wife, and the circle of a little family of which he is sure of being the father. I would only say, that there is a palpable contradiction between the efforts made in America to encourage the Fine Arts and the austerity of the public morals. I would say, that in our actual social state, we have not nor cannot have artists. I would say, in short, that we are not the country of poetry, but of reason; that our soil is more propitious to the culture of science than of art; and that we do not offer pleasure, but that we secure happiness: which is better? I think that to render all perfect it would be well, perhaps, to inoculate our social system with a little *juste milieu.*

THE END.

NOTE ON NEGRO SLAVERY.

———

I₮ there needed a proof how little the possession of sentimental feelings, or even of the higher attribute of benevolence, when unaccompanied by wisdom, fits a human being to rule or direct his fellows, it might be found in the fact, that one of the greatest curses under which the world at present labours, owes its origin to a man, conspicuous for an almost Quixotic philanthropy, in an age when the whole world teemed with brutality. The far-famed Las Casas, the "Apostle of the Indies," the unwearied advocate of the cause of the injured Red men, who were suffering under the persecution of the Pale-faces, which threatened their race with extinction; this very Las Casas, when asked by the king of Spain who was to dig gold for him if the Indians of Hispaniola were freed from their forced labour, this very Las Casas replied, "Import black slaves from Africa!" This reply gave rise to the slave trade, which stocked America with black men, who never came in contact with the whites but to the mutual injury of both parties, either directly or indirectly.

Las Casas was an enthusiast; he had taken up the cause of the Indians, and his object was to be successful. The means of his success were not too scrupulously examined. In order to save the Indians, he probably tried to persuade his conscience that the blacks were not in reality men, but only a species of unhaired monkies, without any souls to save. Even at the present day, there are many sentimentalists to be found amongst the descendants of the Saxon race, in the United States of America, who talk most learnedly on the iniquity of occupying lands for the plough which the Red men once wandered over; and, if their principles were carried into practice, would go to the length of destroying cities and towns, full of white men, in order to leave room for a forest growth, amidst which game might be produced, and thus form a fair hunting-ground, in which the unshackled Indian warrior might take his prey, unmolested. The class of persons who thus sentimentalise are generally well provided for amidst the civilized community, and carry on their speculations without " the winds of heaven visiting their faces too roughly." It were to be wished, that such persons would indulge their fancy for the picturesque on the boards of a theatre, rather than in real life. It is an unfortunate circumstance, that even good objects are more commonly brought about by an

appeal to mere impulses rather than to sound reason:
and thus, when benevolent men first set about the
accomplishment of the abolition of that most ne-
farious traffic, the "slave trade," abundance of
falsehood was mixed up with the details of truth,
in recounting the cruelties practised.   In the height
of their enthusiasm for the blacks, the abolitionists
utterly forgot the miserable condition of the whites;
and if any serious difficulty had arisen as to the
cultivation of the Antilles, it is almost a problem
whether they would not have consented to the
forcible export of Irish labourers, and possibly have
considered it no crime to carry away Moors and
Arabs from the shores of the Mediterranean, in
order to prevent the robbery of negroes from the
shores of the Atlantic, just as Padre Las Casas
tried to save red men at the expense of black men.
     The fight between the slavers and the anti-slavers
is furiously raging; and in many cases both parties
seem to have mutually resolved to throw reason
utterly overboard, in the fear that she may put an
end to the strife.   It is made a matter of impulse—
of feeling—and, with few exceptions, the principles of justice are not so much as alluded to.   Justice is unchangeable, like truth, and can be the
only unerring guide.   The slaveholder alleges,
"I hold, by the permission of the laws to which I
am subject, a certain property in human beings;—
to strip me of my property is to plunder me; to
do this is to break the laws, and therefore I will

resist it. I may, perhaps, agree to it, on compensation being given me; but this shall be only by my own free will, and at my own valuation, or by the valuation of a jury similarly situated with myself." The negro, on the other hand, replies, "I have a property in my own body, which no human laws can defeat; and the law of nature warrants me in regaining my freedom, peaceably, if I can,—if not, by the destruction of the lives of those who hold me in bondage. I care not who was the original thief, or how many hands the article stolen may have passed through, I will seize my own property wherever I may find it, and treat, as an accomplice in the robbery, whoever may attempt to withhold it." Put these words into the mouth of a white, and all the world would recognise their justice. What is there in a black skin to alter their nature?

M. Achille Murat is a strong upholder of the continuance of negro slavery; but, though he makes some just remarks occasionally upon it, he sets out with principles which are a heresy against all that is great and noble in human nature. He argues that, as slavery existed in the beginning of the world, there is no great hardship in its continuing to exist. Throwing aside the principles of justice altogether, he goes upon the principle of power alone, and argues, that a white man, by reason of his intelligence, possessing *power* over a black man, has as much right to use him for his purposes, as he has to catch a wild horse and ride him,

or to kill a lion and strip him of his skin.   Upon this
principle the state of society in New Zealand might
be defended, where a man catches his neighbour
and eats him, because he has the *power* so to do.
He calls negro slavery "a contract," and says, that
a master has as much right over his slave as he has
over his horse,—more; that slavery is a great good,
because hot countries cannot be cultivated without
blacks; and blacks will not work but upon compulsion.   Yet, in another place, he says, that
slavery is expiring in the States of Virginia and
Maryland, because free labour is cheaper, and that,
"in time, such will be the case with all present and
future States, and the Union will be freed from this
domestic plague."   He goes on to assert, that the
slaves are happier than European labourers, and
gives somewhat of an approval to the feudal system
of Austria.   But I must here stop to quote :

"The planter, disengaged from all manual labour, has much more time to cultivate his mind.
The habit of considering himself as morally responsible for the welfare of individuals, gives to his
character a species of severe dignity, which leads
to virtue, and which, tempered by arts, sciences,
and literature, conduces to make of the planter of
the Southern States one of the most perfect models
of the human race.   His house is opened to all
comers with the most generous hospitality, — his
purse but too often with prodigality.   The habit of
being obeyed, gives him a noble pride in treating

with his equals, i. e. with all white men, and an
independent view of politics and religion, which
forms a perfect contrast to the reserve and hypocrisy
which are but too often met with in the north. As
regards his slaves, he is rather their father than
their master, because he is too powerful to be
cruel." Byron, in the "Corsair," describing the
insolence of the Turks* to the Greeks, says:

"And will not strike, because they may."

But I must again quote:
"Compare the elections in the great towns of
the south and the north,—what tumults in the one!
what calmness in the other! In the north, the
inferior classes of society take tumultuous possession of the place of election, and drive away, if
I may so phrase it, by their indecent conduct, all
instructed and enlightened men. In the south, on
the contrary: all the inferior classes are blacks,
slaves, and mutes; enlightened men conduct the
elections tranquilly and rationally, and it is perhaps to that alone is owing the superiority of talent
which has been remarked in the Congress of the
United States in favour of the south." This last
assertion is contrary to the fact.

He goes on to say: "In all countries, and in all

* Individuals of the eastern nations, though frank and
open towards their unresisting slaves, are reserved and
treacherous towards one another.

ages, a great majority of the human race are condemned to subsist by manual labour, and I do not doubt that that portion of society would be far happier, and far more useful, in a state of slavery than otherwise."

The spirit of king-craft is evidently still strong within the bosom of, this. writer. The Tories would do well to import him into England to preach this doctrine of Castes, and of passive obedience. He would doubtless be a strong opponent of the Reform Bill, and a decided advocate for the patriarchal despotism of the Duke of Wellington. Dionysius, when he lost his power over men, took to keeping school, that he might have boys to punish; and even so M. Achille Murat, when turned out of the "Two Sicilies," buys "niggers" in the slave States to keep. together, the remnants of his "severe dignity" and "noble pride." But; thinking it still better to command whites than blacks, as soon as he heard. of the "three days," back he came to Europe to join in. the *mêlée*, and if. occasion offered, to lay claim to any spare crown. which might fit his head. How. exquisite is. his plan for the conducting of elections! All vulgar workmen are to, be excluded, and the enlightened men are to settle the affair. Why, this is the very *beau. ideal* of a rotten borough, which. the Tories—the. whites of England, consider to be. such. a perfect system of representation.

With regard to the doctrine of M. Achille

Murat, that power is the only source of right, it may hold good with regard to the control of men over the inferior animals, but between man and man it is a doctrine truly damnable, and pregnant with monstrous evils. Man is a gregarious animal, and to prey upon his kind would bring about his destruction. Even amongst the inferior animals, who are gregarious, this disposition can rarely be met with; they herd together for mutual protection, and, with the exception of the land crabs in the West Indies, and some similar examples, they abstain from doing injury to their kind. Were they to commence injuring each other, the union would be broken up, and they would be exposed to solitude and all its attendant evils. Let the condition of human beings be imagined,—preying on each other, to make each other a property—a slave! Look at the condition of the hostile tribes of Africa! Can civilization go on while such eternal mistrust endures? Fancy this taking place amongst the whites! M. Achille Murat will reply, that no such thing is intended, that it is merely meant that the whites should exercise power over the blacks, the two being distinct races. I reply, they are all men, the one race inferior to the other, it is true, but still men, and until he can prove that they are only monkeys, they ought to be treated as men, upon the only true rule of human happiness, the principle of "do unto your like as you would your like should do unto you."

For the sake of effect in stirring up men's passions, the abolitionists have endeavoured to exalt the character of the negro far beyond the truth. They have affected to call him their brother, though the evidence of bastardy is made plain to more senses than one. There can be no doubt that at present the negro races are far inferior to the whites, both physically and mentally. To go no farther, look at the fact that, in the island of Jamaica, the numbers of the negroes are to those of the whites and mulattoes nearly as seven to one. They desire to be free; each man of them is physically stronger than a white, yet still they are retained in subjection. Could any thing but gross ignorance bring this to pass? Were the matter reversed; were seven whites held in subjection by one black, how long would it endure? Not a day— not an hour. If this be not evidence sufficient, let us proceed farther. Look at the physical formation of the ordinary negro,—his misshapen limbs and deformed feet; but, above all, his deficiency in that formation of the head, which, at the same time that it constitutes beauty, also confers the power of, and the capability for, the exercise of intellect. The receding forehead denotes the deficiency of brain, and the projected thick lips are unfitted for the proper modulation of the voice, which rolls over them in imperfect sounds, like liquid pouring from a broken-spouted vessel. The very sound of a common negro's voice is ridiculous, like the

3

imperfect chattering of a parrot. They are said
to be skilful as mechanics, but this is, at best,
but a Chinese kind of praise; they can imitate
that which they have seen, but they possess
little of the power of invention.   Who ever
heard of a negro patent or improvement? They
seem to be, in their present state, incapable
of high mental combinations, and all their aspira-
tions are of a contemptible kind; fine clothes,
liquor, and a dance, constitute their chief enjoyments, and their supreme felicity is like that of the
Italians, "*il far niente.*"   Since the race has been
known, there has been no example amongst them
of a *man*, in the emphatic sense of the word.
What has Santo Domingo produced even in the excitement of revolution? Even now, all that requires
thought, in the republic of Haïti, is produced from
the brains of whites and mulattoes.   The annals
of Jamaica bear upon them the history of King
Cudjoe and the Maroon* war; and fearful traditions of his prowess are occasionally related; yet
what was the fact?   That he was a poor miserable
creature, of but little intellect, whose only strength
was in the weakness of his opponents: he had taken

---

* This word is derived from a Spanish word, signifying
"wild," which the Spaniards applied to their fugitive negroes.   The narrator of Drake's voyage to plunder the
Spanish main speaks of the *Symerons,* which word is an
orthographical error.

possession of the cockpits or limestone basins,
leading one into another, from low levels to higher,
through narrow entrances worn by the rush of
waters in the rainy season; and his opponents were
afraid to storm these natural fortresses, dreading
to be picked off, as some of them were occasionally,
though the negro weapons were of the most ordinary kind, and, in many cases, loaded with metal
buttons, for want of bullets, as was proved after
the surrender. Fifty American riflemen would
have destroyed the whole of the Maroons; and
what the British troops failed to do, was afterwards
accomplished by the *fear* alone of some twenty
Spanish hunters and bloodhounds from the island
of Cuba, which, though landed in Jamaica, were
never used. This is a remarkable proof of the
weak intellect of the negroes. They had set at
defiance, and kept at bay, many hundred armed
men, yet, upon the mere talk of a score of dogs
being set upon them, they at once surrendered.
It did not seem to enter into their calculations,
that buttons or bullets would be as effective in the
body of a dog as in the body of a man: a super-
stitious terror, similar to that of their *obeah*, seemed
to seize upon them, and their courage failed them.
Since then they have made attempts at plots, but
invariably without success. They have not firmness of purpose sufficient to ensure a secrecy
upon which their freedom depends. There is no
doubt that they have improved much since they

first came from Africa, and they will gradually improve still more, as is the case with the free negroes of the United States; but such is the *present* character of the black inhabitants of the Antilles, and be it for good, or be it for evil, till knowledge shall have extended still further amongst them, they will continue by their own imbecility the slaves of their white masters. It may be urged, that amongst the white races, abundance of exam-ples may be found, of miserably defective physical formation, and absurd superstition. This is true, but they are not the general characteristics of the race. Amongst the negroes no remarkable instances of genius or wisdom have as yet arisen, that I am aware of.

Let us now examine the character of the white slaveholders, especially in the West India Islands.

In the first place, the bare fact of one human being holding absolute control over another, unless in the case of parents towards children, (and that with much reservation,) much as it tends to inflict mischief on the controlled, serves to inflict still more on the controller. M. Achille Murat asserts, that it gives a man "noble pride." This, I presume, must be upon the same system which the ancient Greeks followed, when they made their Helots indulge in sensual pleasures carried to the length of degradation. But the "noble pride" of M. Achille will be found, on examination, to be merely another form of that love of power, for selfish ends, which induced his father to slaughter so many human beings, in order to become himself paramount; which induced his namesake, at the siege of Troy, to commit so many varied atrocities, which have been handed down to us under the name of heroism. In countries without commerce, where food is produced in abundance, and the labourers are slaves, there is little inducement to use them ill, unless they betray a rebellious disposition. While the authority of the master is unquestioningly obeyed, he has no objection to the physical comfort of his slaves, but his constant care is to prevent that development of mind in them, which must ultimately tend to the subversion of his authority.

Many humane men might doubtless be found amongst the Roman slaveholders individually, but, as a body, they regarded their slaves only as cattle, and they were unmercifully slaughtered whenever feelings of insecurity were excited. In the West India islands, there is a wide difference made between the field negroes and the house negroes. The former are articles of trade, the latter of convenience, and to make them constantly physically wretched would recoil upon their masters, for no man likes a sulky domestic to be near him, and the general intellect of the negroes is of that class which, provided they are well fed and little worked, ever induces high animal spirits. But to return. For what high moral qualities have the white races of the Antilles ever been remarkable? Certainly not for courage or judgment; or their defeat by the miserable Maroons would not have occurred.   Generosity ?   This is the strong hold they would fain take, and they at times quote the play of the West Indian, as containing a personification of their general character.   Let us analyze it.

Mr. Belcœur, or Fine-heart, is a person of strong animal passions, and good-natured when not opposed.   Amply provided with pecuniary means, without any trouble on his own part, his deficiency of intellect has not inflicted on him those physical penalties which are the condition of being born poor, and incapable of intellectual exertion. Born and bred amongst slaves, he has acquired the notion that the few are made to possess the world, and the many to contribute to their comforts, without asking questions, and are bound to consider as a charitable boon all that they are permitted to enjoy, be it much or be it little.   He has no notion of working people but as slaves, and accordingly proceeds " to brush them away with his rattan." Being somewhat astonished to find himself retaliated upon, he gets over the difficulty apparently by reflecting that they are *whites,* and therefore to be treated with more consideration.   Yielding to the sway of animal passions, he sees a handsome woman, and presents her with jewels, the property of another, which had been intrusted to his charge.   Here is a piece of downright dishonesty. It is true that he wished to replace the jewels by

others of greater value; but what then? He happened to be sufficiently rich so to do, but that did
not compensate for the breach of trust. When he
exercised the reckless profusion, which is so unwor-
thily called generosity, he did not stop to reflect
in what his means of compensation were. He was
gulled in a gross manner, and he would have been
equally " generous" with the property of another,
whether he had the power of replacing it or
not. Would he have done this had he known
that there was a necessity for his enduring years of
painful toil in order to replace it? If not, he
might be prodigal, but assuredly not generous,
even supposing the gift to be worthily bestowed.
It is an abuse of terms to call the act of giving
away that which costs nothing, "generosity." It
is like the generosity of children, whose parents
give them money at the church doors to put into
the plate. No privation, no exertion, is entailed
on them by the act, and they know no value in that
which they give, any more than if they had lifted
a pebble from the earth for a deposit. But it
is a still greater abuse of terms to call those acts
by the name of generosity which are closely connected with selfish, and commonly with sensual,
gratification. He who gives up his time, and labour, for the service of another, prompted only by
love, or affection, or respect, is generous; he knows
the full value of what he gives away; but he who
merely gives money, the acquisition of which has

cost him nothing, and the loss of which in no way
interferes with his comforts, is not entitled to the
same credit.   Mr. Rothschild, or Mr. Baring,
might pay twenty-five guineas per quart for green
peas out of season, but it would not be generosity.
If for their own eating, it might be selfish epi-
curianism ; if for the eating of their company,
it might be ostentation : if they were purchased
for a poor invalid, who could eat nothing else,
it would be generosity; but still not comparable
with that of a poor workman, who were to bestow
a week's labour for the same or a similar purpose.
It is so common to confound profuse expenditure, or even waste, with the noble quality of generosity, that it is necessary to make this matter
as explicit as possible. The reckless waste of sailors,
when landing with abundance of prize-money,
has been much lauded, but a case was once related to me of one of the " gallant British tars,"
who refused to give sixpence to the hospital before
leaving his vessel, and when on shore swallowed a
fifty-pound bank note between two slices of bread
and butter, by way of astonishing the lookers-on.
This, surely, was as much ostentation as the act of
Cleopatra when she melted down the pearls for a
royal draught.

   The productions of the West-India islands were
once very valuable articles, and, as marketable
commodities, there was little competition with
them. The land was the property of no large num-

ber of individuals, for whom slaves were forced to
work, and the object was to get as much labour as
possible out of them in a given time. The wear
and tear of human bodies was not regarded, because, in the phrase of the masters, it was cheaper
to buy than to breed. This was upon the principle
of some of the fast-travelling stages, drawn by
horses; the animals are worked so much beyond
their strength as considerably to shorten their lives;
but, as an extra profit can be realized, which is
more than the extra purchase-money of fresh cattle,
it is a good mercantile speculation.   In former
times, the consumption of slave-life in the West
Indies was greater than the replenishment by breed-
ing, but the traffic with the coast of Africa kept
up the number, and doubtless, with regard to the
field negroes, much cruelty existed, in overworking
them, and punishing them for the inability of nature.   But the same persons who overworked their
field negroes might, at the same time, treat their
domestic negroes very kindly, physically speaking.
Altogether, the white slave-owners carried on a
profitable business without any labour, by the exercise of injustice; and what they easily got, they
as easily expended, wherefore the phrase "generous as a West Indian," grew into a proverb. They
wasted what cost them nothing. They were like
the bucaniers, only that they plundered blacks
instead of whites; and the same remark held good
of both, that "what is got over the devil's back is

generally expended under his belly." Rolling in
luxuries, and every kind of abundance, the exercise
of hospitality cost them nothing, but was a mere
giving away of that which they valued not, for that
which they did value. They suffered any one
whose company afforded them pleasure to feed at
their board, heedless of the cruelty whereby their
luxuries were procured. Moral principles they had
none: all that was good in them was impulse, as
well as much that was evil, after deducting the
cruelty exercised in the calculation of trade. It
is true that so long as a planter managed his
own estates, he would exercise no cruelty towards
his slaves which tended to deteriorate his property,
and so far the arguments of the slavers is good,
that a man will no more ill-use his negroes in the
West Indies, than a London brewer will ill-use his
horses; but the agents, who for the most part manage the estates at present, are influenced by no
such motive. Their object is like that of a farmer
of land, to get as large a product as possible, during the time the lease lasts, careless of the condition
the farm may be left in at the expiration of the term.
Such agents are for the most part dishonest men,
who let slip no opportunity of cheating their em-
ployers, and the negroes are more liable to be mis-
used by them than London horses are by hirelings,
because there is a more direct interest in their so
doing. It is a common remark, that if a man dies
possessed of property in the West Indies, his rela-

tives in Europe experience much difficulty in gaining possession of it, as the lax system of morality
induces the feeling, that what is taken away by a
European owner is so much robbed from the islands.
The increasing subdivision of property, and the increased competition of the white population, has a
constant tendency to diminish that quality which
was the substitute for generosity; and the want of
energy for industrious exertion, necessary to compete
with the rivalry of the Eastern Indies and the American continent, together with the deterioration of
the land of long-wrought plantations, gives much
stimulus to the robber-spirit which would rather appropriate the goods of a neighbour than practise
the stoical virtue of self-denial.   Those who have
had the opportunity of comparing the former character of West Indians with their present one, will
agree to the truth of this statement.   Their character never was amiable.   Like spoiled children, they
always smiled when pleased, and, now that they
begin to be curbed, they pout and call names.
Precisely such has ever been the character of their
offspring.   Those who have been doomed to the
task of instructing such as were sent to Europe for
their education, will vouch it.   The children, physically speaking, are rather favourably formed than
otherwise ; there is no fault in their capability, but
the evil may be traced to the mischievous and de-
basing influence of slavery.

So much stress has been laid by the advocates

for slavery, on the apparently undeniable fact, that it is the interest of the owners to use the slaves well; and even well-intentioned men, like Captain Marryat, have laboured so strongly to make out the case,—that it is necessary to be very explicit in setting forth the fallacy. Be it therefore remembered, that the owners are in most cases absent from their property, which is intrusted to the care of interested hirelings, who rarely pay much heed to human sufferings; and even in the case of the owners, the fact is well understood, that the *slave* will only work upon compulsion, and therefore the owner will not inquire too minutely into the conduct of his overseers and drivers. A case was related to me but a short time back, by a gentleman strongly interested in the continuance of slavery, so that no doubt could be thrown on his accuracy. An owner paid a visit to his estate in the island of Jamaica where the negroes were exceedingly ill-used by the overseer. One of the negroes contrived to meet the owner as he was riding along the sea-shore. He complained of the cruelty with which they were treated, and the owner, shaking his head, told him that they were a lazy good-for-nothing set of fellows. The man, then, seeing that his case was hopeless, in a fit of desperation, threw himself into the sea and was drowned. This fact is beyond dispute, and could I in fairness quote my authority, no one would doubt it. As a mass, the field negroes are probably not treated with wanton cruelty,

so long as they will work ; but, notwithstanding,
there are numerous instances of petty Neros amongst
the overseers, labouring under a monomania, which
can only be gratified by the spectacle of human
suffering. Do not such things occur in England
also, in spite of the laws made to prevent them?
Do not those who lack the power to inflict cruelty
on human beings, indulge their propensity on the
inferior animals? Wherefore else was Mr. Martin's
Act made? Such coarse-minded men are precisely those who would seek for the situation of
overseer as a matter of choice, and which nothing
but stern necessity would induce the man of refined
feelings to undertake. From time to time, the
newspapers report instances of barbarous cruelty,
exercised by captains of vessels towards their seamen and apprentices, notwithstanding the existence
of protecting laws. What would be the conduct of
such men, if placed in the situation of irresponsible
power over negroes? The fact is, talk as we may,
those who own slaves, for the purposes of working
them to a profit, do not regard them as human beings, but as cattle, and they increase or shorten
their labour or rations, only with reference to profit,
and without heeding their individual feelings or
comfort beyond the necessity of maintaining them
in health. Amongst the numerous stories told of
negro drollery, which amongst many short-sighted
people is held as an evidence of intellect, is the
following, which bears upon the point I am argu-

ing. An old negro, who had been sold and resold again and again, with the estate to which he belonged, and had thus passed the ordeal of the ownership of individuals of many nations, was asked, by a student of the natural history of man, which nation he liked best. He replied, " Massa, me. like um Spaniard berry much ; me like um Frenchman good berry, not like um Spaniard. Me like English buckra sometime. Me no like um Dutchman. But, Massa, worser an all, me no like um Cotchman ; dam Cotchman no good for um Nigger." " Why so?" asked the interrogator. " Golly, massa," was the reply, " um dam Cotchman him gib poor Nigger him fish wib only one yeye." The fact was, that a frugal native of the North, having made the discovery that his estate was not so profitable as he could wish, became the first inventor of the process of splitting herrings in twain, and thus making one negro ration do the work of two.

Some years back, I was thrown much in company with one of those beings who are, in common parlance, called " ladies," on account of certain factitious circumstances, which are, in the present state of society, made to constitute high caste, without reference to mental qualifications. She was a native of the Antilles, born of English parents, rather agreeable in her manners when pleased, well dressed, possessed of a good shape, and what would, by many persons, be called a pretty face. *Au reste,*

she would " talk conversation," play on the guitar,
the harp, and the piano, and moreover sing a little.
In short, she was considered, when in Jamaica, to
belong to the first and most undeniable society; in
proof of which, the boast of her family was, that
she had refused successively two post captains and
an attorney-general. This lady, on one occasion,
amused a company, of whom I formed a part, with
a narration of her early life in Jamaica, and the
scenes of fashion in which she moved. The won-
ders of her pa's house, and his greatness, were all
duly described, and, amongst other things, a most
extraordinary lap-dog, with all the vicissitudes of
its existence. " The poor thing lost its mother
when only a week old, so I sent for the overseer
to find me a healthy black woman to nurse it. She
at first refused to suckle it, but I told her she
should be whipped, and then coaxed her till she at
last agreed, and the little thing throve wonderfully
well, so that the woman at last became as fond of it
as if it had been her own child." In relating this
most disgusting story, the lady did not seem to be
aware of any impropriety in it, and in answer to a
question from me, she replied, that it was not an
uncommon circumstance. She evidently considered that a lap-dog was quite as important a being
in the scale of creation as a negress, and this without
any apparent consciousness that her act had de-
based a fellow-creature. Her general character
was rather humane than otherwise, and she regu-

larly attended divine worship. The fact is, the whites are accustomed to consider the blacks as inferior animals, and only treat them otherwise when the men seek the negro women as instruments of sensual indulgence. But the most extraordinary scenes of all are presented in the houses where the mulatto girls are accustomed to assemble at evening parties. Perhaps they are accompanied by some of their own class, but the moment one white man enters, every male mulatto vanishes, leaving their pale-skinned masters to be " cocks of the (brown) walk." The climate of the West India islands is certainly not adapted for the exercise of the sterner virtues.

Of late years, the slaves, as a body, have begun to entertain notions of acquiring their freedom, not as of old, by the operation of insurrection, but by the quieter process of law. It is possible that the numerous missionaries who frequented the islands have done much to foster this disposition, not to incite to violence, but to keep up a species of agitation. Missionaries are men, and no doubt like to thrive in their vocation. A black congregation, though not so good as a white one, is better than no congregation at all, and a congregation of negroes is better than one of New Holland, or New Zealand savages, as offering less risk and more profit. Considerable gleanings are to be made from negro ignorance, on which the *obeah* for a long time operated so successfully, and the masters are apt to think that all that goes into the pockets of the missionaries is so much abstracted from their own. They complain that the missionaries are stirring up a lawless disposition amongst their slaves, but by their own acts they show that they themselves are as barbarous and lawless as the most ferocious savages: witness their attacks on the chapels and dwellings of the missionaries.   Whatever may be the motives of the missionaries, whether religious zeal or the love of lucre, which their enemies allege against them, it cannot be denied that they have done much towards humanizing the negroes, and spreading intelligence amongst them, and the negroes are in return attached to them, believing, as they do, that it is through them that they will ultimately regain their freedom.   The white Creoles well know that when the negroes become somewhat more intelligent, they will no longer be able to retain them in slavery, and, for the purpose of impeding their instruction, they have declared an illegal war against the missionaries, whose hatred they have doubtless excited, and whose energies will in consequence be unceasingly exerted to work their downfal.   A gamekeeper belonging to the Marquess of Stafford took away the gun of a burgess of Newcastle, who was sporting on the forbidden grounds, and accompanied the act by words of insult.   The pride of the burgess was hurt, and he vowed, in bitterness of spirit, that he would be revenged.   The slumbering energies of a powerful

3

though humble foe were aroused, and that act of
arbitrary power was the means of wrenching from
the proud nobleman the dictatorship of a borough
which had long been an heir-loom in his family.
Even thus, some stern spirit may be wounded,
amongst those of the missionaries exposed to the insults of the infuriate white Creoles, who, burning for
revenge, may incite the slaves to rise and strike with
" the sword of the Lord and of Gideon." Black men
can fight: they have given evidence of it in many
places. It was an army principally composed of
blacks which left the shores of Chili to accomplish
the liberation of Peru. The negroes of the islands
have physical force enough, whenever they may
possess mental skill to direct it. If ever, under
white leaders, and more especially religious leaders,
they rise into insurrection with arms in their hands,
the episode will not be as that of King Cudjoe.
A general massacre of the whites will make of the
Antilles a species of black federal republic, leaving
to the nations of Europe to consider, whether the
most profitable course would not be, to leave them
to themselves, rather than again take possession of
colonial nuisances by force of arms.

One of the arguments used by the upholders of
slavery, is that these slaves are for the most part in
a better physical condition than the free labourers
of England. That some of the negroes may be
physically better off than some of the English
labourers, I do not doubt; but that mass for mass

they are better off, I do very much doubt. But even if it were as they state, still the condition of the free labourer is preferable, because he has the hope of amelioration, which the slave has not. Whenever the supply of food for English labourers shall be in advance of the population, their condition may become one of great happiness. As regards the slave, whether he be fed well or ill, so long as he remains a slave, it will be the interest of his master to keep him in ignorance, and his condition will be hopeless. The negro notions of what freedom is, are in many cases as absurd as those of some of the whites. Many of the negroes believe that it will consist in living without work, while they will continue to hold their provision grounds, and to receive their rations of herrings and other matters. It has not entered into their reflection, that without work there will be no existing. They imagine that their food will be found for them as a matter of course, and that if they think fit to work, they will be paid money in addition. This want of reflection is the natural result of the condition in which they are kept.

How the question of " slavery or no slavery?" is to be settled, it is difficult to pronounce. The slaver says, " You shall not take away my property!" The moderate men say, " Let the negroes be educated, and when they are so far instructed that they will do no mischief, let them be set free!" " That will answer my purpose!" mutters the slaver to himself, " leave me to instruct them, and I will

take care to retain the fee simple of their bodies as
long as I wish." " They must be set free at once,
at all hazards," exclaims a third party. " My
property!" again shouts the slaver; "touch my
property, touch my life. ˙Compensation! oh, con-
script fathers of the British Senate!" " Who shall
decide upon the question of value?" exclaims a
calculator close at hand. " A jury of ourselves,"
replies the slaver, " and then we can have our own
price." In the mean time, the poor black stands
by awaiting the result of the debate,—anxiously
wishing to know, if that his body appertain to himself or to his master. He wants nothing but intelligence, to enable˙ him to ˙cut the gordian knot
which so many find it difficult to untie. That
the Creoles will quietly submit to any enactment of
the mother country, regarding their property, which
they do not approve, is a hopeless expectation.
Though possessing but little judgment, they have
abundance of irritability, as witness the treatment
of Mr. Jeremie in the Mauritius. Should the legislature set the negroes free, against their will, their
" great rage of heart" will, perhaps, induce them
to commit some barbarities upon the new freemen,
as they have done upon the missionaries, and then,
perchance, all will break forth in broil and general
massacre. They have vapoured much about rebel-
ling against England, and uniting themselves to
America. For my part, I wish Brother Jonathan
no such misfortune, and repute him far too wise to

saddle himself with such annoyances, for the gratification of an ambition which would cost more than
it is worth. Probably the only effectual way to
secure both slaves and masters from the effects of
their mutual hatred, would be to take possession of
the islands, with sufficient troops to keep down both
parties, and then endeavour to make a bargain with
the negroes to purchase their freedom and the
islands together, making the payments by instal-
ments of their annual produce. But this plan
would involve much expense. That the whites and
blacks, when both are alike free, should remain
together on peaceable terms on so small a spot of
earth, is most improbable, and whenever war commenced between them in earnest, it would be to the
utter destruction of the whites. It would be well
to impress this fact upon the latter, as an inducement
not to be too unreasonable in their demands upon a
good-natured people, who have to pay the heavy
penalty of the series of misrule, under which they
have so long groaned. Opening the market to competition would, probably, be the most ready method
of bringing them to their senses. The prospect is
by no means cheering, and the chances are, that a
general massacre of the whites will be the ultimate result. Were England possessed of a wise, just, vigorous,
and above all, a responsible government, this horrible alternative might be avoided; but it is to be
feared, that the imbecility, dishonesty, and want of
responsibility, which have, by long practice, tended

to keep up in the people a disposition to mistrust all governments, will work their usual mischievous effects, and prevent those sound and just
measures from being taken, which intellect, honesty,
and courage, would conceive and execute. A people
long accustomed to be plundered, acquires a habit
of begrudging even necessary expenses. He who
has been a spendthrift in his youth, not uncom-
monly becomes a sordid miser in his old age.
But meanwhile, we must console ourselves with the
Spanish proverb, "Algun dia sera Domingo." Sunday will come at last!

JUNIUS REDIVIVUS.

Note.— The writer of the foregoing essay on Negro Slavery,
is not the translator of the work.

PUBLISHER.

THE END.

J. and C. Adlard, Printers,
Bartholomew Close.

LaVergne, TN USA
31 December 2009
168698LV00004B/47/P